Wow! 365 Vegetable Side Dish Recipes

(Wow! 365 Vegetable Side Dish Recipes - Volume 1)

Judy Massa

Copyright: Published in the United States by Judy Massa/ © JUDY MASSA

Published on November, 24 2020

All rights reserved. No part of this publication may be reproduced, stored in retrieval system, copied in any form or by any means, electronic, mechanical, photocopying, recording or otherwise transmitted without written permission from the publisher. Please do not participate in or encourage piracy of this material in any way. You must not circulate this book in any format. JUDY MASSA does not control or direct users' actions and is not responsible for the information or content shared, harm and/or actions of the book readers.

In accordance with the U.S. Copyright Act of 1976, the scanning, uploading and electronic sharing of any part of this book without the permission of the publisher constitute unlawful piracy and theft of the author's intellectual property. If you would like to use material from the book (other than just simply for reviewing the book), prior permission must be obtained by contacting the author at author@limerecipes.com

Thank you for your support of the author's rights.

Content

365 AWESOME VEGETABLE SIDE DISH RECIPES 9

1. 1015 ONION RINGS Recipe 9
2. AROMATIC SWEET POTATO TAGINE Recipe 9
3. Acorn Squash With Sugar Coated Cranberries Recipe 10
4. Ancho Black Beans And Rice Recipe 10
5. Artichokes Mushrooms And Spinach Casserole Recipe 11
6. Asian Cole Slaw Recipe 11
7. Asian Slaw Recipe 12
8. Asian Style Kale Recipe 12
9. Asparagus Artichoke And Shitake Risotto Recipe 13
10. Asparagus Strudel Recipe 14
11. Asparagus With Blue Cheese Recipe 14
12. Aunt Mames Butter Sauce Corn Recipe ... 14
13. Autumn Beans Recipe 15
14. Avocado And Corn Salsa Recipe 15
15. Awesome Broccoli Cheese Casserole Recipe 15
16. BAKED LIMA BEANS Recipe 16
17. BBQ Baked Lentils For Diabetics Recipe 16
18. BBQ Black Beans With Rum Recipe 17
19. Baba Ghanoush Recipe 17
20. Bacon Cheddar Cauliflower Mashers Recipe 17
21. Bacon Wrapped Asparagus Recipe 18
22. Baked Acron Squash Recipe 18
23. Baked Beans Stovetop Style Recipe 18
24. Baked Breaded Eggplant Slices Recipe 19
25. Baked Garlic Mushrooms Recipe 19
26. Baked Parmesan Tomatoes Florentine Recipe 19
27. Baked Stuffed Avocado Recipe 20
28. Baked Stuffed Vidalia Onions Recipe 20
29. Baked Sweet Onions Recipe 21
30. Baked Tofu Recipe 21
31. Baked Zucchini Fries Recipe 22
32. Beef Stuffed Zucchini Recipe 22
33. Beets Roasted In Wine Recipe 22
34. Biblical Recipes Leeks With Olive Oil

Vinegar Mustard Seed Recipe 22
35. Black Bean Salad With Couscous Recipe .. 23
36. Black Beans And Rice Recipe 23
37. Bok Choy Kraut Recipe 24
38. Braised Baby Bok Choy Recipe 24
39. Braised Eggplants Recipe 24
40. Braised Greens And Garlic Recipe 25
41. Braised Kale Recipe 25
42. Broccoli And Pearl Onion Casserole Recipe 26
43. Broccoli Carrot And Cauliflower Bake Recipe 26
44. Broccoli Cream Cheese Casserole Recipe .26
45. Broccoli Puff Recipe 27
46. Broccoli Stuffing Cake Recipe 27
47. Brussels Sprouts Au Gratin Recipe 27
48. Bulgur And Lentil Stuffed Tomatoes With Yogurt Garlic Sauce Recipe 28
49. Burger Stuffed Onions Recipe 29
50. Butter Beans In Sesame Recipe 29
51. Butterbeans Bacon And Tomatoes Recipe 30
52. Butternut Squash Casserole Recipe 30
53. Butternut Sweet Potato Streusel Recipe 30
54. CABBAGE ON THE GRILL Recipe 31
55. COLLARD GREENS Recipe 31
56. CREAMED GREEN BEANS Recipe 31
57. Cabbage Pickles Recipe 32
58. Cabbage Smothered And Southern Recipe 32
59. Cabbage With Alot Of Flavor Recipe 33
60. Calabacitas Recipe .... 33 ·
61. Carmelized Onion And Gruyere Tart Recipe 33
62. Carrot And Apple Passover Kugel Recipe 34
63. Carrots With Pineapple Recipe 34
64. Cauli Garlic Roast Recipe 35
65. Cauliflower Delight Recipe 35
66. Cauliflower Gratin With Gruyere And Hazelnuts Recipe 36
67. Cauliflower Gruyere Bake Recipe 36
68. Cauliflower Au Gratin Recipe 37
69. Cauliflower With Bacon And Cheese Sauce Recipe 37
70. Cawliflower Curry Recipe 38
71. Charcoal Roasted Beets And Red Onions Recipe 38

72. Chayote Rellano Recipe 38
73. Chile Relleno Casserole Recipe 39
74. Chili Cheese Corn Recipe 40
75. Chinese Restaurant Style Sauteed Green Beans Recipe 40
76. Chipotle Glazed Vegetable Kebabs Recipe 40
77. Christmas Corn Casserole Recipe 41
78. Cider Glazed Roots With Cinnamon Walnuts Recipe 42
79. Classic Baked Beans Recipe 42
80. Cole Slaw Southern Style Recipe 43
81. Collards In Homemade BBQ Sauce Recipe 43
82. Colourful Veggies With Serious Kick Recipe 43
83. Corkys Memphis Coleslaw Recipe 44
84. Corn Casserole Recipe 44
85. Corn Custard Souffle Recipe 44
86. Corn Fritters Recipe 45
87. Couscous And Feta Stuffed Peppers Recipe 45
88. Cowboy Pinto Beans Recipe 46
89. Cranberry Coleslaw Anthonys Home Port Seattle Recipe 46
90. Cranberry Stuffed Winter Squash Recipe . 47
91. Creamed Cabbage Bahama Dish Recipe ... 47
92. Creamed Corn With Bacon And Blue Cheese Recipe 48
93. Creamy Cheesey Broccoli Casserole Recipe 48
94. Creamy Cheesey Confetti Fried Corn With Bacon Recipe 49
95. Creamy Savoy Cabbage Recipe 49
96. Crispy Carrot Casserole Recipe 49
97. Crispy Zucchini Sticks Recipe 50
98. Crock Pot Beans Recipe 50
99. Crock Pot Stuffed Peppers Recipe 50
100. Crockpot Beans Recipe 51
101. Cucumber Feta Salad Recipe 51
102. Cucumber Raita Recipe 51
103. Cucumber And Wakame Seaweed Salad Sunomono Recipe 52
104. Curried Cauliflower And Peas Recipe 52
105. Curried Chickpeas And Spinach Recipe 52
106. Debs Squash Casserole Recipe 53
107. Decadent Cream Braised Brussels Sprouts

Recipe 53
108. Decadent Spinach Gratin Recipe 54
109. Delicious Creamed Cabbage With Bacon Recipe 54
110. Delightful Palak Paneer Recipe 54
111. Dijon Brussel Sprouts Recipe 55
112. Easy Easy Greek Style Green Beans Recipe 55
113. Easy Okra Masala Recipe 56
114. Easy Pesto Cauliflower Recipe 56
115. Easy Stir Fried Spinach Ci Recipe 57
116. Easy,cheesy Cauliflower Recipe 57
117. Egg Plant Casserole Recipe 57
118. Eggplant Al Fresco Recipe 58
119. Eggplant Deluxe Casserole Recipe 58
120. Eggplant Tomato Stack Recipe 58
121. Eggplant Tumbet Recipe 59
122. Eggplant With 3 Sauces Recipe 59
123. Elaines Pepper Stir Fry Recipe 61
124. Elaines Stuffed Bell Peppers Recipe 61
125. Ethiopian Alicha Wot Recipe 61
126. Ethiopian Vegetable Bowl Recipe 62
127. Fabulous Classic Caesar Salad Recipe 62
128. Fall Apart Caramelized Cabbage 63
129. Famous Peoples Carrots Recipe 63
130. Fresh Sweet Corn Cakes Recipe 64
131. Fried Plantains Recipe 64
132. Fryed Cabbage Recipe 65
133. GARLICKY BRAISED KALE WITH SUN DRIED TOMATOES Recipe 65
134. GUACAPICO AKA PICO DE GALLO WITH AVOCADO Recipe 66
135. Gamja Jorim (korean Glazed Potatoes) Recipe 66
136. Garden Zucchini Gratin Recipe 66
137. Garlic Asparagus And Pasta With Lemon Cream Recipe 67
138. Garlic Butter Green Beans Ci Recipe 67
139. Garlic Edamame Soy Beans And Walnuts Recipe 68
140. Garlic Sesame Kale Recipe 68
141. Garlic Spinach Diabetic Recipe 68
142. German Leek Pie Recipe 69
143. Ginger Eggplant Recipe 69
144. Gingered Carrots Recipe 69
145. Gingery Carrots With Raisins Recipe 70
146. Glazed Carrots Recipe 70

147. Great Greek Green Beans Recipe 70

148. Green Bean Casserole Recipe 71

149. Green Bean And Mushroom Casserole Recipe 71

150. Green Beans With Shallots And Pancetta 72

151. Green Beans With Walnuts And Feta Recipe 72

152. Green Beans With Parmesan Bread Crumbs Recipe 73

153. Green Beans With Honey Cashew Sauce Recipe 73

154. Greens Bake Recipe 73

155. Grilled Asian Cabbage Recipe 74

156. Grilled Cabbage Recipe 74

157. Grilled Corn And Black Beans Salad Recipe 74

158. Grilled Corn With Herbs Recipe 75

159. Grilled Corn With Soy Honey Glaze Recipe 75

160. Grilled Corn With Sweet Savory Asian Glaze Recipe 76

161. Grilled Corn With Lime Butter Recipe 76

162. Grilled Eggplant Salad Recipe 77

163. Grilled Onions Recipe 77

164. Grilled Romaine Lettuce Recipe 78

165. Grilled Stuffed Onions Recipe 78

166. Grilled Vegetables With Coffee Bbq Sauce Recipe 79

167. Grilled Veggies With Basil Mayonnaise Recipe 79

168. Grilled Zucchini With Fresh Mozzarella Recipe 80

169. Ground Beef Stuffed Zucchini Bake Recipe 80

170. Guacamole Full On No Holds Barred Recipe 81

171. Guacamole With Roasted Corn And Chipotle In Adobo Sauce Recipe 81

172. Guinness Battered Onion Rings Recipe ... 82

173. Hashbrown Casserole Recipe 82

174. Healthier Creamed Corn With Bacon And Leeks Recipe 83

175. Healthy Oven Fried Vegetables Recipe 83

176. Heart Healthy N Hearty Layered Broccoli Salad Recipe 84

177. Heart Healthy Pumpkin And Black Bean Soup Recipe 84

178. Hijiki No Nimono Recipe 85

179. Holiday Cauliflower Recipe 85

180. Honey Baked Lentils Recipe 85

181. Honey Baked Red Onions Recipe 86

182. Honey Baked Squash Recipe 86

183. Honey Dijon Glazed Baby Carrots Recipe 87

184. Hop In John Recipe 87

185. Hot Cauliflower With Shrimp Recipe 87

186. Hot Corn Recipe 88

187. Hot And Spicy Sauteed Mushrooms Recipe 88

188. How To Make Sauerkraut 89

189. Imam Bayildi Recipe 90

190. Indian Spiced Cauliflower And Potatoes .. 90

191. Indian Style Green Beans And Carrots Recipe 91

192. Indian Style Curry With Potatoes Cauliflower Peas And Chickpeas Recipe 91

193. Individual Cauliflower Gratin Recipe 92

194. Indonesian Bakwan Jagung Recipe 93

195. Italian Eggplant Parmesan Recipe 93

196. Italian Stuffed Zucchini Recipe 93

197. Italian Style Collard Greens Recipe 94

198. Italian Tomato Casserole Recipe 94

199. Italian Style Zucchini Recipe 94

200. Ive Bean To Heaven Recipe 95

201. Japanese Pickled Cucumbers Recipe 95

202. Japanese Style Green Beans Recipe 95

203. Judys Mediterranean Quinoa Salad Recipe 96

204. Kale With Garlic And Dried Cranberries Recipe 96

205. Kale With Garlic And Cranberries Recipe 97

206. Kale Llaloo Recipe 97

207. Korean Baechu Kimchi Recipe 97

208. Korean Bean Sprouts Mung Bean Sprouts Recipe 98

209. Korean Buckwheat Jelly Memil Muk Muchim Recipe 99

210. Korean Pickle Recipe 99

211. Korean Style Kong Namul Muchim Recipe 100

212. Korean Style Shigemchi Muchim Sauted Spinach Recipe 100

213. Korean Gut Churi Kimchi Recipe 100

214. LIMA HAMBURGER PIE Recipe 101

215. Lanas Accidental Healthy Vegan Ginger Stir

Fry 101

216. Lanas Country Style Baked Beans Recipe 101

217. Latkes Potato Pancakes Recipe 102

218. Leek & Goat Cheese Galette Recipe 102

219. Leeks Gratinee Recipe 103

220. Lemon Glazed Carrots Recipe 104

221. Low Carb Shepherds Pie Recipe 104

222. Luffa Squash With Mushrooms Spring OnionsCoriander Recipe 104

223. Magical Greens Recipe 105

224. Mandarin Coleslaw Recipe 105

225. Mango Mix Recipe 106

226. Masala Potaotes Recipe 106

227. Mashed Broccoli And Leeks With Cheese Recipe 106

228. Matzoh Ball And Sweet Potato Stew Recipe 107

229. Mediterranean Kale Recipe 107

230. Mexican Coleslaw Recipe 107

231. Mexican Corn Casserole Recipe 108

232. Mexican Zucchini Casserole Recipe 108

233. Miss Olivias Summer Squash N Zuchini Casserole Recipe 108

234. Molasses Baked Beans Recipe 109

235. Moroccan Spiced Spaghetti Squash Recipe 109

236. My Famous Green Beans Recipe 110

237. Napa Style Roasted Vegetables Recipe ... 111

238. New Years Day Green Beans Recipe 111

239. North African Spiced Carrots Recipe 112

240. Not Really Esquites Recipe 112

241. Not Rolled Rolled Cabbage Recipe 112

242. Onion Gruyere Pie Recipe 113

243. Onion Pie Recipe 113

244. Oven Fried Cauliflower Recipe 114

245. Oven Fried Zucchini Sticks Recipe 114

246. Oven Fried Zucchini In A Crunchy Parmesan Crust Recipe 114

247. Pa Dutch Old Fashioned Green Beans And Bacon Recipe 115

248. Palak Paneer Recipe 115

249. Pan Fried Cabbage Recipe 116

250. Paneer Butter Masala Recipe 116

251. Papas Potato Cabbage Casserole Recipe . 117

252. Parmesan Celery Recipe 117

253. Parmesan Portobellos N Marinara Sauce Recipe 118

254. Parmesan Veggie Stir Fry Ci Recipe 118

255. Pepperoni Zucchini Boats Recipe 118

256. Peruvian Grilled Yucca With Huancaina Sauce Recipe 119

257. Pickled Blackeyed Peas Recipe 119

258. Pickled Jalapenos Recipe 119

259. Pinto Beans Recipe 120

260. Popeye Spinach With Sesame Dressing Recipe 120

261. Potato Tomato And Onion Casserole Recipe 121

262. Pumpkins Kadu Bouranee With Yogurt Sauce Recipe 121

263. Quick Spicy Kimchee Low Carb Tyler Style Recipe 121

264. RED CABBAGE WITH APPLES Recipe 122

265. Ratatouille My Way Recipe 122

266. Ratatouille Recipe 123

267. Red Cabbage Recipe 123

268. Red Lentil Patties Vegetarian Meatballs Recipe 124

269. Refrigerator Pickled Beets And Onions Recipe 125

270. Remys Ratatouille Recipe 125

271. Rich Creamed Corn Recipe 126

272. Rich Squash Casserole Recipe 126

273. Roasted Asparagus Recipe 127

274. Roasted Autumn Vegetables Recipe 127

275. Roasted Cabbage Wedges Recipe 128

276. Roasted Cauliflower & Garlic Recipe 128

277. Roasted Cauliflower Popcorn Recipe 128

278. Roasted Cauliflower Recipe 129

279. Roasted Green Beans Recipe 129

280. Root Vegetables Casserole Recipe 129

281. Rudolph Moms Black Cherry Yam Casserole Recipe 130

282. Rutabaga Gratin With Fennel And Leeks Recipe 130

283. SPINACH WITH OLIVE OIL AND GARLIC Recipe 131

284. Sauted Potatoes And Fish Cakes Gamja Chae Bokkeum Recipe 132

285. Sauteed Brussels Sprouts With Onions And Lemon Zest Recipe 132

286. Sauteed Kale Recipe 132

287. Scalloped Brussel Sprouts Recipe............133
288. Sesame Brussels Sprouts Recipe..............133
289. Skinny Potatoes Recipe 134
290. Slow Cooker Kishke Dumplings Recipe.134
291. Smoky Baked Limas Recipe 135
292. Sour Cream And Mushroom Pie Recipe.135
293. Southern Asparagus Casserole Recipe.....136
294. Southern Collard Greens Theyre Not Just For New Years Anymore Recipe.....................136
295. Southern Collards Recipe 136
296. Southern Corn Pudding Recipe 137
297. Southern Smothered Green Beans Recipe 137
298. Southern Style White Beans Recipe 137
299. Southwestern Fried Corn Recipe 138
300. Spanish Style Grilled Vegetables With Breadcrumb Picada Recipe 138
301. Spicy Chick Peas Recipe...........................139
302. Spicy Chickpeas In Grilled Eggplant Purses Recipe 139
303. Spicy Couscous Moroccan Recipe 140
304. Spicy Curried Chickpeas Recipe 140
305. Spicy Herbed Cauliflower Cheese Recipe 141
306. Spicy Roasted Roots Recipe 141
307. Spiffy Spiced Roasted Carrots Recipe 142
308. Spinach Artichoke Gratin Recipe.............142
309. Spinach Gnocchi Recipe 143
310. Spinach Pauline Recipe 143
311. Spinach Risotto Recipe 143
312. Spinach Stuffed Onions Recipe 144
313. Spinach And Potatoes Aloo Palak Recipe 144
314. Spinach With Chickpeas And Fresh Dill Recipe 145
315. Squash Casserole Recipe 145
316. Squash With Dill Tejfeles Tokfozelek Recipe 146
317. Stir Fried Green Beans With Coconut Recipe 146
318. Stir Fried Cabbage Recipe.........................147
319. Stir Fry Broccoli Stems Recipe 147
320. Stuffed Artichokes Recipe 147
321. Stuffed Eggplant Baked In A Delightful Yogurt Sauce Recipe 148
322. Stuffed Eggplant Recipe 148
323. Stuffed Green Beans Recipe 149

324. Stuffed Red Peppers For Sukkah Recipe 149
325. Stuffed Tomatoes Recipe 150
326. Summer Squash Casserole Recipe 150
327. Summertime Coleslaw Recipe 150
328. Sweet Potato Casserole Recipe 151
329. Sweet Potato Gnocchi With Maple Cinnamon Sage Brown Butter Recipe 151
330. Sweet Potatoes Extraordinaire Recipe....152
331. Swiss Chard Sicilian Style Recipe............152
332. Szechuan Green Bean Recipe...................153
333. Taiwanese Pickeled Cabage Recipe 153
334. Tex Mex Summer Squash Casserole Recipe 154
335. Texas Corn With Onions And Peppers Recipe...154
336. Thai Coleslaw Claim Jumper Recipe.......154
337. Thai Green Rice Recipe............................155
338. Three Bean Casserole Recipe 155
339. Tiny Ham Stuffed Tomatoes Recipe.......156
340. Tomato Blue Cheese Salad Recipe 156
341. Tomato Fritters Greek Style Recipe........157
342. Tzatziki Greek Turkish Recipe 157
343. Tzimmes With Sausage Recipe 157
344. Unexpected Turnip Casserole Recipe 158
345. Unusual Layered Corn Casserole Recipe 158
346. VERY HOT KIMCHEE Recipe 159
347. Vegetable Slaw Recipe 159
348. Vegetable And Shrimp Tempura (for Beginners)...159
349. Veggie Jack Salad Recipe 160
350. Veggie Filled Eggplant Crepes Recipe 161
351. Vidalia Onions And Beef Bouillon On The Grill Recipe 161
352. Wild Mushroom And Matzo Strata Recipe 162
353. Zucchini Bake Recipe 163
354. Zucchini Casserole Recipe 163
355. Zucchini Parmesan Recipe.......................164
356. Zucchini Rice Casserole Recipe 164
357. Zucchini Supper Casserole Recipe 165
358. Zucchini Tomato Gratin Recipe..............165
359. Zuchini Ribbons With Garlic And LemonPepper Recipe 166
360. Aubergines With Cheese Recipe.............166
361. Bourbon Walnut Sweet Potato Mash Recipe 166
362. Easy Crockpot Stuffed Bell Peppers Recipe

167

363. Korean Kimchi Recipe 167

364. Korean Kimchi Pancake Recipe 168

365. Pineapple Topped Sweet Potatoes Recipe
168

INDEX **169**

CONCLUSION **173**

365 Awesome Vegetable Side Dish Recipes

***

1. 1015 ONION RINGS Recipe

Serving: 6 | Prep: | Cook: 5mins | Ready in:

Ingredients

- 3 large Texas 1015 onions
- 2 c. buttermilk
- 1 c. all-purpose flour
- 1 1/2 tsp. baking powder
- 1 tsp. salt
- 1/4 tsp. red pepper
- 2/3 c. water
- 1 beaten egg
- 1 T. vegetable oil
- 1 tsp. lemon juice
- vegetable oil for frying
- salt, if desired

Direction

- Peel and slice onions into separate rings.
- Pour buttermilk into a large shallow pan.
- Add onion rings and soak 30 minutes.
- Combine flour, baking powder, salt, red pepper, water, egg, 1 T. oil, and lemon juice; stir until smooth.
- Heat oil to 375 degrees.
- Remove onion rings from buttermilk and dip into batter.
- Fry in hot oil until golden brown.
- Drain on absorbent paper.
- Sprinkle with salt, if desired
- The cook time is for each batch or load...

- DO NOT OVER FILL FRYER OR THEY WILL BE GREASY AND SOGGY.

2. AROMATIC SWEET POTATO TAGINE Recipe

Serving: 4 | Prep: | Cook: 60mins | Ready in:

Ingredients

- 3 - tablespoon(45 ml) olive oil
- a small amt butter
- 25 to 30 pearl or button onions blanched and peeled
- 2 - pounds sweet potatoes, peeled and cut into bite-size chunks
- generous 1/2 - cup (150 gms) ready to eat prunes pitted...
- 2-3 carrots, cut into bite-size chunks
- 1 - teaspoon (5 ml) cinnamon
- 21/2 -teaspoon (2.5 ml)   ground ginger
- 2- teaspoon(10 ml) clear honey
- 2- cups(450ml) ...vegetable stock
- small bunch   fresh mint, finely chopped
- small bunch coriander
- small bunch cilantro fresh finely chopped
- salt and black pepper to taste

Direction

- Preheat oven to 400 degrees F (200 c)
- Heat the olive oil in a flameproof casserole with the butter and stir in the peeled onions.
- Cook the onions over medium heat for about 5 minutes until they are tender;
- Then remove 1/2 of the onions from the pan and set aside.........
- Add the sweet potatoes and carrots to the pan and cook until vegetables are lightly browned.
- Stir in the prunes with the cinnamon, ginger, and honey, then pour in the stock...
- Bring it to a boil, season it well.

- Cover the casserole and transfer to the oven for 45 minutes........
- Stir in the reserved onions and bake for 10 minutes longer.
- Gently stir in the fresh coriander and mint and cilantro........
- Serve the tagine immediately................enjoy this tasty dish........

3. Acorn Squash With Sugar Coated Cranberries Recipe

Serving: 6 | Prep: | Cook: 70mins | Ready in:

Ingredients

- sugar-Coated cranberries
- 2 cups fresh or frozen cranberries
- Granulated sugar
- 1 cup water
- acorn squash
- 3 medium- sized squash
- 2 Tbsp butter or margarine, melted
- 1/2 tsp salt
- 1/4 tsp ground cinnamon
- 1/4 tsp ground ginger
- 1/4 cup light corn syrup

Direction

- Prepare cranberries: Wash; remove stems (if frozen, do not thaw)
- Prick each berry 2 x's with a pin. I keep clean pins (ones used on turkey to close cavity for stuffing) on hand.
- In saucepan, bring 1 cup sugar & water to boiling. Cook until syrup spins a thread when dropped from spoon. Add cranberries; simmer 20 min. or until syrup jells when dropped from tip of spoon.
- Remove berries one at a time to waxed paper, keeping them separate.
- Let stand at room temp. for several hours or until dry.
- Roll berries in granulated sugar & set aside

- Prepare butter-spice mixture:
- In a small bowl, place melted butter, salt, cinnamon, ginger and corn syrup; stir to combine thoroughly. Set aside.
- Prepare acorn squash:
- Place whole squash in a large microwave-safe baking dish.
- Microwave on high (100% power) for 4 min.
- Cut squash in half lengthwise; remove and discard seeds and stringy fibers.
- Return squash halves to baking dish cut side's down
- Microwave on High for 6 min.
- Rearrange squash halves cut side up.
- Spoon butter-spice mixture into cavity of each squash half.
- Cover with waxed paper; microwave on High for 5 to 6 min. or until squash is tender when pierced with a fork.
- Arrange squash on a large serving platter.
- Fill with reserved sugar-coated cranberries. (By this time, the cranberries should have a crunchy sugar coating)
- Serve immediately.
- Serves 6

4. Ancho Black Beans And Rice Recipe

Serving: 4 | Prep: | Cook: 20mins | Ready in:

Ingredients

- 4 anchos
- 3 c. chicken stock (approx)
- 1/2 t. ground cumin
- 1/2 t. black pepper
- salt
- lard or oil
- 1 c. long-grain rice
- 1 15-oz can black beans
- 1 15-oz can chopped tomatoes, drained

Direction

- Put the rice to soak in cold, salted water.
- Drain and rinse the black beans (get all the blue-black goo off).
- Cover anchos with boiling water, and soak for 30 minutes (use a saucer or bowl to keep them submerged).
- Drain the anchos. Stem, tear open, and get the veins and seeds out, then puree in a food processor with 1/2 c. stock.
- Heat 1 T. of lard in a sauté pan until very hot. Add the puree, cumin, and pepper. Turn the heat to medium low, and sauté, stirring every few minutes, adding chicken stock as necessary to keep it from sticking, until dark, thick, and there is no trace of tannin left when you taste it.
- Drain the rice and rinse until the water runs clear.
- In another pan, heat 2 T. lard until hot. Add the rice, and stir to coat with oil. Add the Ancho paste, mix well, then the tomatoes and 1 1/2 c. of chicken stock. Bring to a boil, cover tightly, and reduce to a low simmer for 15 minutes. Mix in the black beans, cover again, and simmer for an additional 5 minutes. Salt to taste.

---

5. Artichokes Mushrooms And Spinach Casserole Recipe

Serving: 6 | Prep: | Cook: 15mins |Ready in:

Ingredients

- 1/2 cup butter
- 1 cup sliced mushrooms
- 1 1/2 cup chopped onion
- 2 cloves garlic, minced
- 3 (10 oz) packages frozen
- chopped spinach, thawed, well drained and squeeze dry
- 1 tsp Worchestershire sauce
- 2 cans artichoke hearts,
- drained, cut in quarters

- 8 oz cream cheese, softened
- 1/4 cup half & half
- 1/2 tsp salt
- 1/4 tsp pepper
- 1 tsp tabasco
- 8 oz shredded gruyere cheese
- 1/2 cup toasted bread crumbs

Direction

- Melt butter in a heavy skillet over medium heat.
- Add onions, sauté till translucent.
- Add mushrooms and garlic
- Cook till mushrooms release their liquid
- Add spinach & Worcestershire sauce
- Cook till spinach loses its bright green color
- Stir in artichokes
- Add cream cheese, half & half, salt & pepper
- Cook till cream cheese has melted
- Stir in bread crumbs and tabasco
- Pour into a casserole dish
- Sprinkle with Gruyere cheese
- Bake at 375 degree for 15 minutes or till top is golden brown

---

6. Asian Cole Slaw Recipe

Serving: 8 | Prep: | Cook: |Ready in:

Ingredients

- 1 small head napa cabbage, sliced thinly
- 1 bunch green onions, chopped thinly
- 1 pkg chicken flavored ramen noodles, broken up
- salt and pepper to taste
- handful toasted almonds
- For Dressing:
- 1/2 cup veggie oil
- 1/4 - 1/2 cup white wine vinegar (depending on your taste)
- seasoning packet from noodles
- handful toasted sesame seeds

- 1 tsp dark sesame oil

Direction

- Combine all ingredients together to make the dressing.
- Pour dressing over cabbage, onions and noodles and mix well.
- Add salt and pepper to taste
- Let set overnight for seasonings to blend and noodles to soften
- Add almonds before serving

7. Asian Slaw Recipe

Serving: 6 | Prep: | Cook: |Ready in:

Ingredients

- 1 (3-inch) piece ginger, grated fine
- 1/2 cup rice wine vinegar
- 1 tablespoon soy sauce
- 1 lime, juiced
- 2 tablespoons sesame oil
- 1/2 cup peanut butter
- 1 head napa cabbage, sliced thin
- 1 red bell pepper, julienne fine
- 1 yellow bell pepper, julienne fine
- 2 serrano chiles, minced fine
- 1 large carrot, grated fine with a peeler
- 3 green onions, cut on the bias, all of white part and half of the green
- 2 tablespoons chiffonade cilantro
- 2 tablespoons chiffonade mint
- 1/2 teaspoon ground black pepper
- ****
- Optional Additions That I Like:
- Chopped peanuts

Direction

- In a small bowl, or food processor combine ginger, vinegar, soy sauce, lime juice, oil, and peanut butter.

- In a large bowl, combine all other ingredients and then toss with dressing.
- You can save some of the dressing to dress noodles that can be added to this dish along with stir fried pork to make an entire meal.

8. Asian Style Kale Recipe

Serving: 4 | Prep: | Cook: 10mins |Ready in:

Ingredients

- 3/4 pound (1 large bunch) kale*
- 2 to 3 teaspoons sesame oil
- 1 small shallot, minced
- 1 to 2 clove garlic, minced
- 1/4 cup (2 thin) minced scallions, both white and light green parts
- 1 teaspoon finely grated ginger root
- 1 tablespoon low-sodium soy sauce
- 1 tablespoon toasted sesame seeds*, for garnish

Direction

- Wash the kale thoroughly to remove all grit. Discard the tough ribs, and coarsely chop the kale leaves.
- In a large skillet or heavy wok, heat the sesame oil over medium heat. Add the shallot, garlic, scallions and ginger root and cook for about 1 minute to release the aromas. Add the kale a bunch at a time and cook 3 to 4 minutes, or until the leaves have softened a bit but the kale retains its shape. Remove from heat and add the soy sauce. Divide among individual plates, sprinkle with toasted sesame seeds, if using, and serve hot.
- ABOUT COOKED KALE: Some people like their greens on the softer side. I suggest two techniques to achieve that result:
- After the 3 to 4 minutes' cooking time (but before the soy sauce is mixed in), add water, cover and let steam to desired texture.

Continue the recipe with the soy sauce step as stated in the recipe directions.

- OR
- The kale can first be plunged into boiling water and cooked for 3 to 4 minutes, then drained. Proceed with cooking the shallots and then add the kale as stated in the recipe directions.
- NOTE: To toast sesame seeds:
- Heat them in a dry skillet over medium heat or in a 325-degree oven, shaking the pan frequently, until lightly browned and fragrant, 4 to 8 minutes. Watch carefully; they burn easily.

9. Asparagus Artichoke And Shitake Risotto Recipe

Serving: 4 | Prep: | Cook: 45mins | Ready in:

Ingredients

- 5 cups chicken broth
- 1 cup water
- 1 lb thin to medium aspargus, trim and cut 1/4 inch slice, tips - 1-1/4 inch
- 3/4 lb fresh shitake mushrooms, discard stem, slice cap - 1/4 inch thick
- 2 large fresh artichoke hearts
- 2 shallots, finely chopped
- 3/4 cup dry white wine
- 1 Tbsp EVOO
- 1/2 stick unsalted butter
- 1 cup grated Parmesan-Reggiano
- 1-1/2 cups Arborio (Italian) rice
- 2 garlic cloves
- 1 Bay leaf
- 1 Tbsp white vinegar

Direction

- Artichokes: Remove all the outer leaves, choke, and stem of a whole artichoke. Cut heart into 1/4 slices and immediately place in a bowl with juice of 1 lemon, completely

coating the artichoke slices to prevent browning. In a small pot, pour 1/4 cup white wine, 2 smashed garlic cloves, bay leaf, 1-1/2 cups water, & 1 Tbsp./splash white vinegar, and bring to a boil. Add the artichoke hearts with the lemon juice, reduce heat and let simmer for ~ 10 minutes or until tender. Drain and set aside.
- In a 4 quart pot, bring broth and water to a boil, add the asparagus and cook uncovered ~3 to 4 minutes until crisp-tender. Transfer to bowl of iced water with a slotted spoon to stop cooking. Drain and pat dry.
- Keep broth at a very slow simmer, covered.
- In a heavy 4 quart saucepan, heat oil with 1 Tbsp. of butter over med-high heat until foam subsides. Add mushrooms and sauté until browned, ~ 4 minutes. Season with salt and pepper, then transfer to a bowl.
- Cook shallots in 2 tablespoons of butter in a saucepan over medium to med-low heat until tender, ~3 minutes. Add rice, stirring and cook for ~1 minute. Add 1/2 cup white wine, cook while stirring until absorbed, ~1 minute.
- Now add 1 cup of the simmering broth to the rice and cook at a strong simmer while stirring until absorbed, ~ 2 minutes. Continue simmering and adding broth 1/2 cup at a time, stirring frequently. Let the broth be absorbed before making each addition and cook until rice is barely tender and looks creamy, ~ 20 minutes. Reserve leftover broth for thinning later.
- Remove from heat, stir 1/2 cup of cheese, remaining butter, then salt and pepper to taste.
- Gently stir in asparagus, artichokes, and mushrooms. Cover pan and let set for ~ 1 minute. If needed thin rice with some of the leftover broth.
- Serve immediately and garnish as desired with remaining cheese.

10. Asparagus Strudel Recipe

Serving: 16 | Prep: | Cook: 40mins | Ready in:

Ingredients

- 2 -cups water
- 3/4- pound fresh asparagus, trimmed and cut into 1-inch pieces
- 2- medium leeks (white portion only), thinly sliced
- 1-1/4 cups butter, divided
- 2 cups (8 ounces) shredded gruyere or swiss cheese
- 3 -eggs, lightly beaten
- 2- tablespoons lemon juice
- 2- tablespoons minced fresh parsley
- 1- tablespoon minced fresh mint
- 1 -tablespoon minced fresh dill
- 1/3 -cup sliced almonds, toasted
- Dash cayenne pepper
- 32 sheets phyllo dough, (14 inches x 9 inches)

Direction

- In a large skillet, bring water to a boil.
- Add asparagus; cover and boil for 3 minutes.
- Drain and immediately place asparagus in ice water.
- Drain and pat dry. In the same skillet, sauté leeks in 1/4 cup butter for 5 minutes or until tender.
- In a large bowl, combine the asparagus, leeks, cheese, eggs, lemon juice, parsley, mint, dill, almonds and cayenne.
- Melt remaining butter.
- Place one sheet of phyllo dough on a work surface (keep remaining dough covered with plastic wrap and a damp towel to avoid drying out).
- Brush with butter. Repeat layers seven times.
- Spoon a fourth of the vegetable mixture along the short end of dough to within 1 in. of edges.
- Fold long sides 1 in. over filling.
- Roll up jelly-roll style, starting with a short side. Place seam side down on a greased baking sheet.
- Repeat, making three more strudels.
- Brush tops with remaining butter. Bake at 350° for 40-45 minutes or until golden brown.
- Cool for 10 minutes before slicing. Yield: 4 strudels 8 slices each.

11. Asparagus With Blue Cheese Recipe

Serving: 4 | Prep: | Cook: 10mins | Ready in:

Ingredients

- 1 pound asparagus cleaned and tough ends trimmed
- 2 teaspoons red wine vinegar
- 2 tablespoons olive oil
- 2 tablespoons chives minced
- 4 tablespoons blue cheese crumbled
- 1 teaspoon freshly ground white pepper

Direction

- Snap ends off asparagus spears.
- Fill medium skillet with 1 inch water and bring to a boil.
- Add asparagus in single layer and cook 10 minutes.
- Drain well and arrange on a serving plate.
- Stir together vinegar and oil in small bowl.
- Add blue cheese and chives and mix well then pour over hot asparagus.
- Season with white pepper.
- Set aside until tepid then serve.

12. Aunt Mames Butter Sauce Corn Recipe

Serving: 8 | Prep: | Cook: 30mins | Ready in:

Ingredients

- 8 ears yellow corn, husked
- 1 T all-purpose flour
- salt and freshly ground black pepper
- 1 c heavy cream
- 1/2 c cold water
- 2 T bacon grease
- 4 T butter or margarine

Direction

- Cut kernels from the cob and set aside
- Stir together flour, salt and pepper
- Combine with corn.
- Add the heavy cream and water. Mix.
- In a large skillet over medium heat, heat bacon grease and 2 T butter
- Add corn mixture and turn heat down to medium-low, stirring frequently, until it becomes creamy, about 30 minutes.
- Add the remaining 2 T butter right before serving.

13. Autumn Beans Recipe

Serving: 6 | Prep: | Cook: 30mins |Ready in:

Ingredients

- 1 can kidney beans, drained
- 1 can black beans, drained
- 3 cups v-8 juice, more if needed
- 1 cup molasses
- 1/2 cup bacon bits
- 1 tsp garlic powder
- 1 tsp onion powder (1 cup fresh diced onion if you like)
- 1 tsp ground cumin
- 1 tsp ground black pepper
- 1 tsp salt
- 1 tsp turmeric
- 1 tsp ground ginger (i prefer the bite of dry ginger here to fresh)

Direction

- In large pot add all ingredients and bring to boil
- Turn to low heat, cover and let simmer 1/2 hour
- Great options to extend or make more substantial would be to add kielbasa or other favourite sausage, even hot dogs

14. Avocado And Corn Salsa Recipe

Serving: 4 | Prep: | Cook: |Ready in:

Ingredients

- frozen corn
- 1 avocado, cubed
- lime juice
- 1/'2 red onion, peeled and chopped
- coriander leaves (we used parsley as we're not fans of coriander)
- cumin powder
- splash of olive oil
- salt
- spicy hot sauce.

Direction

- In a bowl mix together the ingredients together

15. Awesome Broccoli Cheese Casserole Recipe

Serving: 8 | Prep: | Cook: 45mins |Ready in:

Ingredients

- 1 can cream of mushroom soup
- 1 cup mayonnaise
- 1 egg, beaten
- 1 finely chopped onions
- 3 10-ounce packages frozen chopped broccoli

- 8 ounces shredded sharp cheddar cheese
- salt, to taste
- ground black pepper, to taste
- 2 pinchs paprika
- 1 roll of Ritz crackers
- 1/2 cup butter or margarine

Direction

- 1. Preheat oven to 350 degrees F (175 degrees C). Butter a 9x13 inch baking dish.
- 2. In a medium bowl, whisk together condensed cream of mushroom soup, mayonnaise, egg and onion.
- 3. Place frozen broccoli into a very large mixing bowl, Break up the frozen broccoli.
- Using a rubber spatula, scrape soup-mayonnaise mixture on top of broccoli, and mix well. Sprinkle on cheese and mix well, season. Spread mixture into prepared baking dish,
- 4. Sprinkle on the Crushed crackers mixed with melted butter
- 5. Bake for 45 minutes to 1 hour in the preheated oven.

16. BAKED LIMA BEANS Recipe

Serving: 4 | Prep: | Cook: 60mins | Ready in:

Ingredients

- 1 pkg. or 2 boxes frozen lima beans
- 1 lg. onion
- 1 lg. pepper
- 1/2 c. brown sugar
- 2 tsp. celery seed
- 1 can whole tomatoes
- 1/4 lb. butter
- 1/2 bottle ketchup

Direction

- Cook beans according to package directions; drain.

- Add onions, pepper, limas, brown sugar, celery seed and ketchup.
- Dot with butter. Pour tomatoes over top and bake at 375 degrees for 1 hour with lid on and 1 hour with lid off.

17. BBQ Baked Lentils For Diabetics Recipe

Serving: 8 | Prep: | Cook: 80mins | Ready in:

Ingredients

- 3 1/2 cups water
- 2 cups dried brown lentils
- 2/3 cup diced onion
- 2/3 cup sugar-free ketchup (or 1/2 cup tomato paste + 2 tbsp water)
- 1/3 cup sugar-free maple syrup
- 1/4 cup prepared yellow mustard
- 1/2 teaspoon ground ginger
- 1/2 teaspoon maple extract
- 1/4 teaspoon ground allspice
- 1/4 teaspoon black pepper

Direction

- Preheat oven to 350°.
- Combine water, and lentils in a large saucepan.
- Bring to a boil; cover, reduce heat to medium-low, and simmer 20 minutes.
- Drain lentils in a colander over a bowl, reserving 1 cup cooking liquid.
- Combine lentils and diced onion in a deep, rectangular baking dish.
- Combine the reserved cooking liquid, ketchup, and the remaining ingredients.
- Pour the ketchup mixture over the lentil mixture, stirring to combine.
- Bake at 350° for 1 hour.
- Makes 8 3/4-cup (side dish) servings or 4 1 1/2 cup (main-dish) servings. NI is for side dish size servings!

18. BBQ Black Beans With Rum Recipe

Serving: 8 | Prep: | Cook: 60mins | Ready in:

Ingredients

- 1 cup onions, diced
- 4 cloves of garlic, finely chopped
- 2 jalapeno peppers, seeded and chopped
- 1 tbsp EVOO
- 1/2 cup ketchup
- 1/4 cup molasses
- 1/2 cup dark rum
- 1/4 cup mustard
- 2 tbsp brown sugar
- 2 tbsp worcestershire sauce
- 1 tbsp hot sauce
- 1/2 tsp ginger
- 3 (15 ounce) cans black beans, drained

Direction

- Heat tbsp. of olive oil in large pan.
- Add onion, garlic, and jalapenos to pan.
- Cook five minutes or until onions are tender.
- Stir in ketchup and remaining ingredients except beans.
- Bring to a boil.
- Reduce heat and simmer 5 minutes, stirring occasionally.
- Stir in the beans, and simmer for 1 hour over very low heat stirring occasionally.
- Watch carefully so beans don't stick to the pan.
- Can also add a bit of smoked sausage with the beans.

19. Baba Ghanoush Recipe

Serving: 8 | Prep: | Cook: 30mins | Ready in:

Ingredients

- 3 large eggplants
- 2 cloves garlic, peeled
- salt
- 1/2 tsp. ground cumin
- 1 C. tahini paste (or less)
- juice of 2 small lemons, strained
- 2 Tbsp. finely chopped parsley

Direction

- Place the eggplants under the broiler and cook for 20-30 minutes, turning frequently, until the skins have blistered and charred and the flesh is soft. (Alternatively, if you have a gas range, you can do this over the flame of your stove, but be aware that after they soften, the eggplants will start to leak juice.)
- When cool enough to handle, cut them in half and scoop the pulp out into a sieve.
- Allow to drain for 20 minutes to remove the bitter juice.
- With the side of a broad knife, crush the garlic together with the salt, and chop and mince to form a paste. (Or, pound together with a mortar and pestle.)
- Transfer the garlic paste to a large bowl. Add the eggplant and mash until fairly smooth.
- Add more salt, if desired, and the cumin.
- Gradually add the tahini, alternating with drops of lemon juice, and blending after each addition. The exact quantities are very much a matter of personal taste, and sometimes I leave the tahini out altogether.
- Chill at least an hour.
- Garnish with parsley and serve.

20. Bacon Cheddar Cauliflower Mashers Recipe

Serving: 4 | Prep: | Cook: 30mins | Ready in:

Ingredients

- 1/2 head cauliflower, broken into florets
- 1 tablespoon butter

- 1/4 cup shredded cheddar cheese, Sargento Sharp Wisconsin & Vermont Cheddar with Real bacon Bistro Blend
- Jane's Crazy salt, to taste
- freshly ground black pepper, to taste

Direction

- Place cauliflower florets in a pot of water to cover & bring to boil. Simmer until totally and completely tender and soft. Drain well & transfer to mixer bowl.
- Whip cauliflower with electric mixer; add butter and cheese. Continue to whip until light and fluffy; season with Jane's Crazy Salt and pepper.
- NOTE: Only 55 calories per 1/2 cup serving. Best of all, they sure don't taste diet!

21. Bacon Wrapped Asparagus Recipe

Serving: 3 | Prep: | Cook: 10mins | Ready in:

Ingredients

- 10 fresh asparagus spears, trimmed
- 1/8 teaspoon pepper
- 5 bacon strips, halved lengthwise

Direction

- Place the asparagus on a sheet of waxed paper; coat with nonstick cooking spray. Sprinkle with pepper, turning to coat. Wrap a bacon piece around each spear; secure ends with toothpicks.
- Grill, uncovered, over medium heat for 4-5 minutes on each side or until bacon is crisp. Discard toothpicks.

22. Baked Acron Squash Recipe

Serving: 6 | Prep: | Cook: 45mins | Ready in:

Ingredients

- 2 medium acorn squash, sliced crosswise in 1-inch circles, seeds removed
- 1/2 cup apple cider or apple juice
- 1/4 cup brown sugar
- 1/2 tsp salt
- 1/8 tsp ground cinnamon
- 1/8 tsp ground mace

Direction

- Place squash in a 15 x 10 x 1-inch baking pan.
- Pour cider or juice over squash
- Combine remaining ingredients and sprinkle on top
- Cover with foil
- Bake at 325* for 45 minutes or until squash is tender

23. Baked Beans Stovetop Style Recipe

Serving: 8 | Prep: | Cook: 20mins | Ready in:

Ingredients

- 1 (16oz) can red beans, drained
- 1 (15.8 oz) can great northern beans, drained
- 1 1/4 cups chopped onion
- 3/4 cup chopped green bell pepper
- 2 garlic cloves, minced
- 1 tablespoons margarine
- 1 cup ketchup
- 1/4 cup packed brown sugar
- 1/4 cup maple syrup
- 2 tablespoons worcestershire sauce
- 2 tablespoons liquid smoke sauce
- 2 teaspoons prepared mustard

Direction

- Melt margarine in a medium saucepan over medium heat.
- Add onion, bell pepper, and garlic; sauté for about 4 minutes.
- Stir in ketchup and remaining ingredients; bring to a boil.
- Reduce heat; simmer for about 15 more minutes.

24. Baked Breaded Eggplant Slices Recipe

Serving: 6 | Prep: | Cook: 30mins | Ready in:

Ingredients

- 2 eggplants, washed, unpeeled, ½ inch sliced
- 1 cup bread crumbs
- 1/2 cup Parmesan or other sharp grated cheese
- 2 Tbsp parsley flakes
- 1/4 cup toasted sesame seeds
- ½ cup mayonnaise
- salt and pepper

Direction

- Preheat oven to 400°F
- Arrange eggplant slices on a shallow baking pan and brush them with mayonnaise.
- Sprinkle with salt and pepper, being careful since cheese has salt too.
- In a small bowl mix bread crumbs, grated cheese, parsley and toasted sesame seeds.
- Dip eggplant slices in the bread mixture and coat thoroughly, pressing to stick mixture on both sides.
- Place eggplant slices on a shallow clean and ungreased baking pan and bake for 15-20 minutes or until nicely brown. Turn slices and let brown for 10-15 minutes more.
- They are terrific as a first veggie course as well as side dish for meat or fish.

25. Baked Garlic Mushrooms Recipe

Serving: 4 | Prep: | Cook: 30mins | Ready in:

Ingredients

- 16 large mushrooms
- 8 ounces butter
- 4 garlic cloves finely chopped
- 1 teaspoon salt
- 2 teaspoons freshly ground black pepper
- 8 tablespoons freshly chopped parsley

Direction

- Preheat oven to 350. Lightly grease a shallow baking dish large enough to hold mushroom caps in single layer. Remove stalks from mushrooms and set aside. Place mushrooms in dish and dot each with a dot of butter then season with salt and pepper. Cover dish with foil and bake 20 minutes. Place remaining butter in frying pan together with the garlic and heat until sizzling. Reduce heat and add parsley and chopped mushroom stalks and sauté for 5 minutes. Season with salt and pepper. Drizzle butter sauce over mushrooms and sprinkle with remaining parsley.

26. Baked Parmesan Tomatoes Florentine Recipe

Serving: 4 | Prep: | Cook: 30mins | Ready in:

Ingredients

- 10 oz frozen chopped spinach
- 2 med/small ripe tomaotes
- 1/2 tub fresh mushrooms, sliced
- 2 T butter
- 3 T garlic
- garlic pepper

- seasoned salt
- worcestershire sauce
- juice from a lemon wedge
- dash red pepper flakes
- 2 T real mayo
- 4 T sour cream
- 1/2 c grated parmesan
- 1/2 c shredded mozzerella
- 1/4 c seasoned stuffing mix or bread crumbs
- 1/4 c grated parmesan
- *** As Mian dish, or bigger side for more people, double recipe, and add one onion, and one red pepper, chopped, adding to spinach mixture ***

Direction

- Preheat oven to 350
- Butter small, square casserole dish
- Melt 2 T butter or margarine in large non-stick skillet
- Add spinach
- While spinach is thawing/cooking in skillet, slice tomatoes into 4-5 thick slices each
- Lay on paper towels to drain
- Mix together 1/4 c stuffing or bread crumbs and 1/4 c parmesan, set aside
- Add garlic, seasoned salt, garlic pepper, red pepper flakes, juice from lemon wedge, Worcestershire and mushrooms to spinach
- One all spinach is cooked (about 5minutes), remove from heat
- Stir in mayo, sour cream and 1/2 c parmesan
- Place half the tomato slices on bottom of buttered casserole dish
- Add spinach mixture
- Top with mozzarella
- Top with another layer of tomatoes
- Sprinkle parmesan/stuffing mix over top of tomatoes
- Bake about 30 minutes, until lightly browned and bubbly

27. Baked Stuffed Avocado Recipe

Serving: 4 | Prep: | Cook: 15mins | Ready in:

Ingredients

- 1 large white onion
- 1 tablespoon butter
- 2 large ripe avocado pears halved and stones removed
- 4 ounces chopped almonds
- 4 ounces gruyere cheese diced
- 4 tablespoons grated parmesan cheese
- 2 tablespoons chopped parsley
- 2 tablespoons sherry
- 1 teaspoon salt
- 1 teaspoon freshly ground black pepper

Direction

- Preheat oven to 400.
- Fry onion in butter for 10 minutes.
- Meanwhile scoop flesh out of the avocado skins with a teaspoon taking care not to damage the skins then dice the flesh.
- Add onion to the avocado together with the Brazil nuts, cheeses, parsley and sherry.
- Season with salt and pepper.
- Pile mixture back into the avocado shells and place in a shallow ovenproof dish.
- Bake for 12 minutes.
- Serve immediately.

28. Baked Stuffed Vidalia Onions Recipe

Serving: 6 | Prep: | Cook: 20mins | Ready in:

Ingredients

- 1/2 cup uncooked white rice
- 6 large vidalia onions
- 3/4 pound ground spicy pork sausage
- 1/4 cup chopped green bell pepper
- 1 egg, beaten

- 1 (8 ounce) package cream cheese, softened
- 1/2 teaspoon dried oregano
- 2 tablespoons chopped fresh parsley
- 2 tablespoons butter, melted
- 1/2 teaspoon paprika

Direction

- Preheat oven to 400 degrees F (200 degrees C). Lightly grease a baking dish.
- In a saucepan bring 1 cup water to a boil. Add rice and stir. Reduce heat, cover and simmer for 20 minutes. Meanwhile, bring a large pot of salted water to a boil. Peel onions and slice off the tops; boil for 12 to 15 minutes, or until tender but not mushy. Drain, cool and remove the centers, leaving the shell intact. Chop onion centers and reserve 1/2 cup.
- Place sausage in a large, deep skillet. Cook over medium high heat until evenly brown. Drain and set aside, reserving drippings. Sauté green pepper and 1/2 cup chopped onion in sausage drippings.
- In a large bowl combine green pepper, onion, sausage, egg, 1 cup cooked rice, cream cheese, oregano and parsley. Spoon mixture into onion shells and place in prepared dish. Combine melted butter and paprika; brush tops of onions.
- 5. Cover and bake in preheated oven for 15 minutes. Uncover, and bake an additional 5 minutes.

29. Baked Sweet Onions Recipe

Serving: 4 | Prep: | Cook: 60mins | Ready in:

Ingredients

- 2 large sweet vidalia onions, peeled
- 2 TBSP tomato juice
- 1 1/2 TBSP honey
- 1 TBSP butter or margarine
- 1/2 tsp salt
- 1/8 tsp paprika

Direction

- Cut onions in half crosswise and place, cut side up, in a baking dish.
- Combine remaining ingredients in saucepan on low until butter is melted; stir well.
- Pour over center of each onion half and bake at 350 degrees for 1 hour

30. Baked Tofu Recipe

Serving: 4 | Prep: | Cook: 15mins | Ready in:

Ingredients

- 1 pkg, firm tofu
- 1 table spoon olive oil
- 2 table spoon soy sauce
- 1 teaspoon minced garlic
- 1/2 teaspoon red pepper flake
- 1 teaspoon sesame seed
- 1 1/2 teaspoon sesame oil
- 2 table spoon thinly sliced spring onion
- a pinch of salt & pepper

Direction

- Preheat the oven 450 degree
- Wash the tofu and pat dry
- Cut into 1/2 inch thick slice
- Arrange the sliced tofu onto the roasting pan
- Brush olive oil on top of the tofu
- Sprinkle a pinch of salt & black pepper
- Bake 10 min
- Meantime, mix soy sauce, garlic, red pepper flakes, sesame seed, sesame oil, spring onions.
- Remove from the oven and garnish each tofu with soy sauce mixture.
- Bake 5 more min.

31. Baked Zucchini Fries Recipe

Serving: 16 | Prep: | Cook: 20mins |Ready in:

Ingredients

- 2 cups unseasoned bread crumbs
- 1/2 cup grated parmesan cheese
- 1 t kosher salt
- 1/2 t ground black pepper
- 2 cups flour
- 4 large eggs, beaten
- 6 medium zucchini, unpeeled, but lengthwise into 2" long and 1/4" thick strips

Direction

- Combine bread crumbs, Parmesan cheese, salt and pepper in a bowl or zipper top plastic bag. Place flour in a separate bowl and beaten eggs in another bowl. Dip zucchini sticks first in the flour until lightly coated, then in the beaten eggs. Toss them in the bread crumb mixture until covered. Transfer zucchini to a non-stick baking sheet and bake until coating is crisp, about 20 minutes. Cool slightly before eating. Serve w/ ketchup or tomato coulis.

32. Beef Stuffed Zucchini Recipe

Serving: 5 | Prep: | Cook: 45mins |Ready in:

Ingredients

- 1-1/2 pounds lean ground beef cooked
- 1 white onion chopped
- 1 green bell pepper chopped
- 1/2 teaspoon ground jalapeno pepper
- 1-1/4 cups soft bread crumbs
- 1 egg beaten
- 1 tablespoon parsley
- 1 teaspoon basil
- 1 teaspoon italian seasoning
- 1 teaspoon salt
- 16 ounces tomato sauce

- 2 tomatoes coarsely chopped
- 5 medium zucchini
- 2 cups shredded mozzarella cheese

Direction

- Combine all ingredients except zucchini and cheese then mix well.
- Halve zucchini lengthwise and scoop out seeds.
- Fill with meat mixture then place in baking dish and bake uncovered at 375 for 45 minutes.
- During last 5 minutes sprinkle with cheese and return to oven until cheese is melted.

33. Beets Roasted In Wine Recipe

Serving: 6 | Prep: | Cook: 30mins |Ready in:

Ingredients

- 1 bunch beets peeled and cubed
- 1 cup red wine
- 1/4 cup honey
- 2 tablespoons butter

Direction

- Place beets in saucepan then add remaining ingredients and enough water to barely cover.
- Simmer until tender then pour into baking dish and bake at 350 for 30 minutes.

34. Biblical Recipes Leeks With Olive Oil Vinegar Mustard Seed Recipe

Serving: 4 | Prep: | Cook: 25mins |Ready in:

Ingredients

- .

- 3 large leeks
- 1 tablespoon red wine vinegar
- 1-1/4 teaspoons mustard seeds, toasted
- 2 tablespoons olive oil
- salt and pepper to taste

Direction

- Thoroughly rinse the leeks under running water. Trim and cut them crosswise into 1/2 inch-thick slices. Bring a stockpot of water to a boil, add the leeks, and cook until very soft, 20 to 25 minutes. Drain, then place them in a serving dish and set aside.
- Using a mortar and pestle or an electric spice grinder, finely grind 1 teaspoon of the toasted mustard seeds. In a small bowl, blend the vinegar and the ground mustard. Slowly whisk in the olive oil. Season with salt and pepper. Spoon this mixture over the leeks. Sprinkle with the remaining 1/4 teaspoon whole mustard seeds, and serve at room temperature.

35. Black Bean Salad With Couscous Recipe

Serving: 8 | Prep: | Cook: 10mins | Ready in:

Ingredients

- 1 cup uncooked couscous
- 1 1/4 cups chicken broth
- 3 tablespoons extra virgin olive oil
- 2 tablespoons fresh lime juice
- 1 teaspoon red wine vinegar
- 1/2 teaspoon ground cumin
- 8 green onions, chopped
- 1 red bell pepper, seeded and chopped
- 1 cup seedless green grapes chopped in half
- 1/4 cup chopped fresh cilantro
- 1 cup frozen corn kernels, thawed
- 2 (15 ounce) cans black beans, drained
- salt and pepper to taste

Direction

- Bring chicken broth to a boil in a 2 quart or larger sauce pan and stir in the couscous. Cover the pot and remove from heat. Let stand for 5 minutes.
- In a large bowl, whisk together the olive oil, lime juice, vinegar and cumin. Add green onions, red pepper, cilantro, corn, grapes and beans and toss to coat.
- Fluff the couscous well, breaking up any chunks. Add to the bowl with the vegetables and mix well. Season with salt and pepper to taste and serve at once or refrigerate until ready to serve.

36. Black Beans And Rice Recipe

Serving: 4 | Prep: | Cook: 10mins | Ready in:

Ingredients

- 2 teaspoons olive oil
- 2 white onions minced
- 2 green bell peppers,diced
- 3 garlic cloves minced
- 2 cans black beans drained and rinsed
- 2 teaspoons dried oregano
- 2 teaspoons balsamic vinegar
- 2 red bell peppers diced
- 4 cups hot cooked rice
- 4 tomatoes chopped
- 2 cups shredded sharp cheddar cheese
- hot sauce

Direction

- In large saucepan heat the oil.
- Add onions, green peppers and garlic.
- Sauté for 3 minutes.
- Add black beans and oregano.
- Bring to a boil then cook over medium heat for 5 minutes.
- Add balsamic vinegar and remove from heat.
- Stir in red peppers.

- To serve place rice in individual serving bowls and spoon beans on top.
- Sprinkle with tomatoes, cheese and hot sauce.

37. Bok Choy Kraut Recipe

Serving: 10 | Prep: | Cook: 8mins | Ready in:

Ingredients

- 1 lb bok choy, washed thoroughly and chopped
- 3 garlic cloves, minced
- 1 tbsp prepared horseradish
- 1 tbsp thyme
- 1 tbsp coarse sea salt
- 1 onion, chopped
- 2 ribs celery, chopped
- fresh or dried hot peppers to taste

Direction

- Combine all ingredients in a crock or food-grade bucket, making sure salt is distributed evenly.
- Press mixture down with your fist, wait an hour, or until the salt has drawn out enough moisture to submerge the veggies in brine. If not enough moisture is drawn out, add enough water to almost cover veggies.
- Cover mixture with a non-metal plate and press down. Cover the crock or bucket with a clean t-shirt or piece of fabric and tie a string around that.
- Press the mixture down once a day, and taste every day until it tastes sour enough to you (usually 4-6 days). At this point, transfer the mixture to glass jars and enjoy for up to 2 months in the fridge.

38. Braised Baby Bok Choy Recipe

Serving: 6 | Prep: | Cook: 10mins | Ready in:

Ingredients

- 2 lbs baby bok choy or mature bok choy
- 2 tblsp extra virgin olive oil
- 1/2 cup chopped red onion
- 1/2 tsp salt
- 1/2 tsp white pepper
- 2 tblsp seasoned rice vinegar, available in the Asian section of your grocery store

Direction

- Trim the base of the bok choy, then chop off the leaves. Cut the base in half lengthwise, then cut the halves crosswise on a diagonal into 1/4-inch-thick strips. Cut the leaves crosswise on a diagonal into 1 1/2-inch-wide strips.
- Place a large wok or a pot large enough to hold all the bok choy over medium heat. When wok or pot is hot, add the olive oil and rotate the wok or pot a bit to coat it evenly.
- When the oil is hot, add the onion and stir-fry until softened, 2 to 3 minutes. Add the bok choy and season with the salt and pepper. Cover and cook until tender, stirring occasionally, about 10 minutes. Stir in the vinegar and serve hot.

39. Braised Eggplants Recipe

Serving: 3 | Prep: | Cook: 20mins | Ready in:

Ingredients

- 3 eggplants (the long ones)
- 2 Tbsp of minced garlic
- 2 sweet onions (the small ones)
- 2 Tbsp of oyster sauce
- 2 Tsp of sugar
- 4 Tbsp light soy sauce

- 1/2 Tsp bottled chili bean sauce
- 1 Tsp sesame seed oil
- 125ml or 1/2 cup of cooking oil
- 63ml or 1/4 cup of water
- Bottled minced garlic.

Direction

- Cut the onions into halves and slice thinly.
- Cut off the tips of the eggplants and slice into halves lengthwise.
- Cut each half into 3-4 pieces.
- Pour the cooking oil in a nonstick pan and fry the eggplants.
- Make sure to fry them half-cooked only. The outer side are almost brown.
- Remove the eggplants and place them on paper towels.
- Pour off the cooking oil in the pan until only about 2 Tsp remains.
- Sauté the onions.
- Add the garlic .Sauté until golden brown but make sure not to overcook!
- Add the oyster sauce, sugar, light soy sauce, and chili bean sauce.
- Mix well.
- Add the eggplants. Mix then lower the heat and simmer for about 3 mins.
- Turn off the heat. Drizzle sesame seed oil and give the dish a final stir.
- When serving, garnish with bottled minced garlic on top.

40. Braised Greens And Garlic Recipe

Serving: 4 | Prep: | Cook: 20mins | Ready in:

Ingredients

- 1 lb kale, mustard greens or chard, (about 8 cups)
- 1 Tbs extra virgin olive oil
- 5 cloves garlic, minced
- 1/2 tsp salt

- lemon wedges

Direction

- Wash greens thoroughly by soaking in lots of cold water.
- Drain.
- Chop greens into about 3-inch pieces.
- Heat oil in a large skillet.
- Sauté garlic for 2 minutes.
- Add greens to skillet.
- (They do not have to be dried off, as the water will evaporate during cooking.)
- Cover and cook over medium heat for 10 minutes, stirring once in a while to coat all the greens with garlic and oil.
- Sprinkle with salt.
- Serve with lemon wedges.

41. Braised Kale Recipe

Serving: 8 | Prep: | Cook: 15mins | Ready in:

Ingredients

- 1 tablespoon olive oil
- 2 cups sliced white onions
- 1 teaspoon salt
- 1 teaspoon freshly ground black pepper
- 2 tablespoons minced garlic
- 8 cups firmly packed stemmed torn kale
- 2 cups chicken stock

Direction

- Heat oil in a large skillet over high heat.
- Add onions, salt and pepper then stir fry 2 minutes.
- Add garlic, kale and stock then cook stirring occasionally for 3 minutes.

42. Broccoli And Pearl Onion Casserole Recipe

Serving: 12 | Prep: | Cook: 20mins | Ready in:

Ingredients

- cheese sauce and Vegetables:
- 2 c milk
- 1/4 c flour
- 1/4 c butter
- 3/4 tsp salt
- 1/2 tsp ground pepper
- 1 c shredded gruyere cheese
- 1 c sour cream
- 8 c pre-cut broccoli florets
- 8 oz pearl onions
- Topping"
- 1/4 c Italian bread crumbs
- 1/4 c butter
- 2 Tbs fresh parsley,chopped

Direction

- Heat oven to 350 degrees. Make cheese sauce: heat milk, flour butter, salt and pepper in 2 qt. saucepan, stirring constantly. Boil and stir1 min. Stir in shredded cheese until melted; stir in sour cream. In 3 qt. saucepan, heat water to boiling. Add broccoli; cook about 5 mins or till crisp tender. Remove with slotted spoon and drain well.
- In same saucepan with boiling water, cook onions about 2 mins; drain and peel. Spoon broccoli and onions into a shallow 2qt baking dish. Pour cheese sauce over vegetables.
- In medium bowl, mix melted butter and bread crumbs; spoon over broccoli mixture.
- Bake, uncovered, 15 to 20 mins or till hot and bubbly. Sprinkle bread crumbs with parsley; serve hot!

43. Broccoli Carrot And Cauliflower Bake Recipe

Serving: 12 | Prep: | Cook: 45mins | Ready in:

Ingredients

- 3 cups broccoli (florets)
- 3 cups cauliflower (florets)
- 3 cups carrots (the bag of mini carrots works great for this)
- 1 tbsp mustard powder
- 1 tsp salt
- 1 tsp pepper (fresh ground course)
- 1/4 cup butter
- 3 tbsps flour
- 3 cups cheese (velveeta fat free)
- 1 cup cream (fat free)
- bread Crumb mixture:
- 1 1/4 cups bread crumbs
- 1 tsp italian seasonings
- 1/2 garlic powder
- 1/4 cup butter

Direction

- Stem your vegetables and cut into florets. .
- In small sauce pot add your butter melt, add salt, pepper, mustard, and slowly add in cream - add cheese and allow to melt over low heat.
- Mix veggies in a 6 qt. or large casserole dish - pour cheese mixture over top and bake in a 350 degree oven for 30 min.
- Remove and add top with your bread crumb mixture - which is simply the last 4 ingredients mix together - return to oven for 15 mins. or until golden and bubbly.

44. Broccoli Cream Cheese Casserole Recipe

Serving: 12 | Prep: | Cook: 40mins | Ready in:

Ingredients

- 4 packages frozen broccoli
- 8 ounces cream cheese softened
- 1 stick margarine softened
- 6 slices American cheese
- 1 can cream of celery soup
- bread crumbs for topping

Direction

- Cook broccoli according to package directions then drain.
- Combine cream cheese, margarine, cheese and soup then melt together and mix with broccoli.
- Pour into greased casserole dish and top with bread crumbs.
- Bake at 350 for 40 minutes.

45. Broccoli Puff Recipe

Serving: 6 | Prep: | Cook: 45mins | Ready in:

Ingredients

- 1 10 oz. pkg. frozen chopped broccoli
- 1 can cream of mushroom soup, undiluted
- 2 ozs. sharp American cheese, shredded (about 1/2 c.)
- 1/4 c. milk
- 1/4 c. mayonnaise or salad dressing
- 1 beaten egg
- 1/4 c. fine dry bread crumbs
- 1 Tbsp. margarine or butter, melted

Direction

- Cook broccoli by directions on the package.
- Drain well.
- Place in about a 10 x 6 x 11/2 inch baking dish.
- Stir together soup and cheese, add milk gradually.
- Add mayonnaise and beaten egg.
- Blend well.
- Pour over broccoli.

- Combine bread crumbs and margarine.
- Sprinkle evenly over soup mixture.
- Bake at 350 degrees for 45 minutes.
- Makes 6 servings.

46. Broccoli Stuffing Cake Recipe

Serving: 0 | Prep: | Cook: 45mins | Ready in:

Ingredients

- 2 cups milk
- 4 beaten eggs
- 3 c. herb-seasoned stuffing croutons
- 1 10 oz. pkg. frozen broccoli
- 1/4 tsp. salt
- 1 c. (4 oz.) shredded cheese

Direction

- In sauce pan, heat and stir milk and cheese until blended.
- Gradually stir hot mixture into eggs in mixing bowl.
- Add croutons, broccoli and salt.
- Mix well.
- Turn into greased 1 1/2 quart casserole.
- Bake in a 325 degree oven for 45 minutes.

47. Brussels Sprouts Au Gratin Recipe

Serving: 6 | Prep: | Cook: 30mins | Ready in:

Ingredients

- For the Brussels Sprouts:
- 1 lb. Brussels sprouts, trimmed and quartered
- 3 strips bacon, diced
- 1 cup leeks, slices thinly
- 1 Tbsp. AP flour
- 2 tsp. minced garlic

- ½ cup heavy cream
- ½ cup low-sodium chicken broth
- 1 Tbsp. fresh lemon juice
- ½ cup grated Gruyère or swiss cheese (I like aged)
- For the Crumb Topping:
- 1 Tbsp. EVOO
- 1 cup dry bread crumbs (I use panko)
- ¼ cup (or more) chopped walnuts
- ½ cup grated Gruyère or swiss cheese
- 2 tsp. mince lemon zest
- ¼ cup (optional) minced craisins (dried cranberries)
- Kosher salt and black pepper to taste

Direction

- Preheat oven to 350®. Coat a 2 quart casserole dish with non-stick spray (or butter)
- Trim off the tough leaves and woody stems of the Brussels sprouts, and then quarter them. Blanch sprouts in a pot of boiling water for 5 minutes; drain and set aside.
- Sauté bacon in a skillet over medium heat until crisp. Using a slotted spoon, remove bacon to a paper-towel-lined plate. Add leeks to skillet; cook over medium heat until softened. Stir in flour and garlic; cook ~ 1 minute.
- Stir in broth, cream, and lemon juice; bring to a simmer and cook until thickened, about 2 minutes. Remove the mixture from heat; stir in sprouts, bacon, and ½ cup Gruyere. Transfer mixture to a prepared dish.
- Heat oil for the crumb topping in a non-stick skillet over medium heat. Stir in crumbs and walnuts; cook until crumbs begin to brown. Remove mixture from heat to a bowl; let cool 5 minutes.
- Stir in ½ cup Gruyere, zest, salt and pepper into the casserole dish (add the craisins here if you like). Top Brussels sprouts with bread crumb mixture and bake until crumbs are brown, 25-30 minutes.

---

48. Bulgur And Lentil Stuffed Tomatoes With Yogurt Garlic Sauce Recipe

Serving: 6 | Prep: | Cook: 30mins | Ready in:

Ingredients

- Stuffed Tomatoes:
- 6 large tomatoes (3 lb)
- 1 1/4 teaspoons salt
- 2 tablespoons lentils (preferably French green lentils)
- 1 1/2 cups water
- 1/4 cup extra-virgin olive oil
- 1/2 cup pine nuts
- 1 large onion, finely chopped
- 1/2 cup bulgur (preferably coarse)
- 1 lb swiss chard or spinach, stems discarded and leaves thinly sliced (4 cups)
- 1/4 teaspoon black pepper
- 1/2 cup dried currants
- 1/3 cup chopped fresh flat-leaf parsley
- 2 tablespoons chopped fresh dill
- 2 tablespoons fresh lemon juice
- ~~~~
- Accompaniment: yogurt garlic Sauce (makes 1 cup)
- 1 teaspoon chopped garlic
- 1/2 teaspoon kosher salt
- 1 cup plain yogurt (preferably whole-milk)
- 1 tablespoon fresh lemon juice

Direction

- Make Stuffed Tomatoes:
- Cut off and discard top third of tomatoes and scoop out insides (leave shells intact for stuffing), transferring to a sieve set over a bowl to drain excess liquid. Coarsely chop tomato from sieve and reserve for making braised eggplant.
- Sprinkle insides of tomato shells with 1/2 teaspoon salt and drain upside down on a rack set in a pan while preparing filling.
- Simmer lentils in 1/2 cup water in a small saucepan until just tender, 18 to 20 minutes.

Drain in a sieve, then rinse under cold water and drain well.

- Heat oil in a 5-quart heavy pot over moderate heat until hot, then cook pine nuts, stirring, until golden, about 2 minutes. Transfer with a slotted spoon to paper towels to drain.
- Cook onion in oil remaining in pot over moderate heat, stirring occasionally, until softened but not browned, 6 to 8 minutes.
- Add bulgur, chard, remaining 3/4 teaspoon salt, and pepper and cook, stirring, until greens are wilted, about 2 minutes. Add remaining cup water, then remove from heat and let stand, covered, until bulgur is tender, about 30 minutes.
- Stir in pine nuts, currants, parsley, dill, lemon juice, lentils, and salt and pepper to taste. Spoon filling into tomato shells. Serve with the delightful Yogurt Garlic Sauce. Wow!
- ~~~~
- Make Yogurt Garlic Sauce:
- Mash garlic to a paste with salt using a mortar and pestle (or mince and mash with a heavy knife). Stir together garlic paste, yogurt, and lemon juice.
- **Sauce may be made 1 day ahead and chilled, covered.

49. Burger Stuffed Onions Recipe

Serving: 6 | Prep: | Cook: 20mins | Ready in:

Ingredients

- 6 large cooking onions
- 2 tablespoons vegetable oil
- 1 pound lean ground beef
- 2 tablespoons chopped green pepper
- 2 tablespoons dry bread crumbs
- 1/2 teaspoon chili powder
- 1 teaspoon salt
- 1 teaspoon freshly ground black pepper
- 3 slices American cheese
- 8 ounce can tomato sauce

Direction

- Peel onions then cook in boiling salted water until tender yet firm.
- Drain and cool then slice off top third of each onion.
- Cut out centers to make cups.
- Chop 1/2 cup of the centers and sauté in oil with beef and green pepper for 5 minutes.
- Mix in breadcrumbs, chili powder, salt and pepper then fill onion cups with meat mixture.
- Place stuffed onions in shallow baking dish.
- Top each onion with strips of cheese.
- Pour tomato sauce over all and baste occasionally.
- Bake at 350 for 20 minutes.

50. Butter Beans In Sesame Recipe

Serving: 4 | Prep: | Cook: 5mins | Ready in:

Ingredients

- 4 fl. oz. oil
- 1 rounded teaspoon cumin seeds
- 1 large onion, finely chopped
- 4 oz. sesame seeds, finely ground
- 1 rounded teaspoon ground coriander
- 14 oz. can chopped tomatoes
- 2 level teaspoons salt
- 2 rounded teaspoons brown sugar
- 1 rounded teaspoon chilli powder or hot curry powder
- 1 rounded teaspoon turmeric
- 14 oz. can butter beans, drained
- A little melted butter (optional)
- Chopped coriander leaves

Direction

- In a large frying pan, heat the oil.
- Add the cumin seeds and fry till they crackle.
- Add the onion and fry till soft and coloured a little - about 5 minutes.

- Add the ground sesame. Stir in well. Fry about 3 minutes.
- Add the ground coriander. Fry a further minute.
- Stir in the tomatoes (it will go a weird pink colour at this stage - don't worry).
- Stir in the salt, sugar, chilli or curry powder, and the turmeric.
- Mix well, and cook the sauce about 5 minutes.
- Add the butter beans and heat through.
- To finish, if liked a little richer, stir in a little melted butter.
- Sprinkle with chopped coriander to garnish.

51. Butterbeans Bacon And Tomatoes Recipe

Serving: 6 | Prep: | Cook: 60mins | Ready in:

Ingredients

- 3 bacon slices, chopped
- 1 medium onion, finely chopped
- 1 small green bell pepper, chopped
- 3 garlic cloves, minced
- 1 bay leaf
- 3 medium size tomatoes, chopped (of coarse this is better when tomatoes are in season)
- 4 cups chicken broth
- 4 cups fresh or frozen butterbeans, thawed
- 2 tablespoons minced parsley
- 1 teaspoon salt
- 1 teaspoon pepper
- 1 teaspoon worcestershire sauce
- 1/2 teaspoon hot sauce (your choice)

Direction

- Cook bacon in a Dutch oven until crisp.
- Stir in onion and next 3 ingredients; sauté until vegetables are tender.
- Stir in tomato, and cook for 3 minutes.
- Stir in broth and butterbeans; bring to a coil.

- Cover, reduce heat, and simmer, stirring occasionally, 30 minutes.
- Simmer uncovered, 20 minutes, stirring often.
- Stir in parsley and remaining ingredients.
- Cook stirring often, 5 minutes.
- Discard bay leaf.

52. Butternut Squash Casserole Recipe

Serving: 6 | Prep: | Cook: 30mins | Ready in:

Ingredients

- 1/2 stick margarine
- 2 eggs
- 1 tablespoon vanilla
- 1 teaspoon ground cinnamon
- 1/4 teaspoon ginger
- 3 cups cooked butternut squash
- 1/2 cup granulated sugar
- 1/4 cup brown sugar
- 1/2 cup milk
- Topping:
- 1 cup brown sugar
- 1/3 cup flour
- 1/3 stick margarine
- 1 cup chopped pecans

Direction

- Mix all casserole ingredients together and pour into a greased baking dish.
- Combine all topping ingredients and sprinkle on top of top.
- Bake at 350 for 25 minutes.

53. Butternut Sweet Potato Streusel Recipe

Serving: 12 | Prep: | Cook: 45mins | Ready in:

Ingredients

- 1/4 c butter
- 1/2 tsp cinnamon,1/4 tsp ginger
- 1-1/2 lbs. pre-cut butternut squash
- 2 medium sweet potatoes,cut in 1/2" cubes
- Streusel topping:
- 1/4 c flour
- 1/4 c lt. brown sugar
- 2 Tbs. butter
- 1 tsp ground cinnamon
- 1/2 c pecans,chopped

Direction

- Heat oven to 375. Place butter in 3 qt. shallow casserole, heat in oven 5 to 7 mins or till melted.
- Stir cinnamon and ginger into melted butter. Add squash and sweet potatoes; toss to coat. Cover, bake 30-35 mins or till squash and sweet potatoes are just tender.
- Meanwhile, in medium bowl, combine all topping ingredients. Uncover squash; spoon topping over squash mixture. Bake 10 mins or till topping is brown.

54. CABBAGE ON THE GRILL Recipe

Serving: 4 | Prep: | Cook: 40mins |Ready in:

Ingredients

- 1 medium head cabbage
- 4 teaspoons butter or margarine, softened
- 1 teaspoon salt
- ½ teaspoon garlic powder
- ¼ teaspoon pepper
- 2 teaspoons grated parmesan cheese
- 4 bacon strips

Direction

- Cut cabbage into four wedges; place each on a piece of double-layered heavy-duty foil. Spread cut sides with butter. Sprinkle with salt, garlic powder, pepper and Parmesan cheese. Wrap a bacon strip around each wedge.
- Fold foil around cabbage and seal tightly. Grill, covered, over medium heat for 40 minutes or until the cabbage is tender, turning twice.

55. COLLARD GREENS Recipe

Serving: 8 | Prep: | Cook: 90mins |Ready in:

Ingredients

- 4 bunches collard greens
- 2 lg. ham hocks
- 1 med. onion
- salt and pepper to taste
- .

Direction

- Remove leaves from stems of collard greens and discard stems. Wash thoroughly insuring all grit and grime has been removed from the greens.
- Wash ham hocks and boil with chopped onion until almost done. (Do this ahead of time making sure meat has cooked long enough)
- Add greens, salt, and pepper to ham hocks.
- Bring greens to a boil, reduce heat and cook until greens are tender

56. CREAMED GREEN BEANS Recipe

Serving: 8 | Prep: | Cook: 60mins |Ready in:

Ingredients

- 1 pound or more of fresh green beans. Kentucky Wonder if your lucky.
- 1/2 onion minced
- 1 clove garlic
- basil to taste
- salt
- pepper
- 6 slices of bacon minced
- water to cover
- 1/2 stick oleo
- 2 table spoon flour
- 1/4 cup water
- Carnation Evaporated Milk

Direction

- In a cast iron skillet cook bacon until it renders some fat.
- Add onion and stir.
- Add garlic and stir.
- Add green beans that have been "snapped" into pieces
- Add basil, salt, pepper
- Cover with water and cook on low until done.
- Mix flour with water and add to the bean stock to thicken, add Carnation milk to desired thickness.
- Adjust seasonings.
- Now this and some cornbread... Heaven.

57. Cabbage Pickles Recipe

Serving: 8 | Prep: | Cook: 120mins | Ready in:

Ingredients

- 1 lb white cabbage
- 4 green onions
- 1/2 c vinegar
- 1/4 c dark soy sauce
- 1 Tbsp sugar
- juice from 1/2 lemon
- 1/2 tsp red chili pepper

Direction

- Shred the cabbage, and cut the onions into 1/2 inch long pieces.
- Combine the other ingredients in a large bowl and mix.
- Add vegetables to marinade.
- Cover with a dish that fits just inside the bowl and rests on the cabbage.
- Place weight on the dish, about 2 pounds, and let stand for at least 2 hours.
- Drain before serving.

58. Cabbage Smothered And Southern Recipe

Serving: 8 | Prep: | Cook: 60mins | Ready in:

Ingredients

- 2 SMALL heads of cabbage OR 1 GOOD SIZE MEDIUM CABBAGE (I DON'T USE THE LARGE heads of cabbage)
- 2 LARGE yellow onions
- seasoning (I USE NATURES seasoning)
- black pepper
- salt (ADD TOWARDS THE END OF THE COOKING PROCESS, TASTE BEFORE AND AFTER ADDING salt)
- sugar OR SPLENDA (TO YOUR DESIRED TASTE. PEOPLE DIFFER, SOME LIKE IT SWEET SOME NOT. sugar TAKES THE bitter OUT OF THE cabbage IN MY OPINION)
- MEAT (YOUR CHOICE OF bacon, SMOKED pork (WHICH I USE), ham OR ham hocks).

Direction

- CLEAN YOUR CABBAGE, AND I CUT MINE INTO SMALL QUARTERS.
- IN A LARGE POT; PLACE YOUR CABBAGE, MEAT AND SEASONINGS.
- ADD 1/2 CUP OF WATER (CABBAGE TENDS TO MAKE ITS OWN JUICE)
- BRING TO A BOIL FOR A FEW MINUTES
- TURN DOWN TO A MEDIUM HEAT. PLACE A SEE THROUGH LID ON TOP OF YOUR

POT SO YOU CAN KEEP YOUR SOUTHERN EYE ON THE CABBAGE.

- STIR CABBAGE A FEW TIMES TO HELP THE SMOTHERING PROCESS
- TASTE YOUR CABBAGE HALFWAY THROUGH, YOU MAY HAVE TO ADD A LITTLE BIT OF THIS OR A LITTLE BIT OF THAT. LOL!

59. Cabbage With Alot Of Flavor Recipe

Serving: 4 | Prep: | Cook: 15mins | Ready in:

Ingredients

- Ingredients for serving 8 persons
- 1 head green cabbage
- 1 finely chopped onion
- 1 cup apple juice
- 1/2 cup balsamic vinegar
- 2 cinnamon sticks
- 1/4 cup light corn syrup or honey
- butter for frying
- salt and pepper
- Serve with the ham.

Direction

- This is how you do it
- Slice the cabbage thinly and sauté over medium heat together with the onion for a couple of minutes. Mix in the apple juice, balsamic vinegar, cinnamon sticks and syrup. Cover and let simmer until the cabbage softens. This will take about 15 minutes.
- Remove the lid and season with salt and pepper.

60. Calabacitas Recipe

Serving: 6 | Prep: | Cook: 20mins | Ready in:

Ingredients

- 4 tablespoons olive oil
- 1 red onion, chopped
- 4 garlic cloves, finely minced
- 1½ cups yellow squash, sliced
- 2½ cups zucchini
- 2 cups corn kernels
- 2 scallions, sliced
- 1 cup green chile, chopped
- 1 cup roma tomatoes, diced
- 1 can black beans, drained and rinsed
- ½ cup cilantro, chopped
- salt and freshly ground pepper, to taste
- mixed herbs, to taste (oregano, marjoram, and cumin)

Direction

- Heat 2 tablespoons of the oil in a large skillet or wok and sauté the onion for about 4 minutes over medium-high heat. Add the minced garlic and sauté 2 minutes longer.
- Add the squash and zucchini and sauté 5 minutes more, until softened.
- Add the remaining 1 to 2 tablespoons of oil with the corn, scallions, and green chili and sauté 3 minutes longer.
- Stir in the tomatoes, cilantro, and beans and heat through, about 5 minutes.
- Season with salt and herbs. Serve immediately

61. Carmelized Onion And Gruyere Tart Recipe

Serving: 8 | Prep: | Cook: 40mins | Ready in:

Ingredients

- 1 pie crust, homemade or refrigerated pre-made crust (or puff pastry, as Lolly'a picture here depicts)
- 1 tablespoon (or less) vegetable oil
- 1 tablespoon butter
- 1 pound sweet onions, thinly sliced

- a couple pinches of white sugar
- salt and freshly ground black pepper
- ¼ teaspoon garlic powder
- 4 eggs
- 2 cups half-and-half
- 5 ounces gruyere cheese, grated
- 2 ounces fresh grated parmesan cheese, divided

Direction

- Place pie crust in a 10" glass pie plate or springform pan.
- Using a fork, prick the crust several times on the sides and bottom.
- Sprinkle a light layer of Parmesan cheese over the bottom of the crust.
- Bake at 400° for 8 minutes.
- Remove pan from oven and set aside while preparing the filling.
- To make the filling, heat vegetable oil and butter in a large frying pan and sauté the onions over a fairly high heat for 5 minutes.
- Lower the heat, add a pinch or two of sugar, and cook for an additional 10 to 15 minutes, covered; stir occasionally until the onions are caramelized (this may take up to 30 minutes - you want a rich, brown color to the onions)
- Season with a little salt, pepper and garlic powder
- In a large bowl, lightly beat the eggs
- Stir in the half-and-half and the grated Gruyere cheese.
- Gently fold in the caramelized onions.
- Spoon the onion mixture over the partially baked crust and sprinkle with the remaining Parmesan cheese.
- Bake at 375° for 35 to 45 minutes. Allow pie to set for 10 minutes before cutting and serving. This is crucial, or the tart will not be firm enough to hold its shape when cut.
- Note: This is also very good with added ingredients, such as crab meat, chopped asparagus (sauté a minutes before adding it to the filling), sautéed mushrooms, ham, broccoli pieces, just about anything you would like…experiment with your own flavor

combinations. Add any optional ingredients to the filling just before pouring it into the partially baked pie crust.

---

62. Carrot And Apple Passover Kugel Recipe

Serving: 14 | Prep: | Cook: 25mins |Ready in:

Ingredients

- 1/2 cup vegetable oil
- 2 pounds carrots
- 2 pounds of apples
- 2 tsp. sugar
- 2/3 cup matzoh meal
- 1 tsp. ground nutmeg
- 1 tsp lemon juice
- grated zest of a small lemon
- 1 cup toasted almond slivers

Direction

- Preheat oven to 350. Lightly oil a 2 quart shallow baking dish.
- Peel the carrots and shred them in a food processor - you will net about 8 cups.
- Core and peel the apples. Shred them as well. You'll net about 2 cups.
- Coarsely chop the nuts except for a reserved 1/4 cup to top the dish with.
- Combine all but 1/4 cup of the almonds in a large bowl.
- Transfer the mix to the prepared dish.
- Sprinkle the reserved nuts on top and bake about 25 minutes, until the top just starts to brown.

---

63. Carrots With Pineapple Recipe

Serving: 4 | Prep: | Cook: 25mins |Ready in:

Ingredients

- 3 cups carrots, cut into match sticks
- 3/4 - 1 cup pineapple juice
- 1 tsp. potato starch
- 1/2 tsp. ground ginger
- 1/2 cup pineapple tidbits

Direction

- In a saucepan, combine carrots and 1/2 cup of pineapple juice.
- Bring to a boil.
- Reduce heat, cover, and simmer until tender.
- Meanwhile, in a small bowl, mix together the potato starch, remaining pineapple juice, and ginger.
- Stir into the carrot mixture along with the pineapple tidbits and heat through until the juices thicken.
- Serves 4

64. Cauli Garlic Roast Recipe

Serving: 4 | Prep: | Cook: 30mins | Ready in:

Ingredients

- 2 tsp oregano
- 1 1/2 tsp sea salt
- 1 tsp black pepper
- 3-4 tbsp vegetable broth
- 1 large head cauliflower, chopped
- 20 garlic cloves, peeled and cracked

Direction

- Preheat oven to 450F, line a deep roasting dish with parchment or foil.
- Whisk together oregano, salt, pepper and vegetable broth.
- Add cauliflower and garlic, toss to coat.
- Spread in the dish in one layer.
- Bake 30 minutes, stirring halfway through.

65. Cauliflower Delight Recipe

Serving: 6 | Prep: | Cook: 25mins | Ready in:

Ingredients

- 1 medium or large head of cauliflower, cleaned and broken into smaller, bite size pieces(florets)
- 1 stick butter
- 1 cup sliced green onions
- 1 onion, chopped
- 1 cup celery, chopped
- 1 can cream of celery soup
- 8 oz. sour cream
- 6 slices crisp cooked bacon, crumbled
- 8 oz. sharp cheddar cheese, shredded
- salt and pepper to taste
- 1/2 soup can half and half or milk
- 2 cups medium white sauce, recipe follows
- Your choice: 2 cups crushed Ritz crackers or 2 cups garlic croutons, crushed(I like both equally, I have also used potato chips)
- Medium White sauce:
- 1/4 cup butter or margarine
- 1/4 cup flour
- 1/2 teaspoon salt
- dash pepper
- 2 cups half and half or milk

Direction

- Preheat oven to 350 degrees.
- Prepare casserole dish by spraying with baking non-stick spray or you can use butter and grease bottom and sides.
- Cook Florets by either boiling, steaming or cooking in a microwave oven on high power. (All methods work well!)
- Whatever method you choose, it will take you about 5 to 7minute to cook.
- Drain and place in casserole dish. (You do not have to cook until completely tender, but just about tender)

- In saucepan, sauté onions, green onions, and celery in butter until tender.
- Stir in soup, sour cream and half and half.
- Make the medium white sauce: directions follow
- Add white sauce to saucepan with soup mixture.
- Season cauliflower with salt and pepper.
- Pour sauce over cauliflower.
- Sprinkle crumbled bacon and cheese over top
- Top with cracker or crouton crumbs.
- Bake at 350 degrees for about 15 to 20 minutes or until lightly browned.
- If you like, you can drizzle a little more butter on top of crumbs before baking. (Don't do this if using potato chips)
- White sauce directions (makes about 2 cups of medium white sauce)
- Melt butter or margarine in saucepan over low heat.
- Blend in flour, salt, and pepper.
- Stir in half and half or milk a little at a time.
- Cook and stir over low heat until smooth and thickened.

66. Cauliflower Gratin With Gruyere And Hazelnuts Recipe

Serving: 6 | Prep: | Cook: 30mins | Ready in:

Ingredients

- 1 medium head cauliflower
- 1/2 teaspoon salt
- 1/2 cup crème fraiche
- 3/4 cup grated gruyere cheese divided
- 1/4 teaspoon coarse salt
- 1/2 teaspoon freshly ground black pepper
- 3 tablespoons dry unflavored breadcrumbs
- 2 tablespoons hazelnuts toasted and coarsely chopped
- 2 tablespoons chopped chives for garnish

Direction

- Preheat oven to 375 then butter a baking dish or gratin pan.
- Cut off and discard base of cauliflower then cut the head into small individual florets.
- Bring a large pot of water to a boil and salt generously then add cauliflower and cook 5 minutes.
- Drain florets and pat dry with a clean kitchen towel.
- Place cauliflower in prepared dish and toss with crème fraiche and half of the cheese.
- Season cauliflower with salt and pepper then sprinkle remaining cheese over top.
- Top with breadcrumbs and hazelnuts then bake on center rack of oven for 25 minutes.
- Garnish with chives then serve while warm.

67. Cauliflower Gruyere Bake Recipe

Serving: 4 | Prep: | Cook: 30mins | Ready in:

Ingredients

- 1 head cauliflower,cleaned, cut and cooked
- 1 tablespoon butter
- 1/2 cups bread crumbs
- 2 tablespoons flour
- 3/4-1 cup gruyere cheese, grated or farmer's cheese
- 1 cup sour cream
- 2 eggs
- salt and white pepper to taste

Direction

- Preheat oven to 375°.
- Butter a 9-inch pie pan or oven proof dish.
- In a bowl, stir together the bread crumbs, flour and cheese.
- Pat 1/2 the mixture into the pie plate.
- Arrange the cooked cauliflower in an even layer on top of the bread crumb mixture.
- In a bowl, stir together the sour cream, eggs, salt and white pepper.

- Pour the mixture over the cauliflower.
- Sprinkle with remaining crumb mixture.
- Bake at 375° for 20 minutes.

68. Cauliflower Au Gratin Recipe

Serving: 12 | Prep: | Cook: 20mins | Ready in:

Ingredients

- 2 1/2 lb cauliflower
- 1/2 tbsp lemon juice   ***** see note
- 1/2 qt Béchamel or Mornay sauce PLUS additional 1 ounce --- hot (see recipe)
- 3/4 oz Dry bread crumbs
- 3/4 oz parmesan cheese, grated
- 1 1/4 oz butter, melted

Direction

- Separate the cauliflower into florets.
- Place the cauliflower and lemon juice into boiling, salted water.
- Return to boil, lower heat, and cover.
- Simmer until just tender.
- Do not overcook, as it will cook further in the sauce.
- Drain.
- Butter the bottom of a baking pan or hotel pan and place the cauliflower in it about 2 in deep.
- (Individual ovenproof serving dishes may also be used instead.)
- Cover with the hot sauce.
- Mix together the bread crumbs and cheese and sprinkle evenly over the top.
- Drizzle the melted butter over the top.
- Bake at 350°F for about 20 minutes to heat through.
- Brown the top under the broiler or salamander.
- Note:
- Adding lemon juice to cooking water helps to keep white vegetables white. It may be omitted if desired.
- Variations:

- Substitute cheddar cheese sauce for the béchamel or Mornay, and use grated cheddar cheese instead of parmesan for topping.
- Other vegetables may be prepared au gratin, such as asparagus, Belgian endive, broccoli, Brussels sprouts, celery, celery root, leeks, and turnips.

69. Cauliflower With Bacon And Cheese Sauce Recipe

Serving: 4 | Prep: | Cook: 10mins | Ready in:

Ingredients

- 1 large head cauliflower
- 2 quarts boiling water
- 1 Tbsp. salt
- 8 slices bacon, cut into 1/2-inch pieces
- Cheese Sauce:
- 3 Tbsp. butter or margarine
- 3 Tbsp. all-purpose flour.
- 1 1/2 cups milk mixture boils
- 1/2 cup whipping cream
- 1 tsp. salt
- 1/2 tsp. black pepper
- 1/8 tsp. nutmeg
- 1/2 cup shredded Jarlsberg or mild swiss cheese.

Direction

- Wash cauliflower. Trim and cut into flowerets. Drop into boiling salted water and cook 10 min. or until just barely tender. Drain and place into serving dish. Keep warm.
- Meanwhile fry bacon until crisp over medium heat. Drain and keep warm.
- Prepare Cheese Sauce: Melt 3 Tbsp. butter or margarine in heavy saucepan. Stir in 3 Tbsp. all-purpose flour. Cook over medium heat, stirring for 2 min. Slowly whisk in 1 1/2 cups warmed milk and heat, stirring, until mixture boils. Whisk until smooth. Add 1/2 cup whipping cream, 1 tsp. salt, 1/2 tsp. black

pepper, 1/8, tsp. nutmeg and 1/2 cup shredded Jarlsberg or mild Swiss cheese.

- Pour over cauliflower and top with bacon. Serve immediately.
- To prepare ahead: place cooked cauliflower into buttered ovenproof or microwave proof dish. Top with sauce and bacon. Cover and refrigerate. Reheat at 350°F for 20 min. or until heated through, or place into microwave oven for 5 min. on High power.

70. Cawliflower Curry Recipe

Serving: 4 | Prep: | Cook: 80mins | Ready in:

Ingredients

- 1T ginger puree(1/2T chopped ginger and water)
- 1 lg. cauliflower
- 1/2t ground tumeric
- 1 fresh green chil,sliced crosswise in thin slices
- 1cfirmly packed chopped cilantro
- 11/4t ground cumin
- 21/2t ground coriander
- 11/2t garam masala
- 1T lemon juice
- salt(optional)

Direction

- Cut cauliflower into tiny florets. In a large skillet over med heat, stir-fry ginger puree and turmeric for 2 mins. Adding a few drops of water if mixture begins to stick.
- Add chili and cilantro, stir-frying an additional 2 mins. Add cauliflower and cook for 5 mins, adding a tsp. of water if mixture becomes too dry.
- Add remaining ingredients and 4 tbsp. water
- Stir for 3-4 mins then reduce heat, cover pan, and cook, stirring occasionally, for 40 mins more or till cauliflower is for tender.

71. Charcoal Roasted Beets And Red Onions Recipe

Serving: 6 | Prep: | Cook: 90mins | Ready in:

Ingredients

- 6 small fresh beets trimmed of all but 2 inches of greens and unpeeled
- 2 medium red onions unpeeled
- 2 tablespoons extra virgin olive oil
- 1/3 cup chicken broth
- 3 tablespoons balsamic vinegar
- 1-1/2 teaspoons fresh thyme leaves divided
- 1 teaspoon salt
- 2 teaspoons freshly ground black pepper

Direction

- Prepare a moderately hot charcoal fire in a grill unit that has a cover.
- Place beets and red onions in a cast iron skillet and drizzle with olive oil then place skillet on grill rack over fire and cover the grill unit and roast the vegetables for 1-1/2 hours.
- Remove vegetables from skillet with tongs.
- Add broth, vinegar and 1 teaspoon thyme to the skillet then place over high heat and boil liquid scraping bottom of skillet for about 4 minutes.
- Season with salt and pepper.
- Peel beets and onions when cool enough to handle.
- Slice beets into julienne strips and onions into thin rings then spoon liquid over onions and beets.
- Add remaining 1/2 teaspoon thyme and stir well to combine.
- Heat briefly and serve.

72. Chayote Rellano Recipe

Serving: 6 | Prep: | Cook: 20mins | Ready in:

Ingredients

- 3 chayote squash
- 2 tablespoons vegetable oil
- 1 white onion finely chopped
- 3/4 pound lean ground beef
- 3 cloves garlic minced
- 3 jalapeno chilies seeded and minced
- 3 tomatoes peeled seeded and chopped
- 1/2 teaspoon dried oregano
- 1/2 teaspoon cumin seeds crushed
- 1/2 cup raisins
- 1/2 cup grated parmesan cheese

Direction

- Cut chayote in half lengthwise and remove seed.
- Cook squash in lightly salted water to cover until tender crisp about 25 minutes.
- Drain and scoop out most of the flesh leaving a 1/4" shell.
- Set shells aside and chop flesh.
- Preheat oven to 350.
- Heat oil in a skillet and sauté onion until soft then add ground beef, garlic and jalapenos.
- Cook over medium heat until meat is no longer pink.
- Add tomatoes, oregano, cumin, raisins and reserved chayote flesh then combine well.
- Gently pile mixture into reserved chayote shells and sprinkle with cheese.
- Set in baking dish and bake 20 minutes.

73. Chile Relleno Casserole Recipe

Serving: 6 | Prep: | Cook: 35mins | Ready in:

Ingredients

- 2 pounds pablano chilies (8-12), or 4 cans (4 ounces each) whole peeled green chilies, drained
- 1 tablespoon olive oil or vegetable oil
- 1 onion chopped

- 1 large garlic clove, minced or crushed through a press
- 1/2 teaspoon dried oregano
- 1/2 teasppon ground cumin
- 4 large eggs
- 1 8 ounce package cream cheese, softened
- 1/2 cup milk
- 1/3 cup chopped cilantro
- 1/4 cup AP flour
- 1 teaspoon salt
- 1 1/2 pounds ripe tomatoes (2 large beefsteak or 6 medium), halved, cored, and sliced crosswise 1/4 inch thick.
- 1 cup grated sharp cheddar cheese
- 1 cup grated monterey jack cheese
- 1/2 cup sliced scallions

Direction

- Roast the poblano chilies by placing them directly in the flame of a gas burner turned to high, or about 3 inches below an electric broiler. Turn them frequently until blistered and charred all over. Let them cool for a minute or two, then place in a plastic bag and let cool to room temperature. Rub away the skin with your fingers. Do not rinse (you knew that). Slit the peppers and scrape out the seeds. Cut off the stems and cut the peppers into 2 inch squares.
- Preheat the oven to 350 degrees.
- Lightly oil an 8x12 inch casserole.
- Spoon the oil into a medium skillet and place over moderate heat. Add the onion and sauté to soften, about 3 minutes. Add the garlic, oregano, and cumin; sauté 1 minute longer. If the mixture seems too dry add 1 tablespoon water.
- In a food processor or blender, combine the eggs, cream cheese, milk, cilantro, flour, and salt; blend till smooth.
- Arrange half the poblanos in the baking dish; top with half the tomato slices. Spoon on the onion mixture in an even layer. Scatter 3/4 cup each cheese over the onion mixture. Sprinkle with scallions. Pour 1/2 the egg mixture over all. Arrange the remaining

poblanos on top, and then layer with remaining tomato slices. Pour on the remaining egg mixture and top with remaining cheese.
- Bake for 35 to 40 minutes until deep golden brown and bubbly around the edges. Remove from the oven and let stand for 10 to 15 minutes before serving. Cut into squares and serve hot.

74. Chili Cheese Corn Recipe

Serving: 8 | Prep: | Cook: 30mins | Ready in:

Ingredients

- 4 cups fresh corn kernals or equal amount frozen, thawed and drained
- 1 cup grated cheddar cheese
- 1 8 ounce package cream cheese, softened
- 1 7 ounce can diced green chilies
- 2 teaspoons chili powder
- 2 teaspoons ground cumin

Direction

- Preheat oven to 350 degrees.
- Butter 1 1/2 quart baking dish.
- Mix all ingredients in large bowl and transfer to the baking dish.
- Bake until bubbly, about 30 minutes.
- Serve immediately or to make ahead, cool, cover and refrigerate up to one day.
- Reheat over medium heat.

75. Chinese Restaurant Style Sauteed Green Beans Recipe

Serving: 3 | Prep: | Cook: 10mins | Ready in:

Ingredients

- 1Tbs. less-sodium soy sauce

- 1Tbs honey
- 1Tbs unsalted butter
- 2Tbs extra-virgin olive oil
- 12 oz. green beans,trimmed
- kosher salt
- 1Tbs. minced garlic

Direction

- Combine soy sauce, honey and 1Tbs water in a small dish and set near the stove. Set a shallow serving dish near the stove too.
- In a 10" straight sided sauté pan, heat the butter with the olive oil over med-high heat. When the butter is melted, add the green beans and 1/2tsp salt and toss with tongs to coat well Cook, turning the beans occasionally, until most are well browned, shrunken, and tender,7-8 mins.(The butter in the pan will have turned dark brown.
- Reduce heat to low, add the garlic, and cook, stirring constantly with a heatproof rubber spatula, until the garlic is softened and fragrant, 15-20 seconds. Carefully add the soy mixture (you'll need to scrape the honey into the pan. Cook, stirring, until the liquid reduces to a glazy consistency that coats the beans, 30-45 secs.
- Immediately transfer the beans to a serving dish, scraping the pan with a spatula to get all the garlicky sauce. Let sit for a few minutes and serve warm.

76. Chipotle Glazed Vegetable Kebabs Recipe

Serving: 6 | Prep: | Cook: 8mins | Ready in:

Ingredients

- 2 medium-large zucchini, trimmed, chunked
- 18 small white mushrooms, stems trimmed flat with the caps
- 18 large cherry tomatoes, stemmed
- green sweet peppers, chunked

- onions, chunked
- 3/4 cup Chipotle vinaigrette (recipe follows)
- salt and freshly ground black pepper
- ===================================
==========
- Chipotle vinaigrette
- This dressing is not too fiery hot, and can be used on salads ranging from plain (though not delicate) greens to main-dish salads featuring meat, poultry, or seafood.
- It only takes minutes to prepare.
- 3 tablespoons sherry wine vinegar
- 1 tablespoon balsamic vinegar
- 2 garlic cloves, chopped
- 2 canned chipotles en adobo, chopped
- 2 tablespoons adobo sauce from the chipotle can
- 1/2 teaspoon salt
- 2/3 cup olive oil
- freshly ground black pepper
- *****chipotle chile:
- This hot chile is actually a dried, smoked JALAPEÑO. It has a wrinkled, dark brown skin and a smoky, sweet, almost chocolaty flavor.
- Chipotles can be found dried, pickled and canned in adobo sauce.
- Chipotles are generally added to stews and sauces; the pickled variety are often eaten as appetizers.

Direction

- Cut each zucchini crosswise into 9 equally thick slices.
- Trim the slices to form cubes.
- Divide the vegetables, alternating them, among 6 flat metal skewers.
- Be certain to arrange the flat sides of the zucchini cubes and the stem ends of the mushrooms so they will get the maximum exposure to the fire.
- Light a direct heat charcoal fire and let it burn down to medium-hot (5 seconds to "ouch") or preheat a gas grill to medium-high.
- Position the rack about 6 inches above the heat source.

- When the grill is ready, lightly brush the kebabs with some of the vinaigrette.
- Lay the kebabs on the rack, cover and grill, turning every 2 minutes and basting often with the vinaigrette, until it is used up and the vegetables are lightly colored by the grill, 6 to 8 minutes total.
- Season with salt and pepper and slide the vegetables off the skewers onto plates.
- Serve hot.
- The Chipotle Vinaigrette:
- 1. In a food processor or blender, combine the sherry vinegar, balsamic vinegar, garlic, chipotles, adobo and its sauce, and salt. Process until smooth. With the motor running, gradually add the oil through the hole in the lid: the dressing will thicken. Season with pepper and pulse to blend. Adjust the seasoning and pulse again just before using.
- 2. Use immediately or cover tightly and refrigerate for up to 3 days. The dressing may separate; return to room temperature, then rewhisk to blend.

77. Christmas Corn Casserole Recipe

Serving: 8 | Prep: | Cook: 45mins | Ready in:

Ingredients

- 1/2 onion, chopped
- 1/2 red bell pepper, chopped
- 1/2 green bell pepper, chopped
- 1/2 cup (1 stick) butter
- 2 eggs, slightly beaten
- 1 can creamed corn
- 1 can whole kernel corn, drained
- 1 box "jiffy" corn muffin mix
- 8 oz sour cream
- 2 cups shredded cheddar cheese
- milk
- paprika

Direction

- Sauté the onion and bell pepper in butter.
- Mix together the 2 eggs, 2 cans of corn and the corn muffin mix.
- Add the onions and peppers, and pour all into a 9/ 13 casserole dish.
- Mix the sour cream with a little milk and spread on top of casserole.
- Sprinkle cheese and paprika over all.
- Bake at 325 degrees for 45 minutes or until done.

78. Cider Glazed Roots With Cinnamon Walnuts Recipe

Serving: 6 | Prep: | Cook: 80mins | Ready in:

Ingredients

- 3lbs assorted root vegetables(beets,celeriac,carrots,parsnips,rutabags,turnip)cut into 1" pieces
- 1c apple cider
- 1/4c dark brown sugar.
- 1/2tsp salt,plus more to taste
- 1/4tsp pepper1/2c chopped walnuts
- 1Tbs butter
- 1/8tsp ground cinnamon

Direction

- Preheat oven to 400
- If using parsnips, quarter lengthwise and remove woodsy core before cutting into 1: pieces. Whisk cider, brown sugar, 1/2tsp of salt and pepper in a 9x13" baking dish till sugar is dissolved. Add root vegetables and toss to coat. Cover the baking dish with foil.
- Bake 20 mins. Uncover, stir the vegetables. Continue cooking, uncovered, stirring every 20 mins. or so till the vegetables are glazed and tender, about 1 hour more.
- Meanwhile, place walnuts in a small skillet and cook over med-low heat, stirring

constantly, till fragrant and lightly browned, 2 to 6 mins.
- Remove from heat and add butter, cinnamon and a pinch of salt. Stir till butter melts and nuts are coated. Spread on plate to cool slightly.
- Transfer vegetables to serving dish and sprinkle with cinnamon walnuts.

79. Classic Baked Beans Recipe

Serving: 6 | Prep: | Cook: 20mins | Ready in:

Ingredients

- 4 strips thick-sliced bacon
- 1 cup onion, minced
- 2 can pinto beans, drained and rinsed (15-oz. each)
- 1 can crushed tomatoes (15-oz.)
- 1/2 cup ketchup
- 1/2 cup brown sugar
- 3 Tbsp. worcestershire sauce
- 3 Tbsp. stone ground mustard
- 2 tsp. Tabasco, or to taste
- salt to taste
- 2-3 sliced rye bread, buttered, pulsed in a food processor

Direction

- Preheat the oven to 400*F.
- Sauté bacon in a cast iron skillet over medium heat until crisp.
- Drain on a paper towel lined plate, pour off all but 1 Tbsp. drippings.
- Sweat onions in drippings until soft, 5 minutes.
- Add remaining ingredients (except rye bread crumbs) and bacon pieces.
- Top beans with crumbs and bake until bubbly, 20 minutes.
- Beans may also be baked in individual serving dishes.

- Divide mixture among dishes, top with crumbs and bake

80. Cole Slaw Southern Style Recipe

Serving: 6 | Prep: | Cook: |Ready in:

Ingredients

- 1 large head green cabbage, cored, and very finely shredded
- 3 Kirby (pickling) cucumbers, peeled, seeded and sliced paper thin
- 2 tbs kosher salt
- For Dressing:
- 1/2 c white vinegar
- 1/2 c granulated sugar
- 1/2 tsp salt
- 1 tbs dijon-style mustard
- 1/4 c vegetable oil
- 1/4 c heavy cream
- 2 tbs sour cream
- salt and fresh ground pepper to taste

Direction

- Mix together the shredded cabbage and sliced cucumber in a large colander
- Toss well with the salt and leave to wilt for 20 minutes or overnight
- Squeeze the slaw firmly by handfuls to extract as much liquid as possible, then use your fingers to toss and loosen the squeezed slaw
- Toss it into a large bowl
- Dressing:
- Bring the vinegar, sugar, and salt to a boil in a small saucepan over medium heat, stirring just until the sugar is dissolved.
- Boil for three minutes and whisk in the mustard and oil
- Pour the hot dressing over the reserved slaw and stir well to blend
- Allow to cool slightly before stirring in the heavy cream and sour cream.
- Taste and adjust the salt and pepper

- Refrigerate before serving

81. Collards In Homemade BBQ Sauce Recipe

Serving: 4 | Prep: | Cook: 25mins |Ready in:

Ingredients

- 1 lb collard greens, destemmed and chopped
- 1 1/2 cups ketchup
- 1/2 cup water
- 2 tbsp. brown sugar
- 1 small onion, chopped
- 2 tbsp. lemon juice
- 1 tbsp rice vinegar OR apple cider vinegar
- 1 tbsp. worcestershire sauce
- 1 clove garlic, minced
- 1 tsp. spicy brown mustard
- 1/4 tsp. hot sauce

Direction

- Boil the collard greens for 25 min, meanwhile make the BBQ sauce.
- For the BBQ sauce: In a medium saucepan, combine the rest of the ingredients, bring to a boil. Reduce the heat, cover and simmer for 15 min. Stir occasionally while cooking.
- Drain the collards and toss with the BBQ sauce. Serve warm as a side dish.
- You may have more BBQ sauce than you need. Use as much as you like, store the rest in a zip lock in freezer. Great for using with any meat.

82. Colourful Veggies With Serious Kick Recipe

Serving: 6 | Prep: | Cook: 50mins |Ready in:

Ingredients

- 4 cups vegetable broth
- 2 cups canned diced tomatoes
- ½ cup chopped onions
- ½ cup diced carrots
- ½ cup sliced celery
- 2 cups shredded green cabbage
- 1 tablespoon lemon juice
- ½ teaspoon oregano
- 1 bay leaf
- Pinch black pepper
- 1 ½ cups cooked lentils
- ¼ - ½ tsp Tabasco

Direction

- Bring all ingredients except lentils and Tabasco to a boil.
- Cover, lower heat to simmer 20 minutes.
- Add lentils and Tabasco, stir and re-cover.
- Cook 30 minutes, remove bay leaf, and serve

83. Corkys Memphis Coleslaw Recipe

Serving: 12 | Prep: | Cook: | Ready in:

Ingredients

- 1 medium head green cabbage; shredded
- 2 medium carrots; grated
- 1 green pepper; finely diced
- 2 tablespoons onion; grated
- 2 cups mayonnaise
- 3/4 cup sugar
- 1/4 cup Dijon mustard
- 1/4 cup cider vinegar
- 2 tablespoons celery seeds
- 1 teaspoon salt
- 1/8 teaspoon white pepper
- 1/4 cup Franks or Texas Pete Hot Sauce; optional

Direction

- Mix vegetables in a bowl. Mix remaining ingredients in another.
- Mix together and toss well.
- Cover and refrigerate 3-4 hours.

84. Corn Casserole Recipe

Serving: 6 | Prep: | Cook: 45mins | Ready in:

Ingredients

- 3 cans creamed corn
- 2 eggs slightly beaten
- 1 1/2 C. saltine cracker crumbs
- 2/3 C. margarine
- 2 tsp. sugar
- 2/3 tsp. salt

Direction

- Preheat oven to 350°
- Melt butter and toss cracker crumbs in the melted butter.
- Combine corn, eggs and 1 cup saltines in butter, sugar and salt.
- Pour into a 1 1/2 quart oven proof dish that has been sprayed with cooking spray
- Top with remaining cracker crumbs.
- Bake for 30 minutes covered with aluminum foil.
- Uncover for an additional 15 minutes or until golden brown and is set.

85. Corn Custard Souffle Recipe

Serving: 6 | Prep: | Cook: 65mins | Ready in:

Ingredients

- 1 cup canned or fresh corn (chopped slightly)
- 2 3/4 cup milk
- 1 teaspoon salt
- 1 cup yellow cornmeal

- 1/2 cup sweet butter cut into 1" pieces
- 3 eggs, room temp, separated
- 2 teaspoons sugar or to taste
- 1/4 teaspoon nutmeg.

Direction

- In medium saucepan boil corn in 2 cups of milk, salt.
- Slowly add cornmeal.
- Stir until very thick, remove from heat and stir in the butter.
- Add rest of the 3/4 milk.
- Blend in yolks, one at a time.
- Add sugar.
- This part can be made up to 6 hours ahead of time.
- Then before baking, beat whites, stiff not dry.
- Fold in 1/4 of whites then fold in the rest.
- Pour into 2 quart soufflé dish.
- Bake 10 minutes at 400
- Turn down to 375 for 50-55 minutes.
- Enjoy!

86. Corn Fritters Recipe

Serving: 815 | Prep: | Cook: 10mins | Ready in:

Ingredients

- 2 cups of canned or fresh corn
- 1 egg
- Add milk to liquid from corn to make 1 cup
- 3/4 tsp. salt
- 2 tsp. baking powder
- 1 and 1/2 cups flour

Direction

- Drain 2 cups of canned corn - reserve the liquid
- Add milk to the liquid to make one cup
- Sift 1 and 1/2 cups flour, 2 tsp, baking powder, 3/4 tsp. salt

- In a separate bowl combine 1 egg beaten, milk mix, corn
- Add dry ingredients and mix together
- Drop batter from a Tablespoon into a pot of hot oil
- When lightly brown, turn fritters over and brown the other side.
- Drain on paper towels and serve immediately
- Goes well with chicken or ham

87. Couscous And Feta Stuffed Peppers Recipe

Serving: 4 | Prep: | Cook: 40mins | Ready in:

Ingredients

- vegetable oil cooking spray
- 1-1/4 cups chicken or vegetable broth (fat-free??)
- 2/3 cup couscous
- 1 x-tra large red bell peppers, or yellow, or.....
- 2 tsp EVOO
- 1/2 cup chopped onion
- 6 oz zucchini, quartered lengthwise and sliced thinly across
- 6 oz yellow squash, quartered lengthwise and sliced thinly across
- 1/2 tsp fennel seeds
- 1/2 tsp dried oregano
- 1/2 tsp salt (kosher or sea)
- 1 cup cherry tomatoes, halved
- 15 oz canned chickpeas, drained and rinsed
- 4 oz crumbled feta cheese, ~ 1 cup
- 3 Tbsp tomato paste

Direction

- Preheat oven to 350F, coat a small baking dish with cooking spray.
- In medium saucepan, bring the broth to a boil, add the couscous, cover and remove from the heat, set aside.

- Cut the stems and top 1/2 inch off the bell peppers and scoop out the seeds and white membrane.
- Place peppers upright in a baking dish and roast them for 15 minutes or until they soften, then remove from oven and set aside.
- In a non-stick skillet, heat the EVOO , add the onion, zucchini, yellow squash, fennel seeds, oregano, and salt, then cook over medium heat for 5 minutes or until vegetables are softened.
- Remove skillet from heat, stir tomatoes, chickpeas, and tomato paste.
- With a fork, scrape the couscous into the skillet and toss with the vegetables.
- Stir in the feta cheese.
- Fill the peppers with the couscous/vegetable mixture. Place on the coated baking dish, then bake for 15 minutes.
- Serve immediately.

88. Cowboy Pinto Beans Recipe

Serving: 8 | Prep: | Cook: 120mins | Ready in:

Ingredients

- 1 pound dried pinto beans
- 8 cups water
- 1/4 pound salt pork (as lean as you can find)
- 1 14-ounce can whole tomatoes, with juice
- 4 large cloves garlic, crushed
- 1 large onion, chopped
- 2 tablespoons chili powder
- 1 teaspoon ground cumin
- 3 jalapenos seeded and chopped
- 1 tablespoon worcestershire sauce
- 1 cup barbecue sauce
- 1 teaspoon salt

Direction

- Wash and pick over beans.
- Make several cuts into the salt pork down to but not through the rind.

- Combine all ingredients except salt in a heavy saucepan.
- Bring to a boil then reduce heat to low simmer.
- Cook very slowly covered.
- Stir beans up from the bottom occasionally and add water if they start looking dry.
- Cook for at least 2 hours.

89. Cranberry Coleslaw Anthonys Home Port Seattle Recipe

Serving: 8 | Prep: | Cook: | Ready in:

Ingredients

- 1 cup dried cranberries
- 2 cups red cabbage, thinly sliced (about 1/4 of a cabbage)
- 2 cups green cabbage
- 1/4 cup red onion very thinly sliced
- 1/3 cup apple cider vinegar
- 1/3 cup canola oil
- 1/4 cup granulated sugar
- 1 tablespoon coarse salt (sea salt or kosher salt)
- 1 teaspoon celery seed
- 1/4 cup shredded carrot (optional)

Direction

- In a food processor combine vinegar, oil, sugar, salt and celery seed. Reserve this mixture.
- Put the slicing blade onto the food processor and thinly slice red and green cabbage and red onion. Combine this with the dressing, stirring well.
- Add cranberries, mix and refrigerate several hours, stirring occasionally.
- Drain liquid from the coleslaw before serving.
- This is extremely simple to prepare and involves little preparation or clean-up. Can be made up to two days in advance and keeps well for a week. Enjoy!

90. Cranberry Stuffed Winter Squash Recipe

Serving: 4 | Prep: | Cook: 73mins | Ready in:

Ingredients

- 2 medium winter squash
- 1 Tbs. unsalted butter-- melted salt
- 2 Tbs. unsalted butter
- 1/2 cup finely chopped yellow onions
- 1 Tps. minced garlic
- 2 cups coarsely chopped unpeeled tart apple
- 1/2 cup coarsely chopped fresh cranberries
- 1/2 Tps. ground cinnamon
- 1/4 Tps. freshly grated nutmeg
- 2 cups unseasoned fine dry bread crumbs
- 1 cup grated cheddar, jack or swiss
- 1/4 pound sliced smoked bacon

Direction

- Preheat oven to 400F. Cut the squash in half lengthwise and scoop out seeds and stringy portions. Brush the cut sides of the squash halves with the melted butter and season to taste with salt. Arrange, cut side down, on a lightly greased baking pan. Pour in hot water to a depth of 1/2 inch and bake until barely tender when pierced with a wooden skewer, about 35-45 minutes.
- Melt 2 Tbs. butter in a skillet over medium-high heat. Add the onions and sauté until almost soft, about 4 minutes. Stir in the garlic, apple, and cranberries and sauté until the apples are soft, about four minutes longer. Stir in the cinnamon and nutmeg. In a bowl, combine the apple mixture, bread crumbs, and cheese. Mound in the cavities of the baked squash halves and arrange in a baking dish
- Bake until the squash is tender, the filling is heated through, and cheese melts, about 20 minutes. Meanwhile, fry the bacon in a skillet until crisp. Drain on paper towels, then crumble. Remove the squash from oven,

sprinkle with the crumbled bacon, and serve hot

91. Creamed Cabbage Bahama Dish Recipe

Serving: 6 | Prep: | Cook: 80mins | Ready in:

Ingredients

- 1 - head of green cabbage cut into wedges
- 1 - tablespoon lime juice
- 4- strips of bacon
- 1/4 - pound white cheddar cheese grated
- 2 -tablespoons butter
- 2 - tablespoons flour
- 3/4 - cup milk
- freshly ground black pepper
- salt to taste

Direction

- Place cabbage in a Dutch oven and cover with water,
- Add the lime juice and salt and bring it to a boil.
- Cook the cabbage for one hour or until the leaves become soft. Drain well.
- Preheat oven to 350 degrees f. and line a 9x13 baking pan with the bacon strips.
- Add a layer of the boiled cabbage and a layer of cheese.
- Repeat until all the cabbage and cheese have been used up.
- In a heavy saucepan, melt the butter and stir in the flour.
- When well combined, add the milk, stirring constantly to prevent lumps.
- Add the black pepper, cayenne pepper, and salt and cook until slightly thickened
- Pour the sauce over the top of the cabbage.
- Bake in the oven until the top is bubbly and brown
- About 20 minutes

92. Creamed Corn With Bacon And Blue Cheese Recipe

Serving: 6 | Prep: | Cook: 10mins | Ready in:

Ingredients

- 5 medium ears fresh corn with husks and silk removed
- 4 oz (about 4 slices) of bacon cut into 1/2 inch pieces
- 1 medium shallot, minced
- 1 medium garlic clove, minced
- 1 1/2 c heavy cream
- 1/2 tsp minced fresh thyme leaves
- Pinch cayenne pepper
- 2 oz blue cheese crumbled (about 1/2 cup)
- salt and ground black pepper

Direction

- Cut the kernels from 3 ears of corn and transfer them into a medium bowl.
- Firmly scrape the cobs with the BACK of a butter knife to collect the pulp and milk in the same bowl.
- Grate the remaining 2 ears of corn on the coarse side of a box grater set in the bowl with cut kernels.
- Firmly scrape these cobs with the back of a butter knife to collect the pulp and milk in the same bowl.
- Cook the bacon in a large non-stick skillet over med-high heat until crisp and browned, about 5 minutes.
- Transfer onto a paper towel lined plate to drain.
- Remove and discard all but 2 tbs of the bacon drippings from the pan.
- Add the shallot and cook until softened but not browned, 1-2 minutes.
- Add the garlic and cook until aromatic, about 30 seconds.
- Stir in the corn kernels and pulp, the cream, thyme and cayenne.

- Bring the mixture to a simmer and cook, adjusting the heat as necessary and stirring occasionally, until the corn is tender and the mixture has thickened, 10-15 minutes.
- Remove the pan from the heat and stir in the cheese.
- Adjust the seasonings with salt and pepper and serve immediately.

93. Creamy Cheesey Broccoli Casserole Recipe

Serving: 12 | Prep: | Cook: 35mins | Ready in:

Ingredients

- 1 large bag frozen broccoli florets
- 2 T butter
- 1 dash red pepper flakes
- seasoned salt
- garlic pepper
- juice from a lemon wedge
- 1/4 white onion, finely diced
- 1 small can water chestnuts, drained chopped
- 1 can cream of mushroom & roasted garlic soup (or cream of celery)
- 1 small can mushrooms, drained
- 1/4 c real mayo (I like Dukes)
- 1/4 c sour cream
- 1 well beaten egg
- 8 oz cream cheese, room temp, cut into chunks for faster melting (optional)
- 2 cups Classic Melts Shredded cheese (divided - or whatever blend you like. Use something that melts well. Havartti and other white cheeses are good, too).
- pepperidge Farm herb stuffing mix

Direction

- Cook together on stovetop: broccoli, butter, seasonings, lemon juice, onion, water chestnuts, mushrooms, (I use my large, deep skillet)

- Cook about 10 minutes, broccoli is cooked and onions are soft
- Drain well
- Add to large mixing bowl and stir in all remaining ingredients except half the shredded cheese and the stuffing mix
- Spread in 9x13 Pyrex baking dish
- Cover with remaining cheese
- Sprinkle stuffing mix on top
- Bake at 350 until bubbly, and cheese is melted

94. Creamy Cheesey Confetti Fried Corn With Bacon Recipe

Serving: 6 | Prep: | Cook: 8mins | Ready in:

Ingredients

- 8 bacon slices, chopped
- 4 cups fresh sweet corn kernels (about 8 ears)
- 1 medium-size white onion, chopped
- 1/3 cup chopped red bell pepper
- 1/3 cup chopped green bell pepper
- 1 (8-ounce) package cream cheese, cubed
- 1/2 cup half-and-half
- 1 teaspoon salt
- 1 teaspoon pepper

Direction

- Cook chopped bacon in a large skillet until crisp; remove bacon, and drain on paper towels, reserving 2 tablespoons drippings in skillet.
- Set bacon aside.
- Sauté corn, onion, and bell peppers in hot drippings in skillet over medium-high heat 6 minutes or until tender.
- Add cream cheese and half-and-half, stirring until cream cheese melts.
- Stir in salt, and pepper.
- Top with bacon.

95. Creamy Savoy Cabbage Recipe

Serving: 6 | Prep: | Cook: 15mins | Ready in:

Ingredients

- 1 3/4 pounds savoy cabbage, shredded
- 1 medium onion, finely schopped
- 1/2 cup diced bacon
- 2 tbsp butter
- ground pepper
- nutmeg
- 1 1/4 cups heavy cream

Direction

- 1. Halve the cabbage, cut out the stalk and shred the leaves finely. Sauté the onion and bacon in the butter until onion is translucent and bacon is crisp.
- 2. Add the cabbage, season with salt, pepper and nutmeg to taste and cook briefly. Pour in the cream and reduce the heat to low until the mixture is creamy and the cabbage is tender.

96. Crispy Carrot Casserole Recipe

Serving: 6 | Prep: | Cook: 35mins | Ready in:

Ingredients

- 1 bunch of carrots
- 1 tsp salt
- 1 egg...beaten
- 1/4 tsp pepper
- 1/3 to 1/2 cup Grated cheese
- 1/2 cup cracker crumbs
- 1 1/2 cups milk
- 4 tbsp melted butter or margarine
- 1 tbsp sugar

Direction

- Cook and crush carrots.
- Add egg and grated cheese.
- Beat thoroughly.

- Add milk, sugar, salt, pepper, cracker crumbs and butter.
- Place in lightly greased casserole dish.
- Top with additional buttered cracker crumbs.
- Bake in 375* oven for 35 minutes.

97. Crispy Zucchini Sticks Recipe

Serving: 4 | Prep: | Cook: 10mins |Ready in:

Ingredients

- 4 medium zucchini (about 1-1/2 lb)
- 1/2 cup bread crumbs
- 1/4 cup parmesan cheese
- 1/2 tsp salt
- 1/4 tsp black pepper
- 1/2 tsp cayenne
- 4 tsp italian seasoning
- 2 egg whites
- ranch dressing, optional
- marinara sauce, optional

Direction

- Preheat the oven to 450°.
- Spray a large baking sheet with olive-oil cooking spray.
- Cut each zucchini into 3" pieces. Then quarter each piece into sticks. Set aside.
- Mix the crumbs and next 4 ingredients. Finely grind the Italian seasoning with your fingertips and add to the crumb mix.
- Stir until thoroughly combined.
- Whisk egg whites until almost frothy and pour into a shallow dish. Dip each zucchini stick into the egg, then completely coat with the crumb mixture.
- Place on the baking sheet.
- Spray with the olive-oil cooking spray.
- Bake for 9-10 minutes, until crispy.
- Serve with marinara sauce and/or low-fat ranch dressing for dipping.
- Per serving without sauce or dressing, approximately 96 calories; 2.3 g. fat; 13.7 g.

carbohydrates; 3.7 g. sugars; 2.4 g. fiber; 6.3 g. protein

98. Crock Pot Beans Recipe

Serving: 12 | Prep: | Cook: 240mins |Ready in:

Ingredients

- 1 (3lb) can pork and beans, slight drained
- 1 large onion, chopped
- 1/2 cup bell pepper, chopped
- 1 pound ground beef, lightly browned and drained
- 1/2 pound hot link sausage, sliced thin
- 1 pkg sloppy joe mix
- 1/2 cup barbecue sauce
- 1/2 cup catchup
- 1/2 cup brown sugar
- 2 tablespoons yellow mustard
- 2 tablespoons worcestershire sauce

Direction

- Mix all of the above together
- Cook in crock pot low for approximately 4 hours

99. Crock Pot Stuffed Peppers Recipe

Serving: 2 | Prep: | Cook: 360mins |Ready in:

Ingredients

- 6 large green bell peppers
- 1 pound extra-lean ground beef
- 1 cup rice, uncooked
- 1 large onion, chopped
- 1 large carrot, shredded
- 1 teaspoon beef bouillon granules
- 1/2 teaspoon salt

- 1/2 teaspoon pepper
- 1 can condensed tomato soup
- 1 can water

Direction

- Cut the top off and remove seeds from green peppers. Wash and set aside.
- Combine ground beef, uncooked rice, onion, carrot, bouillon, salt, and pepper in a large mixing bowl. Any other seasonings that you like may also be used - (oregano, parsley, garlic powder, etc.).
- Stuff each pepper about 2/3 full (rice will need room to swell up). Stand the peppers side-by-side in the slow cooker.
- In a small mixing bowl, combine tomato soup and water, and pour mixture over the peppers. Cook on LOW for 6 to 8 hours.

100. Crockpot Beans Recipe

Serving: 6 | Prep: | Cook: 300mins | Ready in:

Ingredients

- 1 15-oz can pork and beans (undrained)
- 1 15-oz can kidney beans, drained
- 1 15-oz can lima beans, drained
- 1 15-oz butter beans, drained
- 1/2 pound bacon, chopped (optional)
- 1 sweet onion, chopped
- 1/2 cup ketchup
- 1/2 cup brown sugar
- 2 Tbs. worcestershire sauce
- 1/2 cup cheddar cheese, grated

Direction

- Mix all the ingredients together. Pour the mixture into a crockpot and cook on low for 5 hours.

101. Cucumber Feta Salad Recipe

Serving: 4 | Prep: | Cook: 10mins | Ready in:

Ingredients

- 1 english cucumber
- 1/2 cup cider vinegar (I prefer rice wine vinegar)
- 1/2 cup water
- 3 Tbsp sugar
- 1 tspn kosher salt
- ~ 1 cup crumbled feta cheese
- fresh mint, chopped, to tasted

Direction

- Very thinly slice the cucumber (with or without skin)
- Spread evenly in a shallow baking dish.
- Combine sugar, salt, vinegar, and water in a small sauce pan.
- Over very low heat, heat the mixture until the salt and sugar dissolve completely.
- Remove sauce pan from heat, allow to cool and then pour over the layered cucumbers.
- Cover the dish and place in refrigerator for at least 3 hours.
- When ready to serve, drain the cucumber slices well.
- Place the cucumber on a serving dish, crumble feta cheese over the cukes, and garnish with mint.
- Enjoy!!

102. Cucumber Raita Recipe

Serving: 2 | Prep: | Cook: | Ready in:

Ingredients

- 2-1/4 cups plain yogurt
- 1 large cucumber peeled and shredded

- 1 fresh hot green chile seeded and finely chopped
- 1/2 teaspoon ground toasted cumin
- 1/4 teaspoon cayenne pepper
- 1/4 teaspoon salt

Direction

- Whisk yogurt in a bowl until smooth and lightened.
- Add cucumber, green chili, toasted cumin and cayenne then stir.
- Chill well and stir in salt just before serving.

---

103. Cucumber And Wakame Seaweed Salad Sunomono Recipe

Serving: 1 | Prep: | Cook: |Ready in:

Ingredients

- 1 small cucumber
- 1 cup wakame seaweed (softened)
- 4 tbsp rice wine vinegar
- 2 tbsp sugar
- 1/2 tsp salt

Direction

- Cut softened wakame seaweed into about 2inch-long pieces. Slice cucumber into thin rounds. Put salt over cucumber slices and set aside for 20 minutes. Squeeze cucumber slices to remove the liquid. Mix vinegar and sugar in a bowl. Add wakame seaweed and cucumber slices in the bowl and mix well.

---

104. Curried Cauliflower And Peas Recipe

Serving: 6 | Prep: | Cook: 20mins |Ready in:

Ingredients

- 1 head of cauliflower
- 1 large onion sliced
- 1 cup frozen peas, thawed
- heavy cream as desired
- minced garlic if desired.
- salt, pepper, curry powder, chicken bouillon powder to taste
- black sesame seeds

Direction

- Cook cauliflower by favorite method until crisp tender.
- In a skillet with some oil or butter, sauté onion until tender.
- Add cauliflower, peas and salt and pepper and curry powder and chicken bouillon to taste.
- Cook till well heated and seasonings blended. Add a few tablespoon of cream to make a thin sauce.
- Sprinkle black sesame seeds on top.
- Serves 4 to 6

---

105. Curried Chickpeas And Spinach Recipe

Serving: 4 | Prep: | Cook: 240mins |Ready in:

Ingredients

- 2 Tbs ghee or vegetable oil
- 1 1/2 cups chopped onions
- 4 cloves garlic, minced
- 1/2 tsp cumin
- 1 pkg frozen chopped spinach or 3 cups chopped kale
- 1 1/2 Tbs curry powder
- 1 tsp ground ginger
- 1 tsp ground coriander
- 1 1/2 cups vegetable broth
- 3 cups cooked chickpeas (canned is fine)
- 1 cup chopped tomatoes
- 1/4 tsp salt or to taste

Direction

- Combine all ingredients in your crockpot and let it cook on low 7 to 8 hours, or on high for 4 hours.
- Use a main dish with a salad or a side dish with poultry or meet

---

106. Debs Squash Casserole Recipe

Serving: 8 | Prep: | Cook: 20mins |Ready in:

Ingredients

- 4 cups cooked yellow squash, mashed
- 1 stick butter
- 1 large onion, sliced
- 4 cloves garlic, minced
- 6 slices of hickory smoked bacon,cooked crisp and crumbled(I use Wrights)
- 1 cup sliced green onions
- 1/2 cup heavy cream
- 1 can cream of mushroom soup
- 1 cup sour cream
- salt and pepper to taste
- 1 cup crushed Ritz crackers
- 8 oz. sharp cheddar cheese, shredded

Direction

- Preheat oven to 350
- Sauté onions and garlic in butter until tender.
- Place squash, sour cream, green onions, soup and cream in a large bowl.
- Mix well and season with salt and pepper.
- Spoon squash into buttered baking dish or casserole dish.
- Top with onion mixture.
- Sprinkle with bacon and cheese.
- Top with cracker crumbs.
- Bake at 350 degrees for 15 to 20 minutes or until nicely browned.

---

107. Decadent Cream Braised Brussels Sprouts Recipe

Serving: 5 | Prep: | Cook: 45mins |Ready in:

Ingredients

- 1 ¼ lb. Brussels sprouts
- 3 Tbs unsalted butter
- ¼ tsp coarse sea salt, plus more to taste
- 1 cup heavy cream
- 1 Tbs fresh lemon juice, or more to taste

Direction

- First things first: buy good sprouts. They should feel firm and have tight, shiny-edged leaves. I like to buy medium-size ones, with heads that measure, say, 1 to 1 ¼ inches in diameter. You could buy littler ones, if you like, but don't buy them any bigger. I find that the larger they are, the stronger – i.e. more bitter – their flavor.
- First, prep the Brussels sprouts. Trim the stem end of each sprout and pull off any ragged or nasty outer leaves. Cut the sprouts in half from stem end to tip, and then cut each half in half again. Ultimately, you want little wedges.
- In a large (12-inch) skillet, melt the butter over medium-high heat. Add the Brussels sprouts and salt. Cook, stirring occasionally, until the sprouts are nicely browned in spots, about 5 minutes or so. I like mine to get some good color here, so that they have a sweetly caramelized flavor.
- Pour in the cream, stir to mix, and then cover the pot. Reduce the heat to low or medium low: you want to keep the pan at a slow simmer. Braise until the sprouts are tender enough to be pierced easily with the tip of a paring knife, about 30-35 minutes. The cream will have reduced some and will have taken on a creamy tan color.
- Remove the lid, and stir in the lemon juice. Taste for seasoning, and adjust as necessary. Let the pan simmer, uncovered, for a minute

or two to thicken the cream to a glaze that loosely coats the sprouts. Serve immediately.

---

108. Decadent Spinach Gratin Recipe

Serving: 8 | Prep: | Cook: 40mins | Ready in:

Ingredients

- 4 tablespoons (1/2 stick)unsalted butter.
- 4 cups chopped yellow oions (2 large)
- 1/4 cup flour
- 1/4 teaspoon grated nutmeg
- 1 cup heavy cream.
- 2 cups milk.
- 3 pounds frozen chopped spinach,defrost (%/10 ounce)packages
- 1 cup freshly grated parmesan cheese
- 1 tablespoon kosher salt.
- 1/2 teaspoon freshly ground pepper.
- 1/2 cup grated gruyere cheese.

Direction

- PREHEAT the oven: 425 degrees
- Melt the butter in a heavy-bottomed sauté pan over medium heat.
- Add the onions and sauté' until translucent, about 15 minutes.
- Add the flour and the nutmeg and cook, stirring, for 2 or more minutes.
- Add the cream and milk and cook until thickened.
- Squeeze as much water from the defrosted spinach as possible.
- Add the spinach to the sauce.
- Add 1/2 cup of the Parmesan cheese, mix well.
- Season to taste, with salt and pepper.
- Transfer the spinach to a baking dish and sprinkle the remaining 1/2 cup Parmesan and Gruyere on top.
- BAKE: 20 minutes until hot and bubbly.
- Serve hot

---

109. Delicious Creamed Cabbage With Bacon Recipe

Serving: 6 | Prep: | Cook: 10mins | Ready in:

Ingredients

- 2 slices bacon, crisp-cooked and crumbled
- 1/2 cup finely diced, cooked country ham
- 1/2 cup chopped onion
- 7 cups shredded green cabbage
- 1/2 cup heavy cream
- pepper to taste

Direction

- In a large pot, layer in order: bacon, ham, onion, cabbage, pepper
- Pour cream over all
- Bring to a simmer, reduce heat to medium
- Cook 10 minutes, stirring gently, occasionally OR until cabbage is soft and liquid is reduced to a niche thick sauce
- Delicious!

---

110. Delightful Palak Paneer Recipe

Serving: 6 | Prep: | Cook: 20mins | Ready in:

Ingredients

- 6 tablespoons olive oil
- 2 cloves garlic, chopped
- 1 tablespoon grated fresh ginger root
- 2 dried red chile peppers
- 1/2 cup finely chopped onion
- 2 teaspoons ground cumin
- 1 teaspoon ground coriander
- 1 teaspoon ground turmeric
- 3/4 cup sour cream

- 3 pounds fresh spinach, torn
- 1 large tomato, quartered
- 4 sprigs fresh cilantro leaves
- 8 ounces ricotta cheese
- coarse sea salt to taste

Direction

- In a large saucepan heat 3 tablespoons of olive oil and sauté garlic, 1/2 tablespoon of ginger, red chilies (optional ingredient) and onion until brown.
- Mix in the cumin, coriander, turmeric and sour cream (add more or less to achieve desired creaminess).
- Add the spinach, handfuls at a time until it is cooked down, about 15 minutes total.
- Remove from heat and allow to cool slightly.
- Pour spinach mixture into a blender or food processor and add the tomato, the remaining 1/2 tablespoon of ginger, and cilantro (add more or less according to taste).
- Blend for 15 to 30 seconds, or until the spinach is finely chopped.
- Pour back into the saucepan and keep warm over low heat.
- In a medium frying pan heat 3 tablespoons of olive oil over medium heat, and fry cheese until browned; drain and add to spinach.
- Cook for 10 minutes on low heat.
- Season with salt to taste.

111.	Dijon Brussel Sprouts Recipe

Serving: 4 | Prep: | Cook: 8mins | Ready in:

Ingredients

- 1 lb. brussel sprouts
- 1 TB melted butter
- 1 TB honey
- 2 tsp Dijon mustard
- 1 medium sweet onion, peeled and chopped or sliced

- 1/2 c. water
- 2 TB of olive oil

Direction

- Trim Brussels sprouts. And cut a small X in the stem end, so they cook evenly.
- Place sprouts, chopped onion and the 1/2 cup water in a medium pan. Drizzle olive oil on top of all. Cover and cook on medium-high heat for approx. 8 or so minutes, or until tender. Pour any excess water out when done. Keep sprouts in pan.
- Add the honey, butter and Dijon mustard on top of the cooked sprouts and onions. Stir gently and reheat to blend. If needed, add more water.
- Sprinkle with salt or pepper, if desired.

112.	Easy Easy Greek Style Green Beans Recipe

Serving: 6 | Prep: | Cook: 20mins | Ready in:

Ingredients

- 1/2 cup chopped onion
- 1 clove garlic, minced
- 1 tablespoon olive oil
- 1 28-ounce can diced tomatoes
- (or, halved grape tomatoes, chopped fresh tomatoes with juice)
- 1/4 cup sliced pitted ripe olives
- 1 teaspoon dried oregano, crushed
- 2 9-ounce packages or one 16-ounce package frozen French-cut green beans, thawed and drained
- (or equivalent of fresh, cooked til tender)
- 1/2 cup crumbled feta cheese (2 ounces)

Direction

- In a large skillet cook onion and garlic in hot oil about 5 minutes or until tender.
- Add undrained tomatoes, olives, and oregano.

- Bring to boiling; reduce heat.
- Boil gently, uncovered, for 10 minutes.
- Add beans.
- Return to boiling.
- Boil gently, uncovered, about 8 minutes or until desired consistency and beans are tender.
- Transfer to a serving bowl; sprinkle with cheese.
- ***NOTE***
- Fresh green beans and tomatoes are always way better than anything canned, and I use them often. If canned is what you have (or a combination of canned / fresh) it's a great recipe to make them taste even better!

113. Easy Okra Masala Recipe

Serving: 4 | Prep: | Cook: 20mins | Ready in:

Ingredients

- 2 Tbs (30 ml) vegetable oil
- 2 medium onions, peeled and finely chopped
- 2 Tbs (30 ml) quick garam masala
- 2 cloves garlic, finely chopped
- 1 Tbs (15 ml) finely chopped fresh ginger
- salt and cayenne pepper to taste
- 2 tomatoes, chopped
- 1 lb (500 g) okra, trimmed and cut into 1-inch (2 cm) pieces
- 2 green bell peppers, cored, seeded, and chopped
- 1/4 cup (60 ml) water
- Quick garam masala
- 1 Tbs (15 ml) ground cardamom
- 1 tsp (5 ml) ground cumin
- 1/2 tsp (5 ml) ground coriander
- 1/2 tsp (2 ml) ground cinnamon
- 1/2 tsp (2 ml) freshly ground black pepper
- 1/4 tsp (1 ml) ground mace
- 1/4 tsp (1 ml) ground nutmeg

Direction

- Heat the oil in a large, heavy skillet over moderate heat.
- Sauté the onions, stirring frequently, until light golden brown.
- Add the garam masala, garlic, ginger, salt, and cayenne pepper.
- Sauté for another 2 minutes, stirring once or twice.
- Add the tomatoes, okra, bell peppers, and water.
- Cover, reduce the heat, and simmer 15 to 20 minutes, until the okra is tender.
- Garam masala:
- Combine the ingredients in a small bowl and stir to combine.
- Makes about 2 tablespoons (30 ml).

114. Easy Pesto Cauliflower Recipe

Serving: 4 | Prep: | Cook: 12mins | Ready in:

Ingredients

- 1 head cauliflower
- 1 bunch basil
- handful of nuts (pine nuts are traditional, but we've used almonds, walnuts, and pistachios)
- 1 clove garlic
- olive oil
- salt
- pepper
- Optional: kalamata olives, chopped

Direction

- Cut cauliflower into chunks, microwave it in a covered dish for about 8 minutes.
- While cauliflower is cooking, put basil, nuts, garlic, salt and pepper in food processor. Drizzle in olive oil until you have a nice thick paste, but nothing too runny.
- A little at a time, drop in cauliflower and blend until smooth.
- Fold in Kalamata olives and serve.

- Yum!

115. Easy Stir Fried Spinach Ci Recipe

Serving: 6 | Prep: | Cook: 5mins | Ready in:

Ingredients

- 1lb fresh baby spinach
- 1 leek, diagonally sliced in 1inch pieces
- 2 cloves garlic
- 1 small can water chestnuts, sliced
- 3oz roasted red pepper, sliced
- 1T soy sauce
- squirt of fresh lime juice
- red pepper flakes and black pepper to taste
- about 2T peanut oil

Direction

- Heat oil, soy sauce, red pepper flakes and lime juice in wok or large stir fry pan.
- Add garlic and leek and cook until just tender, about 1-2 minutes
- Add spinach, water chestnuts and roasted red pepper, stir fry another couple of minutes until spinach is tender.
- Toss with another squirt of lime juice and black pepper before serving.

116. Easy,cheesy Cauliflower Recipe

Serving: 6 | Prep: | Cook: 30mins | Ready in:

Ingredients

- 1 head cauliflower
- 1/2 c water
- 1/2 c mayonnaise
- 1 TB Dijon mustard
- 1/2 c shredded cheddar cheese

Direction

- Cut cauliflower into 8 to 12 large pieces, discarding core; place in microwave casserole dish.
- Add water; cover. Microwave on high 10 mins; drain. Return cauliflower to casserole dish.
- Mix mayo and Dijon...spread over cauliflower; sprinkle with cheese.
- Microwave on high 1-2 mins or till cheese is melted....

117. Egg Plant Casserole Recipe

Serving: 0 | Prep: | Cook: 60mins | Ready in:

Ingredients

- 1 lb. lean ground beef
- 1 chopped onion
- 1 medium size egg plant
- 1/2 c. grated Parmasan cheese
- 8 oz. can of tomato sauce
- 1 teasp. salt
- 1/4 teas. garlic salt
- slices of mozzarella cheese

Direction

- Sauté 1 pound lean ground beef, 1 chopped onion and 1 medium size eggplant.
- When onion is transparent, drain off fat.
- Add 1/2 cup grated Parmesan cheese, 8 ounce can of tomato sauce, 1 teaspoon salt and 1/4 teaspoon garlic salt.
- Mix thoroughly and pour into casserole.
- Top with slices of Mozzarella cheese and bake 1 hour at 325 degrees.

118. Eggplant Al Fresco Recipe

Serving: 6 | Prep: | Cook: 45mins | Ready in:

Ingredients

- * 1 large American eggplant (or 3 Italian eggplants)
- * 2 green bell peppers
- * 1 red bell pepper
- * 2-3 large cloves of garlic
- * ½ cup fruity olive oil
- * sea salt
- * parsley

Direction

- Preheat oven to 350 degrees F.
- Cut the eggplant into ½-inch cubes. Cut the bell peppers into ½-inch squares. Mix them in a large ceramic bowl.
- Add 2 to 3 cloves of finely minced garlic and the finely chopped Italian parsley. Stir in 1 teaspoon of sea salt. Then add the olive oil and mix together with a large spoon.
- Bake uncovered in the oven for 45 to 60 minutes, stirring every 15 minutes. The eggplant should be tender, but not mushy.
- Once the eggplant is tender, remove the bowl from the oven and allow to cool, stirring twice during the cooling. Once the dish is cool, taste test to determine if more salt is required.
- With a slotted spoon, place the eggplant in a ceramic serving dish or pie plate. Garnish with parsley. Serve at room temperature.
- Of course, you have to enjoy *wink*

119. Eggplant Deluxe Casserole Recipe

Serving: 6 | Prep: | Cook: 80mins | Ready in:

Ingredients

- 2 large eggplants, peeled
- 4 strips of bacon cut fine
- 1 large onion minced
- 2 stalks of celery minced (tough strings removed)
- 2 teaspoons of adobe seasoning
- 2 eggs beaten
- 4 tablespoons of finely crushed cracker crumbs
- 1 cup of finely shredded cheddar cheese
- 1/2 teaspoon of salt
- 1/4 teaspoon of pepper
- squeeze of lemon juice
- 1 tablespoon of butter cut in little pieces

Direction

- Peel eggplant, cut in one inch chunks,
- Steam in colander over boiling water until very easily pierced with a fork.
- Mash, season with salt and pepper and a little lemon juice
- Fry bacon in large skillet, slowly.
- When nearly done, push to the edge of the pan; add onion and celery.
- Continue to cook very slowly until the vegetables are clear but not brown.
- Add two tablespoons of cracker crumbs to the eggplant mixture along with the bacon, onion and celery mixture. Mix well.
- Add the adobo seasoning (sub grill seasoning if you want).
- Stir in eggs and cheese.
- Pour into a buttered 1 1/2 quart to 2 quart casserole.
- Sprinkle rest of cracker crumbs on top.
- Dot with butter.
- Bake at 325 degrees for one hour.
- Delicious reheated too!

120. Eggplant Tomato Stack Recipe

Serving: 0 | Prep: | Cook: 30mins | Ready in:

Ingredients

- eggplant cut into slices
- fresh ripe large tomatoes
- fresh basil leaves
- herbs of your choice
- garlic
- mozzarella

Direction

- Cut nice 1/2 -1-inch slices of eggplant
- Put on a baking sheet
- Rub a little olive oil on them
- Rub some garlic on them
- Pop them into a 400' oven
- When they are tender
- Add to each spices of choice, a thick slice of tomato, a basil leaf and a thick slice of mozzarella
- Pop back in the oven until the tomato is warmed through and the mozzarella is melted.

121.   Eggplant Tumbet Recipe

Serving: 8 | Prep: | Cook: 30mins | Ready in:

Ingredients

- 2 eggplants
- 3 potatoes
- 3 red peppers
- 1 onion
- 4 big red tomatoes
- 1 cup extra-virgin spanish olive oil for frying

Direction

- It is a very popular dish in Mallorca Island and a representative sample of Mediterranean cooking style. It is usually cooked and served in the same recipient, a handmade round ceramic pan made of clay and called "greixonera".
- Wash, dry and cut eggplants in ½ inch thick slices. Dip in flour, tapping excess. Put 2

inches olive oil in pan and fry eggplant. Do not brown. Drain on paper towel and set aside.
- Cut peeled potatoes in ½ inch thick slices and fry, drain on paper towel and set aside.
- Cut peppers in 1 inch slices and fry. Drain on paper towel and set aside.
- Peel and cut tomatoes in chunks, brown onion in the rest of the oil in pan and add tomatoes. Let it reduce to a thick sauce.
- Arrange vegetables in a round baking pan, bit enough to accommodate all the vegetables, starting with potatoes, eggplant, peppers and tomato sauce.
- Bake in a preheated 375ºF oven for ½ hour, watching not to burn the top.
- It is best served at room temperature.

122.   Eggplant With 3 Sauces Recipe

Serving: 6 | Prep: | Cook: 45mins | Ready in:

Ingredients

- FOR THE eggplant
- 3 Quarts water
- 3 Tbls salt
- 3 large eggplants (approximately 3 lbs) or equivalent Medium eggplants
- peanut or corn oil, for deep frying
- ************************
- TOMATO/chickpea SAUCE:
- 3 Tbls peanut oil
- 2 whole hot dried Red Chiles
- 1 Tsp whole brown mustard seeds
- 3 cloves garlic, crushed and finely chopped
- 1 (28-ounce) can good-quality whole tomatoes, finely chopped, with the liquid
- 10 fresh curry leaves, if available. (I often substitute mint or basil as an alternative for a different flavor)
- 12 oz cooked and drained chickpeas (Or one 15 oz can rinsed and drained)

- ¾ Tsp salt
- 1 Tsp toasted and ground cumin Seeds
- 1 Tsp toasted and ground coriander
- ¼ Tsp ground turmeric
- ******************************
- yogurt SAUCE:
- 10 Tbls plain yogurt
- 1/4 Tsp salt
- 1/4 Tsp toasted ground cumin Seeds
- ******************************
- TAMARIND CHUTNEY:
- 2 Tbls thick tamarind paste
- 2 Tbls sugar
- ¼ Tsp salt
- ¼ Tsp toasted and ground cumin Seeds
- ***********************
- GARNISH:
- A little sea salt and freshly ground black pepper
- fresh mint or cilantro leaves

Direction

- To prepare the Eggplant:
- Pour 3 quarts of Water into a very large bowl or large pan. Add the Salt and stir well.
- Trim the Eggplants, slicing off the very top and bottom, and then peel them. Cut them, crosswise, into slices about 1 1/4 to 1 1/2 inches thick. Put the slices into the salty water as you cut them. The slices will float. Invert a plate on top of the slices and balance a weight (I use a pint Mason jar filled with Water) on top of the plate. Set aside for 3 to 10 hours.
- To make the Tomato-Chickpea Sauce:
- Heat the 3 Tbls of Oil in a large, lidded skillet on medium high heat. When the Oil is very hot, put in the Chiles and Mustard Seeds. As soon as the Mustard Seeds begin to pop, a matter of seconds, add the Garlic. Stir quickly for a few seconds then add the Curry Leaves, Cumin, Coriander, and Turmeric. Shake pan or stir a few seconds until fragrant. Add Tomatoes Chickpeas and Salt. Stir and bring to a simmer. Cover, reduce the heat to low, and simmer gently for 20 minutes. Cool and

refrigerate if not using within 2 hrs. Remove the Chiles before serving.
- To make the Yogurt Sauce:
- Put the Yogurt in a small bowl and beat lightly with a fork or small whisk until smooth. Stir in the Salt and Cumin. Cover and refrigerate, if not using within 2 hours.
- To make the Tamarind Chutney:
- Combine the Tamarind Paste, Sugar, Salt, and Cumin in a small cup. Mix well. Cover and refrigerate, if not using within 2 hours.
- Up To 4 hrs. in Advance:
- Remove the Eggplant slices from the water and pat them dry.
- Pour enough Oil into a large pan to come to a depth of about ¾ inches. Set over medium heat. Allow time for the oil to get very hot. Put in as many Eggplant slices as the pan will hold in a single layer and fry for 3 to 4 minutes on each side, or until reddish-gold.
- Remove to a large plate or sheet pan lined with a double thickness of paper towels. Fry all the Eggplant slices this way, adding more oil, if needed.
- Do not put fried Eggplant slices on top of each other. I change the paper towels at least once and pat the tops of the slices with more paper towel.
- The eggplants can now be set aside for 3 to 4 hours, if desired
- When ready to serve,
- Preheat the oven to 325 degrees F.
- Spread out the Eggplant slices in a single layer on a baking tray and dust very lightly with salt and black pepper. Place in the oven and heat through, (about 15 mins) If Oil accumulates at the bottom of the tray, pour it out.
- Heat the Tomato-Chickpea sauce.
- Arrange the eggplant slices on a very large platter in a single layer.
- Pour a small ladleful of the tomato-chickpea sauce on top of each slice.
- Center 2 tablespoons of the Yogurt Sauce on top of the Tomato-Chickpea Sauce.
- Put a generous dot of the Tamarind Chutney on top of the Yogurt.

- To Garnish: Sprinkle the entire serving dish with Mint leaves, a little Sea Salt and Black Pepper

123.   Elaines Pepper Stir Fry Recipe

Serving: 4 | Prep: | Cook: 20mins |Ready in:

Ingredients

- 2 whole yellow sweet peppers
- 2 whole green sweet peppers
- 2 whole orange sweet peppers
- 4 large shallots
- 6 to 8 green onions
- mushrooms, no set amount

Direction

- Slice the peppers into long strips.
- Slice the shallots and onions thinly.
- Slice mushrooms to your preference.
- Place on a hot grill, on a baking sheet or tinfoil.
- Cook, turning frequently, until peppers are moderately soft, and the shallots are nicely caramelized.
- Add salt, pepper, whatever- to your taste.

124.   Elaines Stuffed Bell Peppers Recipe

Serving: 6 | Prep: | Cook: 35mins |Ready in:

Ingredients

- .
- 6 –8 green bell peppers
- 1 ½ cups cooked rice (white or brown)
- ½ tsp italian spice
- salt & pepper to taste
- ¼ Vidalia or spanish onion, finely chopped

- 3 to 4 fresh tomatoes
- butter to preference

Direction

- Cut the tops off the bell peppers, and remove the seeds and white sections
- (Since these tops will not be used, freeze and save for a pot of soup or stew later on!)
- Prepare the rice by adding the onion, tomato, Italian spice, salt & pepper
- Slice a few mushrooms for garnish
- Fill the peppers with the rice mixture
- Add a dab of butter on top of each stuffed pepper
- Place three pieces of mushroom on top of the butter
- Bake at 350*F 30 to 35 minutes, or until the peppers are beginning to brown on the edges

125.   Ethiopian Alicha Wot Recipe

Serving: 6 | Prep: | Cook: 35mins |Ready in:

Ingredients

- 1 1/2 cups yellow split peas, rinsed and sorted
- 4 1/2 cups water
- 2 cups diced onion
- 1/4 cup water
- 8 cloves garlic, minced
- 2 teaspoons grated fresh ginger
- 1 tablespoon tomato paste
- 2 tablespoons turmeric
- 1/2 teaspoon cinnamon
- 1/2 tablespoon garam masala
- 1/2 teaspoon cayenne powder
- 1/4 tsp sea salt
- 1/2 tsp black pepper
- 1/2 cup water
- Additional salt and pepper to taste

Direction

- Place split peas in a medium pot, and add water.
- Bring to a simmer and cook, covered, 30 minutes. There will still be some liquid in the pot.
- In another large heavy pot, sweat the onion in about 1/4 cup water until very translucent.
- Add garlic, ginger and tomato paste and sauté two minutes.
- Stir in spices, salt, pepper and remaining water and cook 5 minutes longer, stirring.
- Add the cooked split peas and enough of the cooking liquid to form a thick, gravy-like sauce.
- Cook until everything is well combined and hot. Adjust seasoning to taste.
- Serve over brown rice, couscous or with naan, Injera or pita, if desired.

---

126. Ethiopian Vegetable Bowl Recipe

Serving: 8 | Prep: | Cook: 40mins |Ready in:

Ingredients

- • 1/4 cup vegetable oil
- • 1/2 teaspoon ground ginger
- • 1/2 teaspoon ground turmeric
- • 1/2 teaspoon ground black pepper
- • 1 teaspoon ground cloves
- • 1 teaspoon fenugreek seeds
- • 1 head garlic, minced
- • 1 teaspoon salt
- • 3 large onions, chopped
- • 4 large carrots, cubed
- • 4 large potatoes, cubed
- • 1/4 head cabbage, chopped
- • 2 cups tomato puree
- • 2 cups water
- • salt and pepper to taste

Direction

- Heat the oil in a large skillet over medium-high heat. Stir in the ginger, turmeric, black pepper, cloves, fenugreek, garlic, and one teaspoon salt. Continue to stir until the spices and garlic are well coated in oil, about 30 seconds. Stir in the onions; cook, stirring, until translucent, about 5 minutes. Add the carrots, potatoes, and cabbage; cook, stirring frequently, until the vegetables begin to soften, about 3 minutes.
- Stir in the tomato puree and the water. Continue to cook over very low heat, until vegetables are soft and the tomato sauce thickens, about 30 to 40 minutes. Taste for seasoning and add additional salt and pepper, if needed.

---

127. Fabulous Classic Caesar Salad Recipe

Serving: 4 | Prep: | Cook: |Ready in:

Ingredients

- Fabulous Classic Caesar Salad
- 1 bag (10 ounces) of Hearts of Romaine
- ½ cup of shredded parmesan cheese
- In large bowl, toss the Hearts of Romaine, cheese and herb Croutons Add the dressing to taste and gently toss. Serve immediately.

Direction

- Caesar Dressing
- 2 small garlic cloves mashed to a paste or minced (Tip: place the garlic in a mortar with a pinch of kosher salt and use the pestle to mash it together until you have a past. If you lack a mortar and pestle, place the garlic and a pinch of salt on a cutting board and mince the garlic with a sharp knife until a paste is formed.)
- 2 anchovy fillets, minced, or ½ tsp. of anchovy paste (I do not use this)
- 1 egg cracking into a small bowl (Tip: Because it has a raw egg in it, this dressing must be

refrigerated and used the same day it's made. If you are wary of serving a dressing with raw egg, substitute 1 tbsp. mayonnaise.)

- 2 tbsp. freshly squeezed lemon juice
- 1 tbsp. Dijon mustard
- ¼ tsp. Worcestershire sauce
- ½ cup extra virgin olive oil
- Kosher salt and freshly ground black pepper
- In a small bowl whisk together the garlic, anchovies, egg, lemon juice, mustard and Worcestershire sauce. Add the oil in a stream, whisking until the dressing is emulsified. Season with salt and pepper to taste. Makes about ¾ of a cup.
- Top with Croutons. See separate recipe

128. Fall Apart Caramelized Cabbage

Serving: 8 | Prep: | Cook: 90mins | Ready in:

Ingredients

- ¼ cup double-concentrated tomato paste
- 3 garlic cloves, finely grated
- 1½ tsp. ground coriander
- 1½ tsp. ground cumin
- 1 tsp. crushed red pepper flakes
- 1 medium head of green or savoy cabbage (about 2 lb. total)
- ½ cup extra-virgin olive oil, divided
- Kosher salt
- 3 Tbsp. chopped dill, parsley, or cilantro
- Full-fat Greek yogurt or sour cream (for serving)

Direction

- Preheat oven to 350°. Mix tomato paste, garlic, coriander, cumin, and red pepper flakes in a small bowl.
- Cut cabbage in half through core. Cut each half through core into 4 wedges.
- Heat ¼ cup oil in a large cast-iron skillet over medium-high. Working in batches if needed,

add cabbage to pan cut side down and season with salt. Cook, turning occasionally, until lightly charred, about 4 minutes per side. Transfer cabbage to a plate.

- Pour remaining ¼ cup oil into skillet. Add spiced tomato paste and cook over medium heat, stirring frequently, until tomato paste begins to split and slightly darken, 2–3 minutes. Pour in enough water to come halfway up sides of pan (about 1½ cups), season with salt, and bring to a simmer. Nestle cabbage wedges back into skillet (they should have shrunk while browning; a bit of overlap is okay). Transfer cabbage to oven and bake, uncovered and turning wedges halfway through, until very tender, liquid is mostly evaporated, and cabbage is caramelized around the edges, 40–50 minutes.
- Scatter dill over cabbage. Serve with yogurt alongside.

129. Famous Peoples Carrots Recipe

Serving: 4 | Prep: | Cook: 25mins | Ready in:

Ingredients

- 4 cloves garlic, minced
- 2 tbsp honey
- 1/2 can (6oz) frozen orange juice concentrate, thawed
- 1/3 cup chicken (or vegetable, for vegetarians) broth
- 1 red onion, minced
- 1/2 tbsp dried basil
- 1/2 tsp salt (optional)
- 1/2 tsp Tabasco
- 1 tbsp paprika
- 1 lb carrots, peeled and cut into sticks

Direction

- Preheat the oven to 400F. Line a deep casserole with lightly greased foil (for easy cleanup).

- In a large bowl, combine all the ingredients, tossing the carrots to coat them well.
- Bake for about 25 minutes, or until tender and the glaze is reduced.

130.   Fresh Sweet Corn Cakes Recipe

Serving: 4 | Prep: | Cook: 15mins | Ready in:

Ingredients

- 4 thin slices bacon, diced
- 2 ears fresh sweet corn
- 1 or 2 jalapeno peppers (to your liking), cut in half and seeds removed, then diced finely
- 1 small sweet onion, diced (a good cup or so)
- ½ cup yellow cornmeal
- 1 or 2 tablespoons sugar (depending on how sweet you like your corn cakes)
- 1 teaspoon baking powder
- ½ teaspoon sea salt
- ¼ teaspoon baking soda
- a pinch or more of cayenne pepper (or to your taste)
- 5 tablespoons buttermilk
- 1 medium egg
- 4 ounces grated pepper jack cheese, or Mexican Blend grated cheese
- Topping:
- 2 green onions, sliced (whites and part of the greens)
- 2 ounces crumbled queso fresco cheese
- salsa, optional
- guacamole, optional
- sour cream, optional
- peanut oil (or whatever oil you prefer to fry in)

Direction

- Fry diced bacon in a cast iron skillet (or any heavy skillet that doesn't have a non-stick coating…pans with non-stick coatings will tend to not give you the browning you want for this recipe).

- Remove bacon from skillet and drain on paper toweling, leaving 2 tablespoons bacon grease in the pan.
- Stand corn cobs on end in a deep bowl and use a very sharp knife to run down the sides of the corn, top to bottom, cutting the kernels from the cob; measure out 1 heaping cup of kernels (save any extra for another use).
- In the hot bacon grease in the skillet, sauté the corn, diced jalapeno, and diced onion until onions turn golden, about 10 to 12 minutes; remove pan from heat and set aside.
- In a mixing bowl, combine corn meal, sugar, baking powder, sea salt, baking soda and cayenne pepper.
- In a small bowl, whisk together buttermilk and egg; gently stir into cornmeal mixture just until moistened.
- Add bacon, sautéed veggies and grated cheese to batter, stirring only enough to incorporate all of the ingredients together.
- Return cast iron skillet to medium/medium-high heat, and add oil to generously cover the bottom of the pan.
- When oil is sizzling hot, drop the corn cakes into 4 "patties" in the skillet; fry for approximately 2 minutes, until well browned on bottom; flip corn cakes and fry an additional 2 minutes on the other side.
- NOTE: It is very important to have a very hot oil when you fry the cakes – if the cakes linger too long in the pan to brown, they will become dry. The key is quick, HOT frying!
- Serve immediately, topped with green onions, crumbled cheese, and any other optional toppings

131.   Fried Plantains Recipe

Serving: 4 | Prep: | Cook: 10mins | Ready in:

Ingredients

- 3 large plantains
- 1/4 cup butter or margarine

- 1 tablespoon sugar
- 1/2 teaspoon ground cinnamon

Direction

- Cut each plantain in half crosswise; cut each half lengthwise into 1/4 inch thick slices.
- Melt butter in a large skillet over medium heat.
- Add plantains; sprinkle with sugar and cinnamon.
- Cook 3 to 4 minutes on each side or until golden.
- Drain on paper towels.

132.   Fryed Cabbage Recipe

Serving: 68 | Prep: | Cook: 12mins | Ready in:

Ingredients

- 1 head mountain cabbage
- 6 slices Fat back
- 1/4 tsp salt
- 1/4 tsp black pepper
- crushed red pepper
- sugar
- water

Direction

- Slice cabbage in long thin strips (remove Cobb).Fry fatback mid-high heat in large skillet until golden brown. Remove fatback. Add cabbage let it pile up. Salt & pepper to taste. Use same amount sugar as the salt. Sprinkle 1/4to1/2 tsp. of crushed red pepper on top. Use red pepper +/- for the heat factor you like. Add about 1 tbsp. water cover simmer until cooked down or slightly colored. Stir frequently but keep covered. Serve

133.   GARLICKY BRAISED KALE WITH SUN DRIED TOMATOES Recipe

Serving: 4 | Prep: | Cook: 20mins | Ready in:

Ingredients

- 2 tablespoons extra virgin olive oil
- 5 cloves garlic cut in half then smashed and peeled
- 2 tablespoons finely chopped oil packed sun-dried tomatoes well drained
- 1/2 large bunch kale washed and cut into 1" ribbons
- 1/2 teaspoon salt
- 1 teaspoon freshly ground black pepper
- 1/2 cup chicken stock
- 1/2 teaspoon balsamic vinegar
- 1/2 ounce crumbled goat cheese

Direction

- Heat the olive oil in a soup pot over medium heat.
- Add garlic and sauté stirring for 3 minutes.
- Add tomatoes and stir to combine.
- Add kale tossing to coat well with the oil.
- Season with salt and pepper then continue stirring until kale is wilted.
- Add stock then bring to a boil and reduce to a simmer.
- Cover and cook until kale has softened about 8 minutes.
- Uncover then turn heat to high and boil away the remaining liquid stirring frequently.
- Take pan off heat then season with vinegar and stir to combine.
- Transfer to a small serving dish and top with crumbled goat cheese.

134. GUACAPICO AKA PICO DE GALLO WITH AVOCADO Recipe

Serving: 4 | Prep: | Cook: |Ready in:

Ingredients

- 2 cups onion, coarsely chopped, about 3/8-1/2"
- 2 cups ripe roma tomato, deseeded and coarsely chopped, about 3/8-1/2"
- 3 cup avocados, coarsely diced, about 3/8-1/2"
- 1-2 fresh jalapeno pepper(s), deseeded and chopped (adjust for your heat tolerance)
- 1/4 cup cilantro, chopped, placed loose in measuring cup
- juice of 2 limes
- Generously salt and pepper to taste

Direction

- Mix ingredients in non-reactive bowl and refrigerate for a minimum of 1 hour to allow flavors to blend.
- Serve cold or room temp.

135. Gamja Jorim (korean Glazed Potatoes) Recipe

Serving: 8 | Prep: | Cook: |Ready in:

Ingredients

- •3, 4 medium potatoes, peeled & cubed
- •2 tbsp soy sauce
- •2 tbsp corn syrup (mulyeot)
- •2 tbsp brown sugar
- •3 garlic cloves, finely minced
- •1 tbsp gochugaru (Korean red pepper flakes)
- •1 tsp sesame seeds
- •1 tsp sesame oil (optional)
- •2, 3 tbsp olive oil

Direction

- 1. Peel and cut the 3 medium-sized potatoes into 1/2 inch cubes or a little larger.
- 2. In a heated non-stick frying pan, add the 2, 3 tbsp. olive oil (enough to prevent sticking) and potato cubes. Fry/sauté them for about 7, 8 minutes or until slightly browned and softened.
- 3. Add the soy sauce, gochugaru (red pepper flakes), minced garlic, and brown sugar to the pan. Sauté for another 2, 3 minutes or until ingredients mixed through.
- 4. Lastly, add the corn syrup in tbsp. intervals until a thick glaze starts to coat the potato cubes. Taste continuously until desired taste is met and the potatoes have softened but not broken.
- 5. Cook for a few more minutes if necessary and then transfer to a serving plate. Garnish with sesame seeds or more gochugaru for more spice. Enjoy!
- *There are endless varieties of potatoes to be had out there. We recently saw some great fingerling potatoes at the farmers' market that we missed out on but knew would work great with this recipe. Don't hesitate to experiment and make the dish suitable to your taste preference.

136. Garden Zucchini Gratin Recipe

Serving: 8 | Prep: | Cook: 8mins |Ready in:

Ingredients

- 1 1/2 Tbs butter
- 8 Cups Thinly sliced zucchini OR (combo of 4 cups of zucchini and 4 cups of yellow squash)
- 1 cup sliced white onion
- 2 cloves garlic, minced
- 1/2 cup fat-free half-and-half (of course you can use regular!)

- 4 Tbs reduced-fat cream cheese (of course you can use regular!)
- 3/4 cup panko bread crumbs (Japanese-style bread crumbs), divided (a must)
- 3/4 cup grated parmesan cheese, divided.
- 1/2 teaspoon salt
- 1/4 teaspoon ground black pepper
- nonstick cooking spray

Direction

- Preheat oven to 450 degrees. In a large skillet, melt the butter over medium heat; add zucchini, onion and garlic. Cook, stirring occasionally until vegetables are tender, about 6 to 8 minutes.
- Add the half-and-half and cream cheese to the vegetable mixture; stir to combine, allowing the cream cheese to melt.
- Set aside 4 tablespoons of the panko and 5 tablespoons of the Parmesan cheese. Add the remaining 6 tablespoons of the panko and 5 tablespoons of Parmesan cheese, salt and pepper to the vegetable mixture; stir to combine.
- Coat a 2-quart shallow baking dish with nonstick spray. Spoon mixture into the baking dish. Sprinkle the top with remaining panko and Parmesan cheese.
- Bake until top is golden brown, about 10 to 12 minutes.
- Enjoy!
- 104 calories and 5g of fat per serving!

137.   Garlic Asparagus And Pasta With Lemon Cream Recipe

Serving: 6 | Prep: | Cook: 10mins | Ready in:

Ingredients

- 8 ounces dried rotini
- 1 tablespoon butter
- 2 cups fresh asparagus cut into 2-inch pieces

- 8 baby sunburst squash and/or pattypan squash halved
- 2 cloves garlic minced
- 1/2 cup whipping cream
- 2 teaspoons finely shredded lemon peel

Direction

- Cook pasta according to package directions
- Drain pasta and keep warm.
- Melt butter in a large skillet.
- Add asparagus, squash and garlic.
- Cook stirring frequently until vegetables are crisp-tender then remove with a slotted spoon and add to pasta.
- Combine whipping cream and lemon peel in skillet then bring to boiling and boil 3 minutes.
- To serve pour cream mixture over pasta mixture and toss gently to coat.

138.   Garlic Butter Green Beans Ci Recipe

Serving: 6 | Prep: | Cook: 15mins | Ready in:

Ingredients

- 2lb fresh green beans, cleaned
- 6-8 cloves garlic, minced
- 1 stick butter
- salt and pepper

Direction

- Place beans in large saucepan and add water to just cover.
- Boil, then reduce heat and cook until just tender but still crisp (7-10 min), drain
- In large skillet, melt butter and add garlic.
- Add beans, toss to coat and cook just till heated through.
- Add fresh ground pepper and sea or kosher salt just prior to serving.

- *please note, these are even better if beans are steamed rather than boiled, then tossed in garlic butter*

139. Garlic Edamame Soy Beans And Walnuts Recipe

Serving: 4 | Prep: | Cook: 12mins |Ready in:

Ingredients

- 12-ounce package frozen shelled sweet soybeans (edamame)
- 1 clove garlic, minced
- 1 tablespoon olive oil
- 1/4 cup fine dry bread crumbs or panko (Japanese-style) bread crumbs
- 1/4 cup finely chopped walnuts
- 1/8 teaspoon salt
- 1/8 teaspoon freshly ground black pepper

Direction

- Cook edamame according to package directions; drain.
- In a large skillet cook garlic in hot oil until tender.
- Stir in bread crumbs, walnuts, salt, and pepper.
- Cook and stir over medium heat about 4 minutes or until crumbs and walnuts are lightly browned and crisp.
- Stir in edamame; heat through.

140. Garlic Sesame Kale Recipe

Serving: 6 | Prep: | Cook: 15mins |Ready in:

Ingredients

- 2 bunches kale, trimmed and chopped

- 1 tsp. olive oil
- 2 cloves garlic, minced
- 1/4 tsp. cayenne pepper
- 2 tsp toasted sesame oil
- 2 tsp sesame seeds, toasted

Direction

- In Dutch oven, bring 1 c. water to boil.
- Add kale; cover and cook for 4 min, stirring occasionally.
- Uncover and cook until water evaporates, about 3 min.
- Heat olive oil in heavy skillet over medium heat.
- Sauté garlic and cayenne pepper of 1 min.
- Add kale.
- Cook and stir for 3 min.
- Transfer kale to bowl.
- Toss with sesame oil.
- Season with salt and pepper to taste.
- Garnish with sesame seeds.

141. Garlic Spinach Diabetic Recipe

Serving: 2 | Prep: | Cook: 5mins |Ready in:

Ingredients

- Diabetic Recipes
- garlic Sauteed spinach and onions Diabetic
- Posted: 18 Sep 2007 03:21 PM CDT
- 1 tsp olive oil
- 1 tsp butter or margarine
- 3 c chopped fresh spinach leaves, stems removed
- 1 onion, chopped
- 1 clove garlic, minced

Direction

- Heat olive oil and butter in saucepan over medium heat. Add spinach, onion, and garlic.

- Sauté until spinach is limp and tender. Serve hot.
- Makes 2 Servings.
- Dietary Exchanges: 1 Vegetable and 1 Fat
- Nutrients per Serving:
- 67 Calories
- 1 g Protein
- 6 g Carbohydrates
- 7 g Fat
- 31 mg Sodium
- 3 mg Cholesterol (with butter)

142. German Leek Pie Recipe

Serving: 6 | Prep: | Cook: 35mins | Ready in:

Ingredients

- 1/2 pack butter
- 1 1/2 cup flour
- 1/2 teaspoon salt
- 2 tablespoons water
- 2 cups chopped leeks
- 1/2 onion
- 1 scallion
- 1 cup sour cream
- 3 eggs
- 2 handfuls grated cheese
- optionally: 1 handful ham / sausage cubes
- (+ butter, breadcrums)

Direction

- 1. Prepare the dough: knead butter with flour, salt and water until your dough is elastic. Set in the fridge until you are done with the rest of the preparations.
- 2. Fry chopped leeks in butter or oil, low the heat. Add chopped onion and scallion and simmer until they all are soft.
- 3. Beat egg yolks with sour cream and (optionally) ham chunks. Whip egg whites until they are stiff and stir lightly in the yolk-sour cream mass. Spread butter into your Pyrex dish, sprinkle with few breadcrumbs

and cover with the dough (roll it possibly thin). Put vegetable chunks on the dough layer and pour egg-cream over it. As the last step, pour grated cheese over it and bake (30-40 minutes, 350 f)

143. Ginger Eggplant Recipe

Serving: 4 | Prep: | Cook: 15mins | Ready in:

Ingredients

- 1 large eggplant (Italian, not Japanese)
- salt
- 1/2 c dark soy sauce
- 4 Tbsp mirin
- 1 Tbsp shredded fresh ginger

Direction

- Peel the eggplant, and cut into circles 1/4" wide.
- Cut each circle into 1/4" strips.
- Sprinkle with salt and let stand for 30 minutes to allow the liquid to draw out.
- After 30 minutes, drain and dry with paper towels.
- Combine, soy sauce, mirin, and ginger.
- Marinate eggplant for 3 hours.
- After the eggplant has marinated, place it and the marinade in a shallow pan.
- Broil (in a preheated broiler) for 5-7 minutes. (Or up to 12 minutes if you prefer it softer)

144. Gingered Carrots Recipe

Serving: 4 | Prep: | Cook: 10mins | Ready in:

Ingredients

- 2 pounds carrots scraped
- 2 tablespoons granulated sugar
- 2 teaspoons cornstarch

- 1/2 teaspoon salt
- 1/2 teaspoon ground ginger
- 1/2 cup orange juice
- 2 tablespoons butter

Direction

- Cut carrots diagonally into 1/4" slices.
- Cook carrots in boiling water to cover 7 minutes or until tender then drain.
- Keep warm in a serving dish.
- Combine next 4 ingredients in saucepan then gradually add orange juice stirring well.
- Bring to a boil over medium heat stirring constantly.
- Boil 1 minute stirring constantly then stir in butter and pour over carrots and toss well.

145. Gingery Carrots With Raisins Recipe

Serving: 4 | Prep: | Cook: 35mins | Ready in:

Ingredients

- 1 pound sliced carrots (frozen slices are easy, use fresh if preferred)
- 1/2 cup golden raisins
- 1/2 stick butter
- 1/4 cup honey
- 1 Tbsp lemon juice
- 1/2 tsp ground ginger
- 1/4 cup sliced almonds

Direction

- Cook carrots in a covered saucepan in 1/2 inch of boiling water for 8 minutes then drain.
- Combine carrots, raisins, butter, honey, lemon juice and raisins in a 1 1/2 quart baking dish.
- Bake at 375 35 minutes uncovered, stirring a few times.
- Sprinkle with almonds and serve.

146. Glazed Carrots Recipe

Serving: 8 | Prep: | Cook: 25mins | Ready in:

Ingredients

- 1 packages 16 oz.fresh baby carrots or cut regular size carrots into smaller pieces.
- 1/4 C. butter or margarine
- 1/4 C. packed brown sugar
- 1 envelope ranch salad dressing mix

Direction

- Place carrots in a saucepan; add 1 inch of water.
- Bring to a boil. Reduce heat; cover and cook for 8 to 10 minutes or until crisp-tender.
- Drain and set aside.
- In the same pan, combine butter, brown sugar and salad dressing mix until blended.
- Add carrots.
- Cook and stir over medium heat for 5 minutes or until glazed.

147. Great Greek Green Beans Recipe

Serving: 6 | Prep: | Cook: 18mins | Ready in:

Ingredients

- 1/2 cup chopped onion
- 1 clove garlic, minced
- 2 tablespoons olive oil
- 1 28-ounce can diced tomatoes
- 1/4 cup sliced pitted ripe olives
- 1 teaspoon dried oregano, crushed
- 2 9-ounce package or one 16-ounce package frozen French-cut green beans, thawed and drained
- 1/2 cup crumbled feta cheese (2 oz.)

Direction

- In a large skillet cook onion and garlic in hot oil about 5 minutes or until tender. Add undrained tomatoes, olives, and oregano. Bring to boiling; reduce heat.
- Boil gently, uncovered, for 10 minutes. Add beans. Return to boiling. Boil gently, uncovered, about 8 minutes or until desired consistency and beans are tender.
- Transfer to a serving bowl; sprinkle with cheese. If desired, serve with a slotted spoon.

---

148. Green Bean Casserole Recipe

Serving: 6 | Prep: | Cook: 30mins | Ready in:

Ingredients

- 1 can (10 3/4 oz.) Campbell's® condensed cream of mushroom soup OR Campbell's® Condensed 98% Fat Free Cream of Mushroom Soup
- 1/2 cup milk
- 1 tsp. soy sauce
- Dash ground black pepper
- 4 cups cooked cut green beans
- 1 1/3 cups French's® French fried onions

Direction

- MIX soup, milk, soy, black pepper, beans and 2/3 cup onions in 1 1/2-qt. casserole.
- BAKE at 350°F. for 25 min. or until hot.
- STIR. Sprinkle with remaining onions. Bake 5 min.
- TIP: Use 1 bag (16 to 20 oz.) frozen green beans, 2 pkg. (9 oz. each) frozen green beans, 2 cans (about 16 oz. each) green beans or about 1 1/2 lb. fresh green beans for this recipe.
- For a change of pace, substitute 4 cups cooked broccoli flowerets for the green beans.
- For a creative twist, stir in 1/2 cup shredded Cheddar cheese with soup. Omit soy sauce.

Sprinkle with 1/4 cup additional Cheddar cheese when adding the remaining onions.
- For a festive touch, stir in 1/4 cup chopped red pepper with soup.
- For a heartier mushroom flavor, substitute Campbell's® Condensed Golden Mushroom Soup for Cream of Mushroom Soup. Omit soy sauce. Stir in 1/4 cup chopped red pepper with green beans.

---

149. Green Bean And Mushroom Casserole Recipe

Serving: 10 | Prep: | Cook: | Ready in:

Ingredients

- 2 (15.5 oz) cans of French cut green beans, liquid removed
- 1 pound small Portobello mushrooms, cut into slices
- 1 (10.75 ounce) can roasted garlic, cream of mushroom condensed
- 4 slices of bacon
- 1 cup cheddar cheese, shredded
- 1/2 medium onion, diced
- 1/4 cup olive oil
- 1/3 tsp white pepper
- 3 garlic cloves, finely diced
- 1/2 cup almonds, slivered
- 3/4 tsp seasoned salt, with no msg

Direction

- Preheat the oven to 375 degrees F.
- Fry bacon in a large skillet, over medium-high heat, until crisp. Remove, place onto paper towels and drain. Reduce heat to medium then pour oil into skillet. When oil becomes hot, stir in mushrooms and onion and cook, stirring regularly until the onions become translucent. Add the garlic, and fry for an additional few minutes, until fragrant. Mix in the soup and almonds, then bring to boil. Season with white pepper and salt, then crumble bacon and add

to the mixture. Carefully, stir in the green beans, and place the mixture into a casserole dish.
- Bake, uncovered, for 30 minutes. Remove, and sprinkle Cheddar cheese on the top. Place into the oven for an additional 5 minutes, (until cheese has melted). Allow to stand 5 minutes prior to serving.

150. Green Beans With Shallots And Pancetta

Serving: 4 | Prep: | Cook: 30mins | Ready in:

Ingredients

- 1 pound green beans, ends trimmed, strings removed (if any)
- Salt
- 2 ounces pancetta, diced very small
- 2-3 large shallots, chopped
- 2 teaspoons butter
- Freshly ground black pepper

Direction

- Boil the green beans: Blanch the beans in a large pot of boiling salted water 4 minutes, or until they are crisp tender.
- Note: Test one, if it is "chewy" keep the beans cooking a bit longer. If you are using French cut beans, or extra thin beans, they may not need to cook as long as 4 minutes; start testing them at 1 1/2 to 2 minutes.
- Drain and shock with ice water: Drain and place the beans in a bowl of ice water to stop the cooking. Drain again and set aside. (At this point you can make the beans a day ahead, store in refrigerator.)
- Brown the pancetta: Heat a large sauté pan on medium high heat. Add the diced pancetta and cook, stirring occasionally, until lightly browned, 2-3 minutes. Use a slotted spoon to remove the pancetta from the pan to a plate.

- Add the shallots: Add the shallots to the pan. Cook, stirring often, on medium high heat, in the fat rendered from the pancetta, until lightly browned.
- Add butter and green beans: Add butter to the pan; add the drained green beans and pancetta. Season to taste with salt and pepper.
- Stir constantly until the beans are hot and are well mixed with the shallots and pancetta. Serve immediately.

151. Green Beans With Walnuts And Feta Recipe

Serving: 6 | Prep: | Cook: 10mins | Ready in:

Ingredients

- 8 cups baby green beans, trimmed
- 1 cup)walnuts, roasted and coarsely chopped
- ¼ cup extra virgin olive oil
- 1 tablespoon white wine vinegar
- 1 tablespoon lemon juice
- 1 tablespoon sweet paprika
- ½ teaspoon ground coriander
- ¼ cup coarsely chopped flatleaf parsley
- ¼ cup coarsely chopped coriander
- ½ small red onion, finely chopped
- 2/3 cup feta, crumbled

Direction

- Cook green beans in boiling salted water for 3-5 minutes or until tender to your taste.
- Drain.
- Refresh in iced water.
- Then drain again.
- Combine walnuts with the remaining ingredients except feta.
- Season to taste with sea salt and freshly ground pepper.
- Combine beans and walnut sauce/mixture in a bowl
- Sprinkle with feta.

152. Green Beans With Parmesan Bread Crumbs Recipe

Serving: 4 | Prep: | Cook: 10mins | Ready in:

Ingredients

- 1 tablespoon olive oil
- 1 clove garlic (chopped)
- 1 tablespoon thyme (chopped, or sage)
- 1/4 cup bread crumbs
- 1/4 cup parmigiano reggiano (grated)
- 1 pound green beans (trimmed, steamed)

Direction

- Heat the oil in a pan.
- Add garlic and thyme and sauté until fragrant, about one minute.
- Add the breadcrumbs and Parmigiano reggiano and sauté until golden brown and toasted.
- Remove from heat and toss with the steamed green beans.

153. Green Beans With Honey Cashew Sauce Recipe

Serving: 4 | Prep: | Cook: 15mins | Ready in:

Ingredients

- 1/4 c. coarsely chopped, salted cashews
- 3 TBS butter or margarine
- 2 TBS honey
- 1 lb. green beans, cooked tender and drained or 1 can cut beans, drained

Direction

- In a large skillet, sauté cashews in butter over low heat until lightly browned, about 5 minutes.

- Add honey and cook. Stirring constantly, 1 minute longer. Pour cashew sauce over beans and toss until coated. Spoon into serving dish and serve immediately.

154. Greens Bake Recipe

Serving: 4 | Prep: | Cook: 35mins | Ready in:

Ingredients

- Easy Greens Bake
- 6 free-range eggs, beaten
- 1 bunch (about 1 gallon) fresh greens (kale, collards, swiss chard, spinach, etc.)
- 1 medium onion (or 3-4 scallions), minced
- 1/2 red bell pepper, chopped into 1/4 inch pieces (optional)
- 3 cloves garlic (or 1 stalk green garlic), minced
- 3/4 cup milk of your choice (cow, goat, rice, etc.)
- 2 cups finely shredded cheese of your choice
- 1/2 tsp pepper
- 1 tsp salt, optional
- 1 Tbs olive oil
- .

Direction

- Preheat oven to 350 degrees.
- Wash greens. Strip leaves from stalks. Chop stalks into 1/4 inch pieces and set aside. Chop greens into bite-sized pieces.
- Bring a large pot of water to a boil. Add chopped stalks. Cook until almost tender (collard stalks take longer than spinach or Swiss chard - should take about 5-10 minutes). Add chopped leaves and cook until tender (again, it varies with the greens, about 3-8 minutes.) Drain, then press with a fork to remove as much water as you can. (You can reserve the nutritious water and freeze for later use in soups).
- In the meantime, in a heavy skillet over medium heat, sauté onions and peppers in

olive oil until onions are translucent. Add garlic, sauté about 2 minutes more. (If you want to skip this step, just throw these ingredients in with the stalks and cook them all together, though sautéing brings out the flavor of the peppers and onions better).

- Grease a 9 x 12 casserole. Pour in all the ingredients and mix well. (You can also throw everything in the food processor for a more uniform texture.) The mixture will be thick, and you may need to press it into the corners and smooth the top with a spoon. (Sometimes we mix this up in a bowl and spoon it into regular or mini-muffin cups to make beautiful individual appetizers.)
- Bake for 25-35 minutes, until set in center. Slice and serve warm or at room temperature

155. Grilled Asian Cabbage Recipe

Serving: 3 | Prep: | Cook: 20mins | Ready in:

Ingredients

- 1 lb(1/2 small-med) green cabbage,shredded or 1lb bag shredded cabbage
- 1tsp chili powder,or to taste
- 2Tbs. soy sauce
- 2-3Tbs canola oikl
- 2Tbs white vinegar
- 2Tbs sugar
- 1tsp salt,or to taste
- 2Tbs sesame oil

Direction

- In small bowl, whisk together everything except cabbage. Place shredded cabbage in large bowl, pour on mixture from small bowl and toss well. Place cabbage on very large greased sheet of aluminum foil. Spread it out and seal well

- Place on preheated grill and cook approximately 15-20 mins, turning over every 5 mins till wilted and tender.
- To make a full head of cabbage, make 2 packets.
- To wrap: Bring 2 opposite ends of foil together and fold over tightly. Then seal other 2 ends.

156. Grilled Cabbage Recipe

Serving: 6 | Prep: | Cook: 45mins | Ready in:

Ingredients

- 1 medium green cabbage
- 1 stick butter, soft
- 1/4 cup parmesan cheese, grated
- 1 1/2 tea. garlic powder
- 3/4 tea. onion salt
- 1 Tbsp. sugar
- 6 full strips bacon

Direction

- Mix parmesan cheese, garlic powder, onion salt, and sugar.
- Cut cabbage head into 6 wedges.
- Remove core and brown leaves.
- Spread butter on cut sides.
- Sprinkle parmesan mix on buttered sides.
- Wrap a piece of bacon around each wedge.
- Wrap wedges on 2 layer of foil, completely covered.
- Grill indirectly, or over low heat, for 45 minutes, turning twice.
- Let sit in foil for 10-15 minutes.
- Unwrap and serve.

157. Grilled Corn And Black Beans Salad Recipe

Serving: 6 | Prep: | Cook: 20mins | Ready in:

Ingredients

- 3 ears shucked corn
- 1/2 C fresh lime juice (about 2 limes)
- 1/3 C minced red onion
- 1/3 minced fresh cilantro (I leave this out)
- 3 Tbl. white vinegar
- 2 tsp. sugar
- 2 tsp. ground cumin
- 2 tsp. chili powder
- 1 (15-ounce) can black beans, drained
- lime wedges (optional)

Direction

- Prepare grill.
- Place corn on a grill rack; grill 20 minutes or until corn is lightly browned, turning every 5 minutes. Cool. Cut kernels from corn; place in a bowl.
- Add juice and remaining ingredients; stir gently. Cover and chill 1 hour.
- Garnish with lime wedges, if desired.

---

158.   Grilled Corn With Herbs Recipe

Serving: 6 | Prep: | Cook: 45mins | Ready in:

Ingredients

- 8 ears of corn in the husk
- 1/4 cup chopped mixed fresh herbs such as chives, parsley, basil, sage, and tarragon
- ****
- You will need 6 tablespoons of lime Butter Sauce:
- (It takes only 5 minutes to make this fantastic sauce. Once you see how versatile it is — it works perfectly with the grilled salmon and the grilled corn — you'll want to make it for a whole host of your summer favorites.)
- 1 large garlic clove, chopped
- 1/4 cup fresh lime juice
- 1 teaspoon salt

- 1/2 teaspoon black pepper
- 1 stick (1/2 cup) unsalted butter, melted

Direction

- For Lime Butter Sauce:
- Purée garlic with lime juice, salt, and pepper in a blender until smooth. With motor running, add melted butter and blend until emulsified, about 30 seconds.
- Reserve 6 tablespoons. (Use the rest for Grilled Salmon with Lime Butter Sauce or for some other lucky dish.)
- Lime Butter Sauce Note: Lime butter sauce can be made 1 day ahead and chilled, covered. Stir before using.
- ****
- Prepare grill for cooking over medium-hot charcoal (moderate heat for gas).
- Grill corn (in husks) on lightly oiled grill rack, turning, covered, until kernels are tender, 20 to 30 minutes. Remove corn from grill and let stand until cool enough to handle but still warm, about 10 minutes.
- Discard husks and stem ends from corn. Cut kernels off cobs with a large knife and toss with herbs and prepared Lime Butter Sauce.
- ****
- Oven Preparation Instructions:
- Corn Note: If you aren't able to grill outdoors, corn (in husks) can be roasted directly on middle rack of a preheated 350°F oven 40 minutes. It will give you a nice roasted flavor.
- Discard husks and stem ends from corn. Cut kernels off cobs with a large knife and toss with herbs and prepared Lime Butter Sauce.

---

159.   Grilled Corn With Soy Honey Glaze Recipe

Serving: 8 | Prep: | Cook: 10mins | Ready in:

Ingredients

- 1/3 c honey

- 1/3 c soy sauce
- 8 ears of fresh corn with husks

Direction

- Mix honey and soy sauce together in a 10 inch skillet.
- Bring to a simmer over medium-high heat.
- Reduce the heat to medium and simmer until slightly syrupy and reduced to about 1/2 cup, about 5 minutes.
- Turn off the heat and set aside.
- Prepare the corn by removing all but the innermost layers of husks. The kernels should be covered by, but visible through, the innermost layer.
- Use a scissor to snip off the tassel, or long silk ends, at the tip of the ear.
- Grill corn over a medium hot fire, turning ears every 11/2 -2 minutes, until the dark outlines of the kernels show through the husks and the husks are charred and beginning to peel away from the tip to expose some kernels, about 8-10 minutes.
- Transfer the corn to a platter and carefully remove and discard the charred husks and silk.
- Using tongs, take each ear and roll it in the soy mixture.
- Return the glazed corn to the grill for an additional 1-2 minutes, turning once.
- Serve immediately!!!!!!

---

160. Grilled Corn With Sweet Savory Asian Glaze Recipe

Serving: 6 | Prep: | Cook: 20mins | Ready in:

Ingredients

- 3 tablespoons fish sauce, such as nam pla or nuoc nam *(see below)
- 2 tablespoons water
- 1 1/2 tablespoons (packed) golden brown sugar

- 1/2 teaspoon ground black pepper
- 2 tablespoons (1/4 stick) butter
- 2 tablespoons olive oil, plus additional for brushing corn
- 1 tablespoon thinly sliced green onions, white part only (from about 3)
- 6 ears of corn, husked (**can use thawed frozen corn on the cob - see RoseJ's comments below)

Direction

- Stir first 4 ingredients in small bowl until sugar dissolves. Melt butter with 2 tablespoons oil in small saucepan over medium heat. Add fish sauce mixture and green onions and simmer until sauce begins to thicken, about 2 minutes.
- NOTE: Butter sauce can be made 2 hours ahead. Let stand at room temperature.
- ****
- Preheat grill (medium-high heat).
- Brush corn with oil.
- Grill corn until tender and charred in spots, about 13 minutes.
- Brush corn generously with butter sauce and serve, passing remaining sauce separately.
- ****
- *Fish sauce is a versatile ingredient. It is available in the Asian foods section of many supermarkets and at Asian markets.

---

161. Grilled Corn With Lime Butter Recipe

Serving: 6 | Prep: | Cook: 30mins | Ready in:

Ingredients

- 6 ears corn
- lime butter
- 1 1/2 sticks butter, softened
- 2 tbls. lime juice, fresh
- salt, to taste

Direction

- Cook time does not include soak time
- Peel down husks of corn and remove silk
- Cover corn back up with husks
- Soak corn in water for few hours to overnight
- Heat grill to medium
- Put corn on grill
- Rotate every 5 minutes to avoid burning on one side
- Grill for 30 minutes total
- Lime Butter
- Mash butter and lime juice together with a fork. Add salt

---

162. Grilled Eggplant Salad Recipe

Serving: 4 | Prep: | Cook: 15mins | Ready in:

Ingredients

- 1 med - large eggplant, cut lengthwise into 1/2-inch-thick slices
- 1 large red onion, cut into'/2-inch-thick slices
- 4 roma tomatoes, halved
- 1/2 cup extra virgin olive oil
- 1/2 cup Green Greek olives, pitted and chopped
- 2 tablespoons capers, drained
- 2 tablespoons golden raisins
- 2 tablespoons pine nuts, toasted
- 3 cloves garlic crushed
- 1/4 teaspoon red pepper flakes
- 1/4 cup red wine vinegar
- 2 teaspoons honey
- 1/4 cup finely chopped flat-leaf parsley leaves
- kosher salt & Fresh Ground Back pepper to taste.
-

Direction

- Heat grill to high. Brush the Eggplant, Onion slices, and Tomatoes with 1/4 cup of the Olive Oil and season each vegetable except Eggplant with Salt & Pepper. **
- Grill the Eggplant until golden brown and just cooked through. (6 - 8 minutes per side.) Grill the Onions until golden brown and just cooked through. (3 - 4 minutes per side) Grill the Tomatoes until charred and slightly soft. (2 minutes per side)
- Remove the vegetables from the grill and cut into 1/2-inch pieces. Place the vegetables in a medium bowl and add the Olives, Capers, Raisins, and Pine Nuts.
- Mix together the Garlic, Red Pepper flakes, vinegar, and honey in a small bowl and season with Salt & Pepper. Slowly drizzle in the remaining 1/4 cup Olive Oil and whisk until emulsified.
- Pour the dressing over the vegetables, add the Parsley, and stir gently to combine. Let the salad sit at room temperature for at least 30 minutes and up to 2 hours before serving.
- Suggestion: Grill Halibut Filets and Top with Eggplant Salad before serving.
- ** Salting Eggplant before grilling brings out too much water and retards browning. Grill the Eggplant then season it.

---

163. Grilled Onions Recipe

Serving: 4 | Prep: | Cook: 15mins | Ready in:

Ingredients

- 2 large onions, cut in eighths
- 1/4 cup honey mustard
- 3 tablespoons soy sauce
- 3 tablespoons lemon juice
- 2 tablespoons brown sugar
- 1 teaspoon vegetable oil
- 1/2 teaspoon black pepper

Direction

- Peel onions, leaving root and top button intact. Cut each vertically into 8 wedges. Try to cut

- directly through the root and top. This keeps the wedges together.
- Combine next 6 ingredients [mustard through pepper] together in a small bowl. If you use low sodium soy sauce add 1/8 tsp. of salt.
- Pour the mixture into a large baking dish [large enough that the onions and fish fit in a single layer]. Turn over until all are thoroughly coated.
- Marinate in refrigerator about one hour turning them over half way through. After you remove the food to cook keep the marinade for later use.
- Now you have two choices. You can finish the dish in a grill pan on the stove or on a perforated fish topper on the grill.
- Don't attempt to cook the fish or the onions directly on the grill grate. They will stick or break apart and fall through.
- Get the grill pan or fish topper hot over a medium heat. Then place the onions on the pan for about three minutes on each side. Remove and keep them warm.
- Place the fish (your choice) on the pan and cook for about 5 minutes on each side or until the fish flakes easily when tested with a fork.
- Arrange the fish and onions on a serving tray and drizzle with the mixture left in the marinating dish.

---

164. Grilled Romaine Lettuce Recipe

Serving: 4 | Prep: | Cook: 5mins | Ready in:

Ingredients

- 2 Heads romaine lettuce - cut in half lengthwise and washed.
- 1/2 cup olive oil
- 1/4 cup balsamic vinegar
- 1/2 tsp. dried minced onion
- 1/2 tsp. garlic powder
- 1/4 tsp. oregano

- 1/2 tsp. salt
- 1/4 tsp. pepper

Direction

- Place split heads of Romaine lettuce in a freezer bag .Mix all other ingredients together in a separate bowl and pour in bag.
- Lay bag flat in fridge for 15 minutes.
- Then turn bag over and lay flat again for another 15 minutes.
- Pre heat grill.
- On medium heat, grill Romaine for about 2 minutes on each side.
- Serve warm.

---

165. Grilled Stuffed Onions Recipe

Serving: 6 | Prep: | Cook: 120mins | Ready in:

Ingredients

- * 6 large Spanish onions
- * 2 cups bread cubes (not crumbs)
- * 2/3 cup chicken broth
- * 1/4 pound fresh italian sausage, ground

Direction

- Leave the skins on the onions.
- Cut off root end making a flat bottom.
- Cut off top and save. Hollow out the onion leaving about 3 layers on the outside.
- Combine bread with chicken broth and mix until the chicken broth is completely absorbed.
- Mix in sausage and stuff into onions.
- Place tops back on onions and wrap in aluminum foil. Don't wrap them too tightly or the steam might burst the package.
- Place onions on grill and cook for about 2 hours or until very tender.

166. Grilled Vegetables With Coffee Bbq Sauce Recipe

Serving: 6 | Prep: | Cook: 20mins | Ready in:

Ingredients

- Ingredients for the BBQ Sauce:
- 3/4 cup balsamic vinegar
- 3/4 cup apple cider vinegar
- 2 teaspoons whole pickling spices
- 2 tablespoons olive oil
- 1/2 cup chopped red onion
- 2 finely chopped garlic cloves
- 1 cup ketchup
- 1/2 cup coffee, freshly brewed
- 1/4 cup dark molasses
- 2 tablespoons chili powder
- 3 tablespoons tomato paste
- 2 tablespoons sugar
- Ingredients for the Grilled Vegetables:
- 6 small Japanese eggplants
- 6 small Italian squash (zucchini)
- 1 very large red onion
- 3 large red bell peppers
- 25 mushrooms

Direction

- Directions:
- In a small saucepan, combine the two vinegars with the pickling spices and bring to a boil over high heat.
- Reduce to medium and continue to boil, uncovered, until the mixture is reduced to about 3/4 cup.
- This should take about 8 to 10 minutes.
- Strain the liquid through a sieve into a bowl.
- Discard the spices.
- In a frying pan, heat the olive oil until hot, then add the onion and garlic and sauté until the onion is translucent, about 3-4 minutes.
- Slowly add the reduced vinegar liquid; then add all the remaining
- BBQ sauce ingredients.
- Stir until smooth and thoroughly incorporated.

- Simmer over low heat for 10-12 minutes.
- Remove the pan from the stove and allow to cool.
- Heat up the grill and prepare the vegetables.
- Cut the eggplant and squash lengthwise in two to four pieces depending on their size.
- Slice the onion into six thick slices, about 1/4" thick.
- Cut the bell peppers in half then in quarters; then remove the membranes and seeds.
- Cut off the woody edges of the mushroom stems.
- If the mushrooms are small, leave as is; if large, cut them in half.
- Brush the pieces of vegetables lightly and grill until they're brown but not burnt.
- If the sauce needs thinning add a little more olive oil.
- Serve with brown rice and steamed corn on the cob.

167. Grilled Veggies With Basil Mayonnaise Recipe

Serving: 6 | Prep: | Cook: 8mins | Ready in:

Ingredients

- vegetables Ingredients:
- 2 medium red and/or yellow peppers, cut into 8 wedges
- 2 medium zucchini and/or yellow squash, cut diagonally into 1-inch pieces
- 8 small carrots with 1-inch greens intact
- 6 green onions and/or red scallions, cut into 3-inch pieces
- 2 tablespoons butter, melted
- 1/2 teaspoon coarsely ground pepper
- 1/4 teaspoon salt
- 1 teaspoon finely chopped fresh garlic
- =========================
- basil mayonnaise Ingredients:
- 1/2 cup mayonnaise
- 1 teaspoon finely chopped fresh garlic

- 2 tablespoons fresh lemon juice
- 1/3 cup coarsely chopped fresh basil leaves

Direction

- Heat gas grill on medium or charcoal grill until coals are ash white. Make aluminum foil grilling pan with rectangle of double thickness heavy-duty aluminum foil or use purchased foil pan. Place peppers, squash, carrots and onions in grilling pan. Drizzle with melted butter; sprinkle with pepper, salt and 1 teaspoon garlic. Place on grill. Cover; grill, stirring occasionally, until vegetables are roasted (8 to 12 minutes).
- Meanwhile, stir together all basil mayonnaise ingredients in small bowl. Serve with roasted vegetables.

---

168. Grilled Zucchini With Fresh Mozzarella Recipe

Serving: 4 | Prep: | Cook: 10mins | Ready in:

Ingredients

- 3 zucchini, cut lengthwise into 1/4 inch slices
- 2 tablespoons olive oil
- salt
- Fresh-ground black pepper
- 1/4 teaspoon wine vinegar
- 1 clove garlic, minced
- 1 tablespoon chopped flat leaf parsley
- 1/2 pound salted fresh mozzarella, cut into thick slices

Direction

- Light the grill or heat the broiler. In a large glass or stainless-steel bowl, toss the zucchini with 1 tablespoon of the oil, 1/4 teaspoon salt, and 1/8 teaspoon pepper. Grill or broil the zucchini, turning once, until tender and golden, about 5 minutes per side. Put the zucchini back in the bowl.

- Toss the zucchini with 1/2 tablespoon of the oil, 1/8 teaspoon salt, the vinegar, garlic, and parsley. Let cool.
- Put the mozzarella slices on a serving plate, fanning them out to form a circle. Drizzle them with the remaining 1/2 tablespoon oil and sprinkle them with a pinch of pepper. Fold the zucchini slices in half and tuck them between the pieces of cheese.

---

169. Ground Beef Stuffed Zucchini Bake Recipe

Serving: 8 | Prep: | Cook: 39mins | Ready in:

Ingredients

- 4 - 6 medium sized zucchini's, about 32 ounces or so
- 1-1/2 pounds ground beef or you can use ground chicken, turkey, pork or a combination of beef, veal and pork
- 2-3 cloves garlic, minced
- a dash of cayenne pepper or Tobasco sauce
- 1 medium onion, diced, 2-1/2 ounces or about 1/2 cup
- 1 green bell pepper, diced
- 2-3 large fresh mushrooms, diced or 1/2 cup, diced or about 3 ounces
- 1/2 tin diced tomatoes, drained on paper towel
- salt and pepper to taste
- 3/4 cup freshly grated parmesan cheese

Direction

- Cut zucchini in half lengthwise.
- Scoop out pulp, leaving 1/4" of flesh intact.
- Discard pulp.
- You can use a teaspoon to scrape out the pulp and seeds, then once most of the pulp has been removed, use the spoon to scrape out any remaining seeds.

- Place zucchini shells on a greased, foil-lined rimmed baking sheet. Sprinkle zucchini with salt and pepper.
- Sauté the meat, garlic, cayenne or Tabasco sauce, onion, green bell pepper and mushrooms, seasoning to taste with salt and pepper.
- Drain any fat.
- Add diced tomatoes and gently fold.
- Fill zucchini with mixture.
- Cover with foil and bake at 350º 30-35 minutes or until zucchini is tender.
- Uncover, top with cheese and bake to melt cheese, about 10 - 15 minutes.
- Makes 6 servings
- Per Serving: 143 Calories
- I think I'd probably use another type of cheese next time. The parmesan doesn't melt enough. Cheddar, mozzarella, Tex Mex or even Swiss cheese might be nice. If you're counting calories, low fat or skim milk cheese can also be used. This recipe is great served as a side dish with any meal. It is also nice served with a gravy.

---

170. Guacamole Full On No Holds Barred Recipe

Serving: 4 | Prep: | Cook: 10mins | Ready in:

Ingredients

- 3 medium sized ripe avocados
- 1 medium size white onion
- 1 medium size red onion
- 1- 6 cloves of fresh garlic
- 3 small bird-eye chilli peppers
- A large bunch of chopped cilantro or coriander leaves
- 3 tablespoons of lime juice
- 1 tablespoon of lemon juice
- 1/2 teaspoon of salt
- 1/2 teaspoon of cracked black pepper

Direction

- As each item is prepared, place all contents in a suitable plastic container or in your food processor/blender.
- Cut avocados in half and then remove stones.
- Fully scoop out flesh of each half and then chop roughly into 1cm/1/2 inch cubes.
- Coarsely chop both onions into small cubes.
- Crush 1 to 6 cloves of garlic, according to taste.
- Slice and de-seed 1-3 birds' eye chillies, according to preference.
- Finely chop a bunch of cilantro/coriander leaves.
- Put all of the ingredients so far into a plastic container or into your blender.
- Add the lime and lemon juice.
- Finally add the salt and black pepper.
- Then either mash/stir manually or using the lowest setting or burst mode on your blender until you have a semi-smooth mixture.
- For best results, serve after 2 hours in the fridge or immediately if time is of the essence.
- (I prefer the light use of a blender as it produces a finer texture but you can simply mash the ingredients in the plastic container if you wish.)

---

171. Guacamole With Roasted Corn And Chipotle In Adobo Sauce Recipe

Serving: 4 | Prep: | Cook: 30mins | Ready in:

Ingredients

- 4-6 ripe avocados (about 1 1/2 pounds), halved, pitted, peeled (I used Haas)
- 2 tablespoons fresh lime juice
- 2-3 ears of fresh corn
- 2-3 plum/roma tomatoes, seeded, diced
- 4 green onions, chopped

- 1/4 - 1/2 cup canned chipotle chile with adobo, finely chopped (can use more or less because they pack a fiery punch)
- 1/2 cup sour cream
- 1/2 cup cilantro, chopped

Direction

- Put your corn in the oven at a preheated 400 F for 30 minutes. Leaves the shucks and silks in place and place on the oven rack.
- Remove corn and let cool until you can handle it without injury - about 15 minutes. Shuck and de-silk.
- ~~~~
- Mash avocados with lime juice in medium bowl.
- Using sharp knife, remove corn kernels from cob and add to avocado mixture.
- Stir in tomato and green onions.
- Combine chipotle and sour cream in small bowl; whisk to blend. Stir cream mixture into avocado mixture. Season with salt.
- **Can be made 4 hours ahead. Place plastic wrap directly onto surface of guacamole and refrigerate. Bring to room temperature before serving.

172. Guinness Battered Onion Rings Recipe

Serving: 4 | Prep: | Cook: 20mins | Ready in:

Ingredients

- 4 cups vegetable oil, for frying
- 2 cups flour
- 1/4 teaspoon cayenne pepper
- 1 teaspoon baking powder
- 2 teaspoons cornstarch
- 1/2 teaspoon salt, plus more for seasoning
- 1/2 teaspoon ground white pepper
- 1 (12-ounce) bottle Guinness, at room temperature

- 1 large yellow onion, peeled and cut into 1/2-inch thick rings

Direction

- In a deep stockpot or deep-fryer, preheat oil to 360 degrees F.
- Place 1/2 cup of the flour and the cayenne pepper in a resealable plastic bag or paper bag and set aside.
- In a medium mixing bowl, combine the remaining flour, the baking powder, cornstarch, salt, and white pepper. Whisk in Guinness until smooth.
- Place the onion rings in the bag containing the flour mixture and toss to coat well. Working in batches, transfer the floured onion rings to the beer batter, making sure that each ring is thoroughly coated with the batter. Remove the rings from the batter and allow excess batter to drip off from the onion rings and immediately place in the preheated oil. Fry, in batches, until golden brown, turning rings as needed, about 2 to 3 minutes per batch. Remove the onion rings, place on a paper towel-lined plate, and season with salt. Repeat with remaining onion rings. Serve hot.

173. Hashbrown Casserole Recipe

Serving: 11 | Prep: | Cook: 60mins | Ready in:

Ingredients

- 2 lbs. of frozen hash browns
- 1 pt. of sour cream
- 1/2 c. of chopped onions
- 2 c. of grated cheddar cheese
- 1/2 c. of melted margarine
- 1 can of cream of chicken soup
- 1 tsp. of salt
- 1/4 tsp. of pepper

Direction

- First you want to add all the ingredients in a bowl.
- Mix well.
- Add to a buttered casserole dish.
- Bake at 350 degrees approx. 45 min.
- Enjoy!

174. Healthier Creamed Corn With Bacon And Leeks Recipe

Serving: 6 | Prep: | Cook: 20mins | Ready in:

Ingredients

- Healthier creamed corn with bacon and leeks
- ~~~~~~
- Cooking Light Magazine, 2002
- The combination of sweet corn and smoky bacon gives this uncomplicated dish sublime flavor. It's a delicious way to put fresh end-of-summer corn to use. Cooking Light Magazine, 2002
- 6 ears corn
- 2 cups 1% low-fat milk
- 1 tablespoon cornstarch
- 1 teaspoon sugar
- 1/2 teaspoon salt
- 1/4 teaspoon freshly ground black pepper
- 4 slices bacon
- 1 cup chopped leek
- Preparation
- Cut kernels from ears of corn to measure 3 cups. Using the dull side of a knife blade, scrape milk and remaining pulp from cobs into a bowl.
- Place 1 1/2 cups kernels, low-fat milk, cornstarch, sugar, salt, and pepper in a food processor; process until smooth, scraping sides.
- Cook bacon in a large cast-iron skillet over medium heat until crisp, turning once.
- Remove the bacon from pan, reserving 1 teaspoon drippings in pan; crumble bacon.

- Add leek to pan, and cook 2 minutes or until tender, stirring constantly.
- Add pureed corn mixture, remaining 1 1/2 cups corn kernels, and corn milk mixture to pan; bring to a boil.
- Reduce heat, and simmer for 3 minutes or until slightly thick, stirring constantly.
- Sprinkle with the crumbled bacon just before serving.

Direction

- PLEASE SEE ABOVE.

175. Healthy Oven Fried Vegetables Recipe

Serving: 4 | Prep: | Cook: 12mins | Ready in:

Ingredients

- 1/4 c. fine dry bread crumbs
- 1 T. parmesan cheese
- 1/8 t. paprika
- 2/3 c. 1/4" sliced mushrooms
- 2 T. Italian salad dressing
- 2/3 c. 1/4" thick sliced onion rings
- 2/3 c. 1/4" thick sliced cauliflower

Direction

- Preheat oven to 450 degrees.
- Spray a baking sheet with cooking oil spray.
- Set aside.
- Stir together breadcrumbs, parmesan cheese and paprika in a 9" pie plate until well mixed.
- Place vegetables in a medium bowl.
- Drizzle salad dressing over vegetables and toss till coated.
- Roll vegetables in crumb mixture till coated.
- Place the coated vegetables in a single layer on the baking sheet. Bake for 10-12 minutes or until golden.
- NUTRITION FACTS:
- Serving Size: 1

- Servings per Recipe: 4
- Calories 101
- Calories from Fat 58
- Total Fat 6g
- Saturated Fat 1g
- Mono Fat 0g
- Cholesterol 1mg 0%
- Sodium 340mg 14%
- Total Carbs 9g 3%
- Dietary Fibre 1g 5%
- Sugars 1g

176. Heart Healthy N Hearty Layered Broccoli Salad Recipe

Serving: 4 | Prep: | Cook: | Ready in:

Ingredients

- 6 cups chopped broccoli flowerets
- 1 small red onion, very thinly sliced
- 1 1/2 cups (6 ounces) grated 50% light cheddar cheese
- 2/3 cup dried, sweetened cranberries or raisins
- 1/2 cups sliced canned beets (drained-rinsed)
- 1/2 cup plain fat free yogurt
- 3 tablespoons honey
- 2 tablespoons Light (no fat)mayonnaise
- 2 tablespoons apple cider vinegar
- 1/4 cup unsalted, dry roasted, hulled sunflower seeds or chopped walnuts
- 1ounce (2 tablespoons) 50% less fat bacon pieces

Direction

- In a large, glass serving bowl, layer broccoli, onion and cranberries. In a small bowl, whisk together yogurt, honey, mayonnaise and vinegar. Drizzle the yogurt dressing over the layered salad. Layer cheese on top. Cover and refrigerate until ready to serve. Sprinkle with sunflower seeds and bacon pieces just before serving.

- Nutritional Facts:
- Calories: 230
- Fat: 12 g
- Saturated Fat: 4.5 g
- Cholesterol: 25 mg
- Sodium: 350 mg
- Calcium: 25% Daily Value
- Protein: 14 g
- Carbohydrates: 29 g

177. Heart Healthy Pumpkin And Black Bean Soup Recipe

Serving: 4 | Prep: | Cook: 30mins | Ready in:

Ingredients

- Heart Healthy pumpkin and black bean Soup
- 1- 1/2 tablespoon extra-virgin olive oil
- 1 medium onion, finely chopped
- 4 cups canned or fresh low-sodium
- Swanson's 98% fat free chicken stock
- 1 can (14 1/2 ounces) diced tomatoes in juice
- 1 can (15 ounces) black beans, drained
- 2 cans (15 ounces) pumpkin puree
- 1/2 cup light cream
- 1 teaspoon curry powder
- 1/2 teaspoons ground cumin
- 1/4 teaspoon cayenne pepper
- coarse salt
- fresh chives for garnish

Direction

- Heat soup pot over medium heat. Add oil.
- When oil is hot, add onion.
- Sauté onions 5 minutes.
- Add broth, tomatoes, black beans and pumpkin puree.
- Stir to combine ingredients and bring soup to a boil.
- Reduce heat to medium low and stir in cream, curry, cumin, cayenne and salt, to taste.

- Simmer 5 minutes, adjust seasonings and serve garnished with chives.

178.   Hijiki No Nimono Recipe

Serving: 4 | Prep: | Cook: 20mins | Ready in:

Ingredients

- Dried hijiki (seaweed)
- dried shitake mushrooms
- sesame seeds
- 1 TBSP low sodium soy sauce (shoyu in japanese)
- 1 TBSP rice vinegar
- 1 TBSP sugar
- 1 TSP mirin (sweet japanese wine)
- 1 TBSP dashi powdered soup mix (available at japanese grocery)
- water
- frozen edamame beans (not in the shell)

Direction

- Soak dried Hijiki in cold water for 1/2 hour - will increase about 10 times in size so be sure to use a big enough bowl.
- Soak mushrooms in warm water for about 15-20 minutes.
- Toast sesame seeds for about 5 minutes in a dry pan and set aside.
- Pour soy sauce, vinegar, mirin, sugar and dashi in a measuring cup.
- Fill the rest of the cup with water.
- Drain and rinse seaweed.
- Remove mushrooms from water. Cut off stems and slice.
- Place all ingredients including liquids in a medium sauce pan and cook on medium heat until all the liquid is gone, stirring occasionally- about 20 minutes.
- Sprinkle with toasted sesame seeds.
- *serve with rice and seafood-see above pic*

179.   Holiday Cauliflower Recipe

Serving: 8 | Prep: | Cook: 20mins | Ready in:

Ingredients

- 1 large head cauliflower, broken into florets
- 1 can mushrooms, drained
- 1/4 cup green bell pepper, diced
- 1/4 cup butter
- 1/3 cup all-purpose flour
- 2 cups milk
- 1 teaspoon salt
- 1/4 teaspoon cayenne pepper
- 1 cup cheddar or swiss cheese, shredded
- 2 tablespoons pimento, diced

Direction

- Cook cauliflower in boiling salted water just until tender-crisp. Drain.
- In large skillet, sauté mushrooms and green pepper in butter.
- Blend in flour. Cook until bubbly.
- Gradually stir in milk.
- Cook until thickened.
- Stir in salt, cayenne, cheese and pimento. Stir until cheese is melted.
- Arrange half the cauliflower in bottom of greased 2 quart casserole.
- Cover with half the sauce.
- Repeat.
- Bake at 325 degrees for 20 minutes or until bubbly.

180.   Honey Baked Lentils Recipe

Serving: 8 | Prep: | Cook: 60mins | Ready in:

Ingredients

- 2 1/3 cups lentils (1 lb)
- 1 small bay leaf
- 5 cups water
- 2 teaspoons salt
- 1 teaspoon dry mustard
- 1/4 teaspoon ground ginger
- 1 tablespoon soy sauce
- 1/2 cup chopped onions
- 1 cup water
- 1/3 cup honey

Direction

- In a Dutch oven or saucepan combine lentils, bay leaf, 5 cups water and salt.
- Bring to a boil.
- Cover, reduce heat, and simmer for 30 minutes.
- Discard bay leaf.
- Preheat oven to 350 degrees F.
- In a bowl combine dry mustard, ginger, soy sauce, onions and 1 cup water.
- Add to lentils.
- Pour honey on top.
- Cover tightly.
- Bake for 1 hour.
- Serve over rice.

181. Honey Baked Red Onions Recipe

Serving: 8 | Prep: | Cook: 15mins | Ready in:

Ingredients

- 3 large red onions
- 1/3 cup honey
- 1/4 cup water
- 3 tablespoons melted butter
- 1 teaspoon paprika
- 1 teaspoon ground coriander
- 1/2 teaspoon salt
- 1/8 teaspoon cayenne pepper

Direction

- Peel and cut onions in half crosswise.
- Place cut side down in shallow baking dish just large enough to hold all onions in one layer.
- Sprinkle with water then cover with aluminum foil.
- Bake at 350 for 30 minutes.
- Turn onions cut side up.
- Combine remaining ingredients.
- Spoon half of mixture over onions.
- Return to oven and bake uncovered 15 minutes.
- Baste with remaining honey mixture and continue baking 15 minutes longer.

182. Honey Baked Squash Recipe

Serving: 2 | Prep: | Cook: 40mins | Ready in:

Ingredients

- 2 small acorn squash halved width wise and deseeded
- 3 tablespoons butter
- 3 ounces honey
- 4 ounces dried figs chopped
- 1 ounce chopped almonds
- 1/2 teaspoon ground cinnamon
- 1/4 teaspoon freshly ground nutmeg

Direction

- Preheat oven to 350. Place squash cut sides down in shallow ovenproof dish and add enough boiling water to come to a depth of 1/2 inch. Cover with foil and bake 25 minutes. Place butter in a small saucepan and melt over low heat then add the honey, figs, almonds, cinnamon and nutmeg and mix well. Carefully pour off water from baking tin containing squash and turn squash cut sides up. Fill the hollows with fig mixture then return to the oven uncovered and bake 15 minutes longer. Serve immediately.

---

183. Honey Dijon Glazed Baby Carrots Recipe

Serving: 6 | Prep: | Cook: 1mins | Ready in:

Ingredients

- 3 Tbs. honey
- 3 Tbs. Dijon mustard
- 1 package frozen baby carrots, I slice mine so they cook quicker.

Direction

- Prepare carrots using the method you normally use (boil, steam, etc. until fork tender).
- Drain excess water.
- Set carrots aside in a separate bowl.
- Return pan to stove and add honey and mustard.
- Heat until bubbly, then return carrots to honey mixture, coat evenly with the sauce and cook for one minute.
- Serve immediately.

---

184. Hop In John Recipe

Serving: 8 | Prep: | Cook: 240mins | Ready in:

Ingredients

- 1 lb. of dried black eyed peas
- 2 smoked ham hocks or one meaty ham bone (great use of leftovers)
- 2 medium yellow onions chopped
- 3 cloves of minced garlic
- 1 bay leaf
- 1 cup of long grain rice

- 1 can of diced tomatoes with chile peppers, keep the juice
- 1 1/2 chopped bell pepper, red is prettiest for the holiday but I use green to economize
- 3 ribs of celery chopped
- 1 serrano pepper, minced, seeds and veins removed
- 2 teaspoons of favorite Cajon seasoning (The BAM man is my favorite)
- 1/2 tsp of dried thyme leaves
- 3/4 tsp of cumin
- 3/4 tsp of salt
- 4 green onions, diced, tops and all

Direction

- In a large Dutch oven combine the peas, your ham bone and 6 cups of water.
- Add one half of one of the onions along with 1 big tsp. of the chopped garlic.
- Add the bay leaf.
- Bring to a boil, reduce the heat and simmer gently for 2 to 2 1/2 hours.
- Remove the ham bone and cut off the meat and dice.
- Drain the black-eyed peas.
- Discard the bay leaf.
- Bring 2 1/2 cups of water to boil
- Add rice and cover and simmer until the rice is nearly done about 15 minutes.
- Mince the remaining onions/garlic and add to the rice along with peas, tomatoes, peppers, celery, seasoning, thyme, cumin and salt.
- Cook another 10 minutes until the rice is tender.
- Stir in chopped ham and diced green onions.
- Serve with additional Crystal Hot sauce on the side.
- Cracklin' cornbread, collards are a must.

---

185. Hot Cauliflower With Shrimp Recipe

Serving: 6 | Prep: | Cook: 10mins | Ready in:

Ingredients

- 1 large cauliflower
- 2 cups milk
- 1/2 medium onion, minced
- 2 sprigs dill, chopped
- 4 tablespoons butter
- 4 tablespoons flour
- 1 teaspoon salt
- 1/4 teaspoon white pepper
- 2 cups cooked and shelled shrimp, chopped
- 1/4 cup heavy cream, whipped
- 12 cooked and shelled shrimp, whole
- 2 tablespoons minced dill

Direction

- Trim cauliflower, wash thoroughly and cook whole in boiling salted water;
- Make the sauce. Combine milk, onion and dill, and bring to a boil;
- Melt butter, stir in flour and cook 3 minutes, stirring constantly;
- Stir hot milk into flour mixture and cook, stirring constantly, until thickened and smooth;
- Cook 2 minutes longer to thicken;
- Season with salt and pepper. Add chopped shrimp and cook over low heat until heated through;
- Fold whipped cream into sauce;
- Place hot cauliflower on hot serving dish and pour sauce over it. Decorate with whole shrimp and dill.

186.   Hot Corn Recipe

Serving: 6 | Prep: | Cook: 35mins | Ready in:

Ingredients

- 1 stick butter
- 1 (8 ounce) package good quality cream cheese
- 2 (12 ounce) cans shoe peg white corn*
- 1 (4 ounce) can chopped green chilies, drained

- salt to taste
- pepper to taste
- 1 or 2 jalapeno pepper, finely chopped (optional)

Direction

- Melt butter in a small saucepan over low heat.
- Add cream cheese and stir until melted.
- Remove from heat.
- Combine cheese mixture with remaining ingredients in a 2 quart baking dish
- Add jalapeno peppers, if desired, for an extra spicy taste.
- Bake uncovered for 35 minutes at 350 degrees
- *NOTE: I have used frozen shoepeg corn, and I cook it in very little water for a few minutes, just to defrost. After draining it, I add it to the cream mixture.

187.   Hot And Spicy Sauteed Mushrooms Recipe

Serving: 4 | Prep: | Cook: 15mins | Ready in:

Ingredients

- 1/2 cup butter, divided
- 1 pound fresh mushrooms (I use baby bellas), sliced
- 1/2 cup green bell pepper, chopped
- 1/2 cup red bell pepper, chopped
- 1/4 cup green onions, thinly sliced
- 2 cloves garlic, minced
- 1/4 cup red wine
- 1/2 teaspoon Cajun or creole seasoning
- 1/4 teaspoon cayenne pepper
- 1/4 teaspoon ground black pepper

Direction

- In large skillet, melt 4 tablespoons butter.
- Sauté mushrooms until tender.
- Remove mushrooms from pan and set aside.
- Add remaining butter to skillet.

- Add green pepper, red pepper and green onions. Sauté until softened.
- Add garlic and sauté 1 minute.
- Add wine and seasonings.
- Return mushrooms to skillet and simmer 2 to 3 minutes.

188.   How To Make Sauerkraut

Serving: 12 | Prep: | Cook: | Ready in:

Ingredients

- 1 1/2 – 2 lbs. fresh cabbage, organic whenever possible
- 1 1/2 – 2 tsp. sea salt

Direction

- Rinse cabbage in cool water. Remove the coarse outer leaves and discard. Remove and rinse a few unblemished leaves and set them aside. Rinse the cabbage again in cool water and place on cutting board.
- Using a large knife, quarter the cabbage and remove the core. Thinly slice the cabbage with a knife or mandoline slicer then transfer cabbage to a large bowl.
- Add 1 teaspoon of the salt and, with your hands, massage it into the cabbage. When the cabbage starts to look wet and shiny, taste it. You should be able to taste the salt without it being overwhelming (in other words it should be a little salty but still taste good). Add more salt, a little at a time, if needed to get that 'salty but not too salty' flavor and a good amount of brine. Continue to massage until the cabbage becomes wet and limp and brine begins to pool in the bottom of the bowl. When you can squeeze the cabbage with two hands and the brine runs freely into the bowl, you're ready for Step 4. If you've put in a good effort and don't have much brine, cover the bowl and allow it to sit for 45 minutes. Massage again until the liquid runs freely when you squeeze a handful of cabbage in your hands.
- Transfer the cabbage to a clean 1 quart mason jar or crock a few handfuls at a time, stopping to press the cabbage into the bottom of the jar using your hand to work out any air pockets before you add more cabbage. Repeat this adding and pressing until all of the cabbage has been packed tightly into the jar. You should have some brine on top of the cabbage once it's all been pressed into the jar. Leave 2-3 inches of headspace in the jar so you have enough room for the next step. If you have too much cabbage, place some in another clean jar (yeah for extra kraut!) to make a second batch.
- Place the zip-top freezer bag into the jar and use your fingers to spread it out so that it covers as much of the cabbage leaf as possible. Fill the bag with cool filtered water and seal it while pressing out as much of the air as possible. Tuck the top of the bag into the jar. If using a lid with an airlock, screw lid on tightly, fill airlock to 'Fill' line with water and snap airlock cap in place. If not using an airlock, very loosely screw lid onto jar (so that gases created during fermentation can escape) or cover with a clean kitchen towel.
- Place vessel on a baking sheet or pan out of direct sunlight and cool (55-75°F) to ferment for 4-14 days. Dark is best but it needs to be somewhere where you won't forget about it! Check your ferment daily to be sure everything is under the brine. Remember: "If it's under the brine, everything's fine!"
- If you see air pockets or notice that the brine is not completely covering the cabbage, carefully remove the lid and zip-top bag and with clean hands, gently press the cabbage down to return everything to below the brine.
- Taste test your kraut starting at Day 4 by carefully removing the bag with clean hands. Use a plastic or wooden fork to gently push the cabbage leaves aside and remove a small taste. It's ready when it has a pleasing pickle-y flavor without the strong acidity of vinegar, the cabbage has softened a bit but retains some crunch and the cabbage is more yellow than

green and slightly translucent (like it's been cooked). If it's not ready, rinse the bag under running water and carefully place it back in the bag so that all of the cabbage is below the brine. Taste again in another day or two to see what you think.

- When it's pleasing to your tastebuds (and/or less than a pH of 4.6 as measured with a pH strip), skim off any scum from the surface and transfer your finished kraut into clean glass jar, tamping it down with your clean hand, a tamper or handle of a wooden spoon. Pour any leftover brine into the jar. Optionally, top with a small circle of parchment paper by lightly pressing it onto the surface. Tighten the lid then refrigerate for up to 6 months to 1 year.

---

189. Imam Bayildi Recipe

Serving: 6 | Prep: | Cook: 10mins |Ready in:

Ingredients

- 4 medium aubergines (eggplants)
- 3 tablespoons olive oil
- 1 onion, finely chopped
- 2 garlic, cloves crushed
- 1 green pepper (capsicum)
- 1 red pepper (capsicum)
- parsley, good handful chopped
- 3 large tomatoes, blanched, skinned and coursely chopped
- 1/2 teaspoon ground cinnamon
- black pepper
- salt
- 1/2-1 teaspoon sugar
- 1/2 lemon, juice of

Direction

- Heat oven to 375°F.
- Slice each aubergine in half lengthwise.
- Scoop out the flesh from the aubergines and chop.

- Blanch the aubergine shells in boiling water for 2 minutes then drain upside down.
- Heat 3 tbsp. of oil in a pan and sauté the onion until soft and golden.
- Add crushed garlic and fry for 2 minutes.
- Add parsley, chopped aubergine, tomatoes, green and red pepper, cinnamon, salt and black pepper and cook for about 5 minutes.
- Add lemon juice and sugar to taste.
- Arrange the aubergine boats in a baking dish and fill each one with the filling.
- Cover the dish with aluminium foil.
- Bake in the oven for about 25 minutes.

---

190. Indian Spiced Cauliflower And Potatoes

Serving: 0 | Prep: | Cook: |Ready in:

Ingredients

- 1 (1 3/4-lb) head cauliflower, cut into 3/4-inch-wide florets
- 1 1/4 lb Yukon Gold potatoes, peeled and cut into 1/2-inch cubes
- 5 tablespoons vegetable oil
- 1/2 teaspoon cumin seeds
- 3/4 teaspoon salt
- 1 medium onion, finely chopped
- 2 garlic cloves, finely chopped
- 2 teaspoons minced fresh jalapeño, including seeds
- 2 teaspoons minced peeled fresh ginger
- 1 teaspoon ground cumin
- 1/2 teaspoon ground coriander
- 1/4 teaspoon turmeric
- 1/4 teaspoon cayenne
- 1/2 cup water
- Accompaniment: lemon wedges

Direction

- Put oven rack in upper third of oven and place a shallow baking pan on rack. Preheat oven to 475°F.
- Toss cauliflower and potatoes together in a bowl with 3 tablespoons oil, cumin seeds, and 1/4 teaspoon salt. Spread in hot baking pan and roast, stirring occasionally, until cauliflower is tender and browned in spots and potatoes are just tender, about 20 minutes.
- While vegetables are roasting, cook onion, garlic, jalapeño, and ginger in remaining 2 tablespoons oil in a 12-inch heavy skillet over moderate heat, stirring frequently, until very soft and beginning to turn golden, 8 to 10 minutes. Add ground cumin, coriander, turmeric, cayenne, and remaining 1/2 teaspoon salt and cook, stirring constantly, 2 minutes. Stir in water, scraping up any brown bits from bottom of skillet, then stir in roasted vegetables. Cook, covered, stirring occasionally, 5 minutes.

---

191. Indian Style Green Beans And Carrots Recipe

Serving: 4 | Prep: | Cook: 20mins | Ready in:

Ingredients

- 3/4 pound fresh green beans cut into 3/4" pieces
- 2 teaspoons mustard seed
- 1 teaspoon ground coriander
- 1/4 teaspoon salt
- 1/4 teaspoon ground ginger
- 1/4 teaspoon ground cumin
- 2 medium carrots sliced
- 1 small white onion cut into thin wedges
- 2 teaspoons olive oil
- 1 tablespoon lemon juice

Direction

- In large saucepan with a steamer rack steam beans over boiling water covered for 10 minutes.
- Meanwhile stir together mustard seed, coriander, salt, ginger and cumin then set aside.
- Add carrots and onion to beans them steam 10 minutes.
- Meanwhile heat oil in medium skillet then cook spice mixture over medium heat until seeds pop.
- Stir in hot vegetables and lemon juice then toss to mix and heat through then serve while hot.

---

192. Indian Style Curry With Potatoes Cauliflower Peas And Chickpeas Recipe

Serving: 8 | Prep: | Cook: 40mins | Ready in:

Ingredients

- 2 tablespoons curry powder (sweet or mild)
- 1 1/2 teaspoons garam masala
- 1/4 cup vegetable oil
- 2 medium onions , chopped fine (about 2 cups)
- 12 ounces Red Bliss potatoes , scrubbed and cut into 1/2-inch pieces (about 2 cups)
- 3 medium cloves garlic , minced (about 1 Tbsp.)
- 1 tablespoon finely grated fresh ginger
- 1 - 1 1/2 serrano chiles , ribs, seeds, and flesh minced ()
- 1 tablespoon tomato paste
- 1/2 medium head cauliflower , trimmed, cored, and cut into 1-inch florets (about 4 cups)
- 1 can (14 1/2 ounces) diced tomatoes , pulsed in food processor until nearly smooth with 1/4-inch pieces visible
- 1 1/4 cups water
- 1 (15 ounce) can chickpeas , drained and rinsed

- salt
- 8 ounces frozen peas (about 1 1/2 cups)
- 1/4 cup heavy cream or coconut milk

Direction

- Toast curry powder and garam masala in small skillet over medium-high heat, stirring constantly, until spices darken slightly and become fragrant, about 1 minute.
- Remove spices from skillet and set aside.
- Heat 3 tablespoons oil in large Dutch oven over medium-high heat until shimmering.
- Add onions and potatoes and cook, stirring occasionally, until onions are caramelized and potatoes are golden brown on edges, about 10 minutes. (Reduce heat to medium if onions darken too quickly.)
- Reduce heat to medium.
- Clear center of pan and add remaining tablespoon oil, garlic, ginger, chili, pea and tomato paste; cook, stirring constantly, until fragrant, about 30 seconds.
- Add toasted spices and cook, stirring constantly, about 1 minute longer. Add cauliflower and cook, stirring constantly, until spices coat florets, about 2 minutes longer.
- Add tomatoes, water, chickpeas, and 1 teaspoon salt; increase heat to medium-high and bring mixture to boil, scraping bottom of pan with wooden spoon to loosen browned bits.
- Cover and reduce heat to medium.
- Simmer briskly, stirring occasionally, until vegetables are tender, 10 to 15 minutes.
- Stir in peas and cream or coconut milk; continue to cook until heated through, about 2 minutes longer.
- Adjust seasoning with salt and serve immediately.

---

193. Individual Cauliflower Gratin Recipe

Serving: 4 | Prep: | Cook: 30mins | Ready in:

Ingredients

- 1 (3-pound) head cauliflower, cut into large florets
- few sprigs of fresh thyme
- 6 tablespoons unsalted butter, divided
- 3 tablespoons all-purpose flour
- 1 - 1 1/2 cups half & half
- grated nutmeg, to taste
- kosher salt & white pepper, to taste
- 1 cup freshly grated gruyere or(Swiss/Emmentaler Cheese)
- 1/2 cup freshly grated parmigiano-reggiano, divided
- 1/4 cup fresh bread crumbs

Direction

- Preheat the oven to 375 degrees F.
- Place the cauliflower and thyme sprigs in a steam basket over a pot of boiling water. Cover and steam the cauliflower florets for 10-15 minutes, until tender but still firm. Drain.
- Meanwhile, melt 3 tablespoons of the butter in a medium saucepan over low heat. Add the flour, stirring constantly with a wooden spoon for 2 minutes. Slowly pour the half & half into the butter-flour mixture and stir until it comes to a boil. Boil, whisking constantly, for 1 minute, or until thickened. Off the heat, add salt, white pepper, nutmeg, the Gruyere, and half the Parmesan.
- Pour a little sauce on the bottom of each small baking dish. Place the drained cauliflower on top and then divide the rest of the sauce evenly on top (you might have a little sauce left over).
- Combine the bread crumbs with the remaining 3 tablespoons of butter (melted) and sprinkle over the gratin. Sprinkle with the remaining Parmigiano-Reggiano.

- Bake for 25 to 30 minutes, until the top is browned. Serve hot or at room temperature.

194. Indonesian Bakwan Jagung Recipe

Serving: 6 | Prep: | Cook: 20mins | Ready in:

Ingredients

- i can of sweet corn
- 1 egg
- 1/2 cup of sugar
- 1 cup of flour
- pinch of salt and pepper
- 1 teaspoon of ground coriander seed powder

Direction

- Mix all ingredients
- If it's too runny add a little more flour
- Fry one tbsp. to make one corn cake
- Fry until golden brown
- Serve with chilli sauce

195. Italian Eggplant Parmesan Recipe

Serving: 6 | Prep: | Cook: 30mins | Ready in:

Ingredients

- 1 medium eggplant
- 2 tablespoons grated parmesan cheese
- 2 eggs
- 1 teaspoon parsley flakes
- 1 clove of garlic, crushed
- salt and pepper to taste
- bread crumbs
- 1 cup speghetti sauce

Direction

- Peel eggplant, cut into 1/2 inch slices.
- Combine cheese, eggs, parsley, garlic, salt and pepper.
- Dip into cheese mixture and into bread crumbs.
- Brown quickly on both side; drain on paper towel.
- Place layer of sauce in 1 qtr. baking dish; add eggplant.
- Repeat layers.
- Bake at 375 degrees for 30 minutes.

196. Italian Stuffed Zucchini Recipe

Serving: 4 | Prep: | Cook: 30mins | Ready in:

Ingredients

- 4 medium zucchini halved lengthwise
- 2 tablespoons regular olive oil (not extra virgin)
- 3/4 cup finely minced onions
- 3 large cloves garlic
- 3 eggs beaten
- 1/2 cup chopped tomato
- 3/4 cup grated parmesan cheese
- 2 tablespoons chopped parsley (optional)
- 2-3 tablespoon fresh chopped basil (crucial!)
- 1/2 teaspoon salt
- 1 teaspoon freshly ground black pepper
- 1/4 teaspoon plain bread crumbs

Direction

- Scoop out inside of zucchini.
- Chop scooped zucchini into bits and cook in oil with onions and garlic until onions are soft.
- Combine sautéed ingredients with tomatoes cheese, herbs, eggs, salt and pepper.
- Fill each zucchini with mixture and dust with breadcrumbs and some extra cheese.
- Bake at 375 for 30 minutes in a lightly oiled glass baking dish.

197. Italian Style Collard Greens Recipe

Serving: 4 | Prep: | Cook: 25mins | Ready in:

Ingredients

- 1/2 pound collard greens, stemmed and washed
- 1 teaspoon olive oil
- 1 cup coarsely chopped celery
- 3/4 cup coarsely chopped onion
- 2 large cloves garlic, minced
- 1 can (14 1/2 ounces) no-salt-added stewed tomatoes, undrained
- 2 teaspoons dried Italian seasoning
- 1 can (15 ounces) white beans (such as cannelloni, Great Northern or navy), rinsed and drained

Direction

- Take collard greens and pat them dry then chop them coarsely.
- In a large saucepan heat oil over medium heat and then add celery, onion and garlic to the saucepan, cooking and stirring for 5 minutes. Take chopped greens, stewed tomatoes with juice and seasoning and add them to the saucepan and cook and stir, breaking the tomatoes up, until the greens have become wilted.
- Bring the mixture to a boil over high heat and once it begins to boil reduce the heat to low and allow the mixture to simmer covered for 15 minutes. Add the beans to the mixture and allow it to simmer covered for about 5 more minutes.

198. Italian Tomato Casserole Recipe

Serving: 4 | Prep: | Cook: 5mins | Ready in:

Ingredients

- 1 tsp. olive oil
- 1/4c. seasoned bread crumbs
- 1 lb. tomatoes, sliced ½" thick
- ¼ c. fresh basil leaves, sliced
- ¼ tsp. pepper
- 1 c. shredded mozzarella
- fresh basil for garnish

Direction

- Mix oil with bread crumbs. Spread in shallow microwave safe dish. Microwave on high 1 minute, uncovered, stirring once, until lightly browned. Set aside. Arrange overlapping rows of tomato slices in the dish. Sprinkle with basil and pepper. Then top with the shredded mozzarella. Top with bread crumbs. Microwave on high, uncovered, 4 minutes or until cheese is melted and tomatoes are heated through. May take longer. Garnish with fresh basil.

199. Italian Style Zucchini Recipe

Serving: 8 | Prep: | Cook: 45mins | Ready in:

Ingredients

- zucchini, sliced about 1/4" or a little more
- Use medium to large zucchini only -NOT big fat seeded ones-yeck-dry and tough- don't let anyone palm them off on you!
- onions, sliced thinly......sweet or yellow...you choose
- tomato sauce (not pasta sauce)
- italian seasoning
- Mozzarrella, shredded

Direction

- Slice zucchini and onion and par-cook separately in the microwave.
- Do not overcook zucchini slices, you want them to be a little crunchy in the finished product.
- In a casserole or baking pan, depending on the quantity you're making: place a layer of zucchini and then a layer of onion
- Pour some tomato sauce over the zucchini and onion, you don't have to cover it completely
- Sprinkle some Italian Seasoning over the tomato sauce to your taste
- Sprinkle a good amount of cheese over the Italian Seasoning and then repeat layers until zucchini and onion are used up.... ending with cheese.
- Bake at 350 for 45 minutes to an hour or until hot and bubbly

200. Ive Bean To Heaven Recipe

Serving: 8 | Prep: | Cook: 45mins | Ready in:

Ingredients

- 2 slices thick bacon diced
- 1 medium white onion diced
- 15 ounces canned pork and beans drained
- 1/2 cup dark brown sugar
- 1/2 cup ketchup
- 1 tablespoon liquid smoke
- 1/4 teaspoon garlic powder

Direction

- In a medium saucepan cook bacon pieces until they just begin to brown.
- Remove bacon from pan and drain but retain grease.
- Add onion and sauté until tender.
- Add remaining ingredients and bring to slow boil.

- Simmer 30 minutes.
- Allow to cool for one hour before serving.

201. Japanese Pickled Cucumbers Recipe

Serving: 4 | Prep: | Cook: 30mins | Ready in:

Ingredients

- 5 Japanese cucumbers
- 2 tsp kosher salt
- ½ Tsp wasabi powder
- ¼ cup seasoned rice vinegar
- ½ Tsp soy sauce

Direction

- Using a vegetable peeler or mandolin, cut cucumbers into long thin strips and place into a colander.
- Toss cucumbers with salt and let drain for 15 minutes.
- Rinse cucumbers under cold water, then squeeze handfuls of the cucumbers to remove excess water; pat dry.
- Stir together the wasabi powder, vinegar, and soy sauce until wasabi powder is dissolved. Toss the cucumbers with the sauce and let sit for a few minutes for flavors to mingle.
- Serve within 2 days.

202. Japanese Style Green Beans Recipe

Serving: 4 | Prep: | Cook: 15mins | Ready in:

Ingredients

- 1Tbs. canola oil
- 11/2 tsp. sesame oil
- 1 lb. fresh green beans

- 1Tbs soy sauce
- 1Tbs toasted sesame seeds

Direction

- Warm a large skillet over med. heat. When skillet is hot, pour canola oil and sesame oil in skillet and then place green beans in skillet. Stir beans to coat with oil. Cook until beans are bright green and slightly browned in spots, about 10 mins.
- Remove from heat, stir in soy sauce and let sit 5 mins. Transfer to platter and sprinkle with toasted sesame seeds.

203. Judys Mediterranean Quinoa Salad Recipe

Serving: 18 | Prep: | Cook: 20mins | Ready in:

Ingredients

- 1 14 oz. package quinoa
- 1 ½ quart water
- 4 large cloves garlic, crushed
- ½ cup green onions, chopped
- ¾ cup carrots, diced small
- ½ cup celery, chopped small (include the tops, adds additional flavor)
- 3 tbls fresh mint, chopped
- 2 tbls cilantro, chopped
- 1 cup flat-leaf parsley, chopped
- 2 cups arugula
- Zest from 2 large lemons
- ½ cup freshly squeezed lemon juice (2 large lemons)
- ½ cup extra virgin olive oil
- ½ cup toasted pine nuts
- 1 cup dried cranberries
- ½ cup black olives, pitted
- ½ cup crumbled feta cheese (I used the basil and tomato flavored feta)
- salt and freshly ground pepper to taste
- NOTE: This recipe serves 18 if you are serving a 1/3 cup of this salad as a side dish.

Direction

- Rinse quinoa thoroughly by running fresh water over the quinoa in a pot and draining. "Rinsing is recommended to wash away any naturally occurring bitter tasting saponins remaining after processing.*" Place quinoa and water in a saucepan and bring to a boil, then reduce heat and simmer until all of the water is absorbed (10-15 mins.). When done, the grains will be translucent and the outer germ layer will separate. You will end up with approximately 3 cups of cooked quinoa.
- Add the lemon zest while the quinoa is still warm, this will enhance the flavour of the natural oils from the lemon zest. Let quinoa cool to room temperature, then transfer to a serving bowl.
- After quinoa has cooled to room temp, mix in the garlic and scallions thoroughly, then add the remaining chopped herbs, vegetables, dried cranberries, and toasted pine nuts. Finally, mix in the feta cheese and kalamata olives and season with salt and freshly ground pepper.
- Refrigerate for at least 1 hour before serving to allow the flavours to meld and develop.
- "*Saponins are soap-like substances that occur on the outside of the quinoa grains. It is believed they are put there by nature to deter insects and birds." "Quinoa was a staple a staple of the ancient Incas and means" the mother grain". It's high in iron and has a distinctive flavour and fluffy texture. You can use it in casseroles, pilaf, salads, and in baking recipes. Have fun creating your own recipes with this wonderful grain. Judy

204. Kale With Garlic And Dried Cranberries Recipe

Serving: 8 | Prep: | Cook: 15mins | Ready in:

Ingredients

- 2 pounds kale (preferably Russian Red), stems and center ribs discarded and leaves coarsely torn
- 1 or 2 tablespoons minced garlic
- 5 tablespoons olive oil
- ½ cup dried cranberries (2 ounces)

Direction

- Cook kale in a 6-quart pot of boiling salted water (1½ tablespoons salt for 4 quarts water), uncovered, until almost tender, 5 to 7 minutes.
- Drain in a colander, then immediately transfer kale to an ice bath to stop cooking. When kale is cool, drain but do not squeeze.
- Cook garlic in oil in same pot over medium heat, stirring, until fragrant, about 30 seconds.
- Add kale, dried cranberries, ¾ teaspoon salt, and ⅛ teaspoon pepper and cook, tossing frequently with tongs, until kale is heated through and tender, 4 to 6 minutes.

---

205. Kale With Garlic And Cranberries Recipe

Serving: 8 | Prep: | Cook: 15mins | Ready in:

Ingredients

- 2 lbs. kale, stems & center ribs discarded, leaves coarsely torn
- 1 tbsp. minced garlic
- 5 tbsp. olive oil
- 1/2 cup dried cranberries
- 3/4 tsp. salt
- 1/8 tsp. pepper

Direction

- In 6-qt. pot of boiling water, cook kale, uncovered, until almost tender (5-7 minutes)
- Drain, transfer to cold water bath so stops cooking
- When cool, drain - do not squeeze

- In same pot, over medium heat, cook garlic in oil, until fragrant
- Add kale, dried cranberries, salt and pepper, tossing frequently, until kale tender 4-6 minutes

---

206. Kale Llaloo Recipe

Serving: 6 | Prep: | Cook: 25mins | Ready in:

Ingredients

- 1 tablespoon butter
- 3 slices bacon, roughly chopped
- 1/2 cup diced vidalia onion
- 1 (1 1/2-pound) bunch kale, chopped
- 1/2 cup coconut milk
- 1 cup beef broth
- salt and freshly ground black pepper

Direction

- In a large sauté pan, add butter and bacon and cook over medium heat until bacon begins to crisp and renders its fat. Add onions and cook until softened, 5 to 8 minutes. Add kale and sauté until it wilts and combines with the onion and bacon. Add coconut milk and broth and continue to cook until kale softens, another 10 minutes. Season with salt and pepper, to taste.

---

207. Korean Baechu Kimchi Recipe

Serving: 20 | Prep: | Cook: | Ready in:

Ingredients

- • 1 large Napa or Chinese cabbage
- • 1 gallon (4 ltr) water
- • ¾ cup (175ml) coarse pickling or sea salt

- • 1 small pod of garlic, peeled and finely minced.
- • One 2-inch (6cm) piece of fresh ginger, peeled and minced. (optional)
- • ¼ cup (60ml) fish sauce, optional.
- • ½ cup Korean type chili powder or chili flakes. This will be hot so reduce if needed.
- • 1 bunch green onions, cut into 1-inch (3cm) lengths (use white and green parts)
- • 1 medium daikon radish, peeled and grated (the long white radish).
- • 2 teaspoons raw sugar or honey, to taste.
- • 3 or 4 seeded Bird's Eye peppers, optional.
- • ¼ cup finally chopped cucumber.
- • ¼ cup rice wine vinegar or just dry white wine. Avoid strong flavored vinegar, like malt.

Direction

- Slice the cabbage lengthwise in half, then slice each half lengthwise into 3 sections. Cut away the tough stem chunks and discard.
- Dissolve the salt in the water in a very large container, then submerge the cabbage under the water. Put a plate or something on top to make sure it stays submerged, then let stand for at least 2 hours. Agitate 3 or 4 times. If you have a hot date you can leave it longer.
- While the cabbage is soaking mix the other ingredients in a very large SS or glass bowl.
- Drain and rinse the cabbage then shake loose any excess water.
- If you're all suited up you can add the cabbage to your spice mixture and gently mix it together. Rest a bit and mix some more. Try not to break up the cabbage but mix well.
- Pack the kimchi in a clean glass jar or jars large enough to hold it and the liquid (make sure the cabbage is covered with liquid) and cover it tightly. Let stand for one to two days in a cool place out of direct sunlight.
- Check the kimchi after 1-2 days. If it's bubbling a bit, it's ready and should be refrigerated. If not, let it stand another day, when it should be ready. You can loosen the lid just a tad to release any built up gasses but

aim the mouth of the jar away from your face. Good.
- Once fermentation starts, serve or store in the refrigerator.
- I like to leave this for a week or so to let the flavors develop and combine but "new" kimchi is delicious. In Korea they used to put this in stone jars and bury it for years against a bad crop year, so it lasts. I've never had a batch in the fridge for more than about a month and it does get a bit stronger with time but if you like kimchi it's still great.
- This is a combination side dish/condiment and often has toasted sesame seeds sprinkled on it when served. Bahp jom joo-seh-yo (pass that food please).

---

208. Korean Bean Sprouts Mung Bean Sprouts Recipe

Serving: 4 | Prep: | Cook: 5mins | Ready in:

Ingredients

- 1 bag bean sprouts (mung bean sprouts usually near the alfalfa sprouts)
- 1/2 -1 teas sesame oil for quick stir fry.
- 1/2 teas of sesame seeds (optional)
- 1/2 tea salt
- optional chili pepper flakes or korean garlic chili paste.

Direction

- Wash sprouts under cold water for a couple of minutes and drain well.
- In wok or sauté' pan heat sesame seed oil till hot but not smoking, (you can add sesame seeds in now till golden if desired)
- Throw in the beansprouts and fry till slightly wilted, just a couple of minutes.
- Take off heat and salt to taste and add optional chili peppers if you like spicy.

209. Korean Buckwheat Jelly Memil Muk Muchim Recipe

Serving: 8 | Prep: | Cook: 20mins | Ready in:

Ingredients

- 2 cups buckwheat powder
- 8 cups water
- 1 cup chopped kimchi
- 1 Tbsp toasted sesame seed
- 1 Tbsp sesame oil
- 1/4 cup chopped green onions.
- 1 Tbsp minced garlic
- 1 1/2 Tbsp soy sauce

Direction

- Mix buckwheat power and water in large sauce pan.
- Keep it for 2 hours in room temperature.
- Mix well, then start boil with high heat. Keep stir starch mixture until it gets thicker. Stir in one direction.
- Keep stir in one direction until the bubble starts to form, add salt; keep stir about 13-15 minutes not to scorch.
- Turn the heat to very low, then cover the lid and steam 7-8 minutes until Muk is ready.
- Transfer the jelly into a 9x13 baking dish, and let it cool about 3-4 hours.
- Cut the buckwheat starch jelly in half. Cut into 0.7cm-thick slices.
- Chop the kimchi (shake off its stuffing); Squeeze the liquid out. Mince the green onions and garlics finely.
- Add chopped green onions, garlic, crushed sesame seeds, and sesame oil to soy sauce to make seasoned soy sauce.
- Put the sliced jelly and squeezed kimchi in a large bowl and mix with seasoned soy sauce. Serve on a plate and sprinkle with crushed laver.

210. Korean Pickle Recipe

Serving: 10 | Prep: | Cook: | Ready in:

Ingredients

- 10 Persian cucumber
- 1/2 radish
- 1 carrot, peeled
- 2 stalks celery
- 20 clove of garlic
- 4 jalapenos
- 1 large onion
- 2 cup soy sauce
- 2 cup water
- 2 cups vinegar
- 2 tablespoons salt
- 1/2 cup sugar
- 1 tablespoon sliced ginger

Direction

- Cut the vegetables into bite size pieces-half size of your 2nd finger
- Put 3 tablespoons of salt on cucumber, carrot, radish, celery, garlic, jalapenos and let stand about 15-20 minutes
- Put 2 tablespoons of salt & 1 tablespoon of vinegar, 1 teaspoon of sugar on sliced onions and let stand 15-20 minutes
- Meantime, in a pot, add water & soy sauce then boil, once boiling,
- Turn off the heat, then add vinegar, sugar, salt and sliced ginger
- Remove water from the salted vegetables using cotton towel. (To make a good Jangajji, vegetable should be dried or salted, thereby reducing their moist, before preservation)
- Put the dried vegetable in a jar and pour the pickling sauce over.
- Keep it 2 -3 days, then it is ready to eat.
- *To last long, remove the pickling juice using colander and boil and let it cool, then pour the juice over the pickle every 7-10 days.

211. Korean Style Kong Namul Muchim Recipe

Serving: 8 | Prep: | Cook: 20mins |Ready in:

Ingredients

- 1 bag of Kong na-mul (Korean beansprouts)
- 2 cup water
- 2 teaspoon salt
- 1 teaspoon toasted sesame seeds.
- 1 tablespoon sesame oil
- 1 teaspoon minced garlic.
- 1 green onion, thinly sliced
- 1 teaspoon red pepper flakes (optional)

Direction

- Wash the bean sprouts in cold water, removing any empty husks. Place them in a pot and add 2 cups of water& 1 teaspoon of salt. Do not fill the pot.
- Cover, bring to a boil and cook about 5 minutes. (Do not lift the lid to check if the pot is boiling because an unpleasant, fishy odor will fill your kitchen.)
- Remove the pot from the heat, rinse the sprouts in cold water and drain.
- Combine the sprouts, green onions, garlic, sesame seeds, oil, and 1 teaspoon of salt and red chili flakes in a bowl. Serve warm or chilled.

212. Korean Style Shigemchi Muchim Sauted Spinach Recipe

Serving: 4 | Prep: | Cook: 3mins |Ready in:

Ingredients

- 1 bunch spinach
- 1 tablespoon minced garlic
- 1 teasppon salt
- 1 teaspoon sesame seed oil
- toasted sesame seeds

Direction

- Remove the roots from the spinach, then give them a thorough rinse to get rid of as much dirt as possible.
- Bring a medium pot of water to the boil, then add the spinach, a pinch of salt and make sure it is submerged for a few minutes (or till wilted but not completely cooked)
- Drain spinach and rinse thoroughly in cold running water
- Drain well, then take small handfuls and squeeze out as much water as you can, whilst being careful not to mush the spinach entirely.
- Roughly cut into easy-to-eat lengths, then put into a bowl, along with garlic, salt to season and the sesame seeds and sesame oil.
- Toss through evenly, then store in an airtight container once cooled.

213. Korean Gut Churi Kimchi Recipe

Serving: 4 | Prep: | Cook: |Ready in:

Ingredients

- 1 Chinese cabbage
- 1 teaspoon vinegar
- 2 cloves garlic
- 1 tablespoon salt
- 1 teaspoon hot pepper
- 1 tablespoon sugar
- 1 tablespoon soy sauce

Direction

- Chop cabbage into thin pieces. Mix it with crushed garlic and hot pepper, soy sauce and vinegar. Add salt and sugar and keep for fermentation for at least 1 hour. Season with sesame oil. In this Korean food recipe, the fiber in cabbage prevents intestinal cancer. Pepper and garlic help to lower blood cholesterol and aid in blood clotting. During the process of fermentation, microorganisms are produced, which are very beneficial to the human body.

---

214. LIMA HAMBURGER PIE Recipe

Serving: 4 | Prep: | Cook: 30mins |Ready in:

Ingredients

- 2 tbsp fat
- 1/2 small minced onion
- 1 can condensed tomato soup
- pepper to taste
- salt to taste
- 1 1/2 lb ground beef
- 2 1/2 cups lima beans

Direction

- Melt the fat in a skillet. Add the ground beef and onion; fry until the onion is tender and the beef is no longer pink. In a baking dish, combine the lima beans, tomato soup, salt and pepper. Top the beans mixture with the ground beef and onion mixture. Top with a piece of pie dough. Bake in a 400 degree oven for 20 to 30 minutes until heated through and the pastry crust is golden brown.

---

215. Lanas Accidental Healthy Vegan Ginger Stir Fry

Serving: 4 | Prep: | Cook: 10mins |Ready in:

Ingredients

- 1 tablespoon cornstarch
- 1 clove garlic, crushed
- 1 teaspoons chopped fresh ginger root

- 3-4 Tbs. EVOO divided =EVOO is extra virgin olive oil
- 1 1/2 cups cut white or other sweet potato
- (I had white and they were incredible)
- 1/2 cup chopped carrots
- 1 cup yellow or other squash rounds
- 3/4 cup red bell pepper
- 1 to 2 tablespoons low sodium soy sauce
- 4 tablespoons water
- 1 cup chopped onions
- salt and fresh pepper to taste (if desired)

Direction

- In a bowl, blend cornstarch, garlic, and 2 tablespoons EVOO until cornstarch is dissolved.
- Add 1 teaspoon ginger; mix.
- To heated skillet or wok (with EVOO), add carrots, sweet potatoes, peppers, squash, (onions last).
- Add water as needed.
- Cook vegetables in EVOO (to your desired crispness level), stirring constantly to prevent burning.
- Stir in soy sauce and water.
- Add sauce (mixed) and cook for a couple more minutes.
- Cook in medium heat, stirring very often, until vegetables are tender but still crisp.

---

216. Lanas Country Style Baked Beans Recipe

Serving: 12 | Prep: | Cook: 60mins |Ready in:

Ingredients

- LANAs COUNTRY STYLE baked beans
- ==========================
- 1 can kidney beans
- 1 can pinto beans
- 1 can butter beans
- 1 can pork & beans

- 1/4 c. bar b cue sauce
- 1/4 c. ketchup
- 6 slices bacon
- 1 c. chopped ham
- 2 sm. onions, chopped
- 1/2 c. dark brown sugar (packed)
- 1/4 cup syrup or molasses
- 1 c. catsup
- 2 tbls. prepared mustard
- If you like.. 'hot' don't forget to add the 'hot' :-)
- ===================================

Direction

- Drain kidney, pinto, pork, and butter beans. Mix well.
- Fry bacon, but don't brown it too crisp. (Reserve a good tablespoon of the bacon drippings for flavor).
- Put beans, bacon and onions in casserole. Add sugars, syrup, catsup, sauce, reserved drippings, and mustard.
- Mix well and bake at 325 degrees for 1 hour.

---

217. Latkes Potato Pancakes Recipe

Serving: 6 | Prep: | Cook: 10mins | Ready in:

Ingredients

- 1 medium yellow onion
- 3 large yukon gold potatoes (about 2 1/2
- lbs.), peeled
- kosher salt, to taste
- 6 tbsp. finely chopped chives
- 3 tbsp. plain matzo meal
- 2 large eggs, lightly beaten
- Freshly ground white pepper, to taste
- canola oil for frying
- sour cream or applesauce

Direction

- Working over a bowl, grate some of the onion, followed by some of the potatoes, on the large-hole side of a box grater. Repeat until all the vegetables are used up.
- Sprinkle mixture with salt and transfer it to a sieve set over a bowl. Squeeze out as much liquid as possible from mixture, allowing it to collect in bottom of bowl. Transfer mixture to another bowl and cover surface with plastic wrap; set aside. Set reserved potato liquid aside to let the milky white starch settle. Pour off liquid from starch. Transfer starch to mixture along with the chives, matzo, eggs, and salt and pepper. Gently mix.
- Pour enough oil into a skillet that it reaches a depth of 1/4"; heat over medium-high heat. Working in small batches, form mixture into balls, using about 1/4 cup of the mixture for each, and place them in the oil. Flatten each ball gently with a spatula to form 3"–4" pancakes. Fry, turning once, until golden brown, crisp, and cooked through, about 8 minutes. Transfer the pancakes to a paper towel–lined plate to drain. Serve the potato pancakes with sour cream or applesauce.

---

218. Leek & Goat Cheese Galette Recipe

Serving: 8 | Prep: | Cook: 30mins | Ready in:

Ingredients

- Galette dough:
- 2 cups all-purpose flour
- 1/2 tsp kosher salt
- 1 tb granulated sugar
- 12 tb cold butter, cut into small pieces
- 1/3 - 1/2 cup ice water, as needed
- ~
- for the filling:
- 6 large leeks, including inch of green
- 3 tb unsalted butter
- 1 tsp chopped fresh thyme

- 1/2 cup dry white wine
- 1/2 cup crème fraîche
- kosher salt + white pepper + black pepper
- 1 egg, beaten
- 3 tb chopped parsley
- 4 oz (herbed) goat cheese, less or more to taste
- eggwash, for brushing pastry

Direction

- Preheat oven to 400F.
- For the dough:
- Mix the flour, salt, and sugar together in a bowl. Cut in the butter by hand, food processor or using a mixer with a paddle attachment, leaving some pea-sized chunks.
- Sprinkle the ice water over the top by the tablespoon and toss with the flour mixture until you can bring the dough together into a ball. Press into a disk and refrigerate if the butter feels soft at all.
- To form a galette, roll it out on a lightly floured counter into a 14-inch irregular circle about 1/8 inch thick. Fold it into quarters and transfer it to the back of a sheet pan or a cookie sheet without sides, then unfold it - it should be larger than the pan (as you'll be folding it in on itself once it's filled). Chill until ready to fill.
- For the Filling:
- Thinly slice and wash the leeks. You should have about 6 cups.
- Melt butter in medium skillet. Add leeks, thyme, and 1/2 cup water. Stew over medium heat, stirring frequently, until leeks are tender, about 12 minutes. Add wine and continue cooking until reduced; then add the crème and cook until it coats the leeks and little liquid remains. Season with salt and plenty of pepper. Let cool 10 minutes then stir in beaten egg and 2 tbsp. of the parsley.
- Spread leek mixture on top of rolled galette dough, leaving a 2 inch border around the edge. Crumble the goat cheese on top, then fold the dough over the filling (fold it over a little or a lot, up to you). Brush with egg wash and bake until crust is browned, 25-30

minutes. Garnish with remaining parsley. Bon appétit!

---

219. Leeks Gratinee Recipe

Serving: 4 | Prep: | Cook: 40mins | Ready in:

Ingredients

- 8 medium leeks, split lengthwise, washed and trimmed to the pale green part, use the tough uppper dark green part for making stock
- 8 slices of prosciutto
- 3 tbsp of unsalted butter
- 3 tbsp of flour
- 2 1/2cups of chicken broth heated (add a boullion cube to canned stock to strengthen the flavor component-no salt needed to flavor sauce if you do this)
- 5 to 6 passes of nutmeg on your microplane rasp (1/8 tsp of nutmeg)
- 1 cup of grated gruyere cheese
- 1/2 cup of plain bread crumbs

Direction

- Trim, wash leeks.
- Put them in a shallow sauce pan and cook them in enough boiling water until the leeks are tender but not mush. About 10 minutes.
- Drain and cool the leeks.
- When you can handle them, wrap each leek in a slice of prosciutto and place in a well-buttered baking dish.
- Preheat oven to 375 degrees.
- Make a roux by combining the melted butter and flour over low heat. Cook a few minutes.
- Add the chicken stock and the nutmeg.
- Continue cooking until it thickens.
- Pour the sauce over the leeks, sprinkle with the cheese and the bread crumbs; bake uncovered until brown and bubbly about 15 to 20 minutes.

220. Lemon Glazed Carrots Recipe

Serving: 6 | Prep: | Cook: 15mins | Ready in:

Ingredients

- 2 pounds baby carrots, the fresh already cleaned ones.
- 3 tablespoons butter
- 3 tablespoons brown sugar
- 2 - 3 tablespoons fresh-squeezed lemon juice, according to taste
- 1/4 teaspoon salt
- 2 tablespoons finely chopped parsley

Direction

- Place a steamer basket in a 3- or 4-quart pot; add 1-inch water to pot.
- Place carrots in basket and bring to a boil over Medium-High heat.
- Cover pot; reduce heat to Medium-Low and cook 10 to 15 minutes or until tender.
- Drain.
- Return empty cooking pot to Medium heat.
- Add butter; melt and blend with sugar, 2 tablespoons lemon juice and salt.
- Stir and cook until sugar dissolves. If desired, stir in additional lemon juice, to taste.
- Add carrots and parsley; toss to coat. Serve hot.
- I always end up adding more butter... I love my butter!

221. Low Carb Shepherds Pie Recipe

Serving: 8 | Prep: | Cook: 30mins | Ready in:

Ingredients

- 2 Bunchs cauliflower

- 2 Packages Ground turkey sausage or you can still use hamburger
- 1 Can tomato sauce
- 2 Tablespoons Sofrito Frozen seasoning bacon bits
- 1 Ounce mozzarella cheese
- 1 Ounce Parmesean cheese
- 2 Pinch pepper black
- 1 Ounce heavy cream
- 3 Pinch sea salt
- 4 Tablespoons butter

Direction

- Steam 2 heads of cauliflower until they are fork tender.
- Brown ground turkey and drain. Place back in pan and add the tomato sauce, salt and pepper to taste, 2 tablespoons of sofrito (you can find this in the freezer section of your supermarket usually together with the Goya products, it's a frozen mixture of red peppers, green peppers, onions, garlic, parsley, and cilantro.) and 1 package of sazón, also in your Goya section. 1 little packet FULL of flavor.
- Mix well in meat. Drain cauliflower and mash with your potato masher. Sprinkle salt and pepper to taste and add heavy cream and butter. Mash like mash potatoes. Spread turkey along the bottom of a baking dish, sprinkle mozzarella cheese on top, then add your layer of mashed cauliflower and sprinkle with parmesan cheese.
- Bake at 350 for about 20 minutes or until top is golden brown.
- Spoon out and serve!

222. Luffa Squash With Mushrooms Spring OnionsCoriander Recipe

Serving: 4 | Prep: | Cook: 15mins | Ready in:

Ingredients

- 1 lb 10 oz luffa squash, peeled
- 2 tablespoon groundnut (peanut) or sesame oil
- 2 shallots, halved and sliced
- 2 garlic cloves, finely chopped
- 1 1/2 cups button (white) mushrooms, quartered
- 1 tablespoon mushroom sauce
- 2 teaspoons soy sauce
- 4 spring onions (scallions), cut into 3/4 inch pieces
- fresh coriander (cilantro) leaves and thin strips of spring onion, to garnish

Direction

- Cut the luffa squash diagonally into 3/4 inch thick pieces.
- Heat the oil in a large wok or heavy pan.
- Stir in the halved shallots and garlic, stir-fry until they begin to turn golden color, then add the mushrooms.
- Add the soy sauce and the squash.
- Reduce the heat, cover and cook gently for a few minutes until the squash is tender.
- Stir in the spring onion pieces, garnish with coriander and spring onion strips, and serve with white rice.

223. Magical Greens Recipe

Serving: 6 | Prep: | Cook: 10mins | Ready in:

Ingredients

- 3 cups greens such as spinach, kale, chard or a combination
- 1/4 cup vegetable stock
- 1 tablespoon finely chopped shallots
- 1 teaspoon salt
- 1 teaspoon freshly ground black pepper

Direction

- Wash greens and remove any tough stalks then cut into 2" lengths.

- Bring stock and shallots to a simmer in a skillet over medium high heat.
- Cook 1 minute then add greens, salt and pepper.
- Toss quickly until greens are barely wilted.

224. Mandarin Coleslaw Recipe

Serving: 8 | Prep: | Cook: | Ready in:

Ingredients

- 1 cup fat free mayonnaise (I am not a big fan of the fat free, so I used Hellman's light version- feel free to use the full- fat variety)
- 2 tbsp. sugar
- 1 teaspoon vinegar (I used apple cider vinegar)
- 1/4 tsp. salt
- 1/4 tsp. black pepper (I used 1/2 tsp. of freshly ground)
- 8 oz. of Publix coleslaw (I used the full 16 oz. bag because I don't like a soupy or overly sweet coleslaw)
- 1 (11 oz.) can mandarin oranges, drained
- ****
- I added:
- 1/2 cup chopped red bell pepper
- 1 jalapeno pepper, seeded and chopped (if your pepper's not that hot like mine, could add two)
- 2 tbsp. of Italian parsley, chopped

Direction

- Combine mayonnaise, sugar, vinegar, salt and pepper.
- Place coleslaw in salad bowl with bell pepper, jalapeno and parsley.
- Toss with dressing until thoroughly blended.
- Gently fold in oranges.
- Place in refrigerator to marry flavors for at least one hour.
- Toss well; serve.

225. Mango Mix Recipe

Serving: 8 | Prep: | Cook: |Ready in:

Ingredients

- 1-2 mangoes
- 1 red medium onion
- 1 1/2 cups of corn
- 1/3 cup fresh cilantro
- 1 can black beans (drained and rinsed)
- 3 T lime juice
- 3 T Mongolian Fire oil (by House of Tsang, available at most grocery stores)

Direction

- The above ingredient quantities are estimates (as I make this without measuring anything, and am just going by memory)
- Peel and chop mangoes into 1/4" chunks
- Chop cilantro finely
- Add all ingredients in bowl and mix. Let sit awhile.
- Serve slightly chilled

226. Masala Potaotes Recipe

Serving: 4 | Prep: | Cook: 52mins |Ready in:

Ingredients

- 3 - 4 large baking potatoes (peeled and cut into 1 or 2 inch cubes)
- 2 Tblsp of olive oil
- curry powder to taste (home made or any favorite brand)
- 1 tsp of garam masala
- salt & pepper to taste

Direction

- (Preheat oven to 375F.)
- In a large mixing bowl, put in all the ingredients, mix and toss thoroughly.
- Spread them in one layer on a sprayed or buttered baking tray.
- Bake for 25 minutes, take out of the oven, toss and turn the pieces around keeping one single layer for them to cook evenly.
- Put back in the oven and bake for another 25 to 30 minutes or just until tender when pierced with a fork.
- Serve with your favorite meat, poultry of even fish dish as a side.
- You will get hooked on this one.

227. Mashed Broccoli And Leeks With Cheese Recipe

Serving: 4 | Prep: | Cook: 15mins |Ready in:

Ingredients

- 1 1/2 pound broccoli, cut into 1-inch chunks, including stems
- 1 large leek, roughly chopped
- 2 cloves garlic, smashed
- 1 1/2 cups vegetable or chicken broth
- 1/4 cup plain yogurt or light sour cream
- salt and pepper, to taste
- 1/2 cup grated cheddar cheese

Direction

- In a large pot, combine broccoli, leek, garlic and broth. Bring to a boil and simmer, covered, over low heat until broccoli is tender, about 15 or 20 minutes.
- Remove from heat and puree in the pot with an immersion blender (be careful not to spatter!), or transfer to a food processor or blender and puree. (I like to leave a few chunks though, for texture)
- Stir in yogurt or sour cream and season to taste with salt and pepper. Sprinkle each serving w/ a bit of grated cheese.

228. Matzoh Ball And Sweet Potato Stew Recipe

Serving: 12 | Prep: | Cook: 60mins | Ready in:

Ingredients

- 1 recipe matzoh balls- yours or a box mix
- 2 lbs sweet potatoes peeled and sliced
- 1 lb carrots peeled and sliced
- 1 box pitted prunes
- 1, 16 oz can crushed pineapple drained and reserve the juice
- 1/2 cup brown sugar
- 1 tsp salt or to taste
- pepper to taste

Direction

- Prepare you matzoh balls and set aside
- Cook sweet potatoes tender but not overly soft and set aside
- Cook carrots and set aside
- Soften prunes in boiling water and drain and set aside
- Then in a large casserole dish place the cooked sweet potatoes, carrots, prunes and crushed pineapple.
- Sprinkle with brown sugar, salt and pepper to taste
- Add the matzoh balls and pour on the reserved pineapple juice
- Bake in a 350F about 30- 40 minutes until well heated, basting several times.

229. Mediterranean Kale Recipe

Serving: 2 | Prep: | Cook: 20mins | Ready in:

Ingredients

- 15-20 large kale leafs (torn into pieces)
- 1/2 medium red onion (chopped)
- 2 tbsp. salted butter
- olive oil to coat
- 1-2 oz. Greek style feta cheese
- 1-2 tbsp. balsamic vinegar

Direction

- Heat a large cast iron skillet over medium to high heat.
- Once heated, add butter, melt, and coat skillet.
- Toss in onion and cook for roughly 3 minutes or until they start to become tender.
- Start adding kale a little at a time. As it cooks down add more.
- Once all of the kale has been added, add olive oil to coat or to your liking.
- Cook for roughly 10-12 minutes or until kale has cooked down and looks wilted. Some browning is OK.
- Finish by adding the balsamic and feta to the skillet and lightly tossing the kale while cooking for 5 more minutes.
- Plate and serve. I served this with pasta and garlic bread.

230. Mexican Coleslaw Recipe

Serving: 6 | Prep: | Cook: | Ready in:

Ingredients

- 2 cups very thinly sliced green cabbage
- 1-1/2 cups peeled and grated carrots
- 1/3 cup chopped cilantro
- 1/4 cup rice vinegar
- 2 tablespoons extra-virgin olive oil
- 1/4 teaspoon salt

Direction

- Place cabbage and carrots in a colander then rinse thoroughly with cold water to crisp.
- Let drain for 5 minutes.

- Meanwhile whisk cilantro, vinegar, oil and salt in a large bowl.
- Add cabbage and carrots and toss well to coat.

231. Mexican Corn Casserole Recipe

Serving: 12 | Prep: | Cook: 60mins | Ready in:

Ingredients

- 4- eggs
- 1- can (15 1/4 ounces) whole kernel , drained
- 1- can (14 3/4ounces) cream style corn
- 1 1/2 -cups cornmeal
- 1 1/4- cups buttermilk
- 1- cup unsalted butter at room temperature
- 8- ounces chopped green chiles
- 2- medium onions , chopped
- 1- teaspoon baking soda
- 1 1/2- cups shredded pepper-jack cheese--
- 1 1/2- cups shredded cheddar cheese -
- opt........jalapeno and sweet red pepper rings for garnish

Direction

- Preheat oven to 325 degrees F.
- Grease a 13x9 x2 inch baking dish
- Beat eggs in a large bowl, add kernel corn, cream style corn, cornmeal, buttermilk, butter, chilies, onions and baking soda mix well
- Stir in 1 cup each of the shredded cheeses
- Pour mixture into baking dish
- Bake uncovered for 60 minutes
- Top with remaining 1 cup of cheeses
- Let stand for 10-15 minutes before serving
- Garnish with pepper rings
- Makes 12-15 servings

232. Mexican Zucchini Casserole Recipe

Serving: 8 | Prep: | Cook: 45mins | Ready in:

Ingredients

- 4 cups shredded zucchini
- 1/4 cup fine chopped onion
- 2 jalapeno peppers seeded and finely chopped
- 4 eggs
- 1/4 cup vegetable oil
- 1-1/2 cups baking mix
- 1/2 cup grated cheddar cheese
- 1/4 teaspoon salt
- 1/2 teaspoon freshly ground black pepper

Direction

- Preheat oven to 375.
- In large bowl mix zucchini, onion and pepper.
- In a smaller bowl beat eggs with oil until combined.
- Add to vegetable mixture and stir until combined then add baking mix and cheese.
- Stir well until baking mix is fully moistened then season with salt and pepper.
- Pour into greased rectangular pan and top with more grated cheese and bake 45 minutes.
- Remove from heat and cool slightly then cut into squares and serve warm.

233. Miss Olivias Summer Squash N Zuchini Casserole Recipe

Serving: 8 | Prep: | Cook: 45mins | Ready in:

Ingredients

- 1 stick butter
- 1 large onion, finely chopped
- 1 medium carrot, grated

- ½ large green bell pepper, finely diced (add small amounts of other colors of bell pepper if desired)
- 2 pounds small yellow squash, sliced
- 1 pound small zucchini, sliced
- 3 cups pepperidge Farm herb Seasoning, divided
- 1 (10 ¾ ounce) can cream of chicken soup
- 1 (10 ¾ ounce) can cream of mushroom soup
- ½-cup mayonnaise
- ½-cup sour cream
- Seasoned salt of your choice
- 1 cup Sargento?s Italian 6 cheese blend shredded cheese
- ½ stick butter, melted

Direction

- Preheat oven to 350 degrees.
- Spray a 9x13 baking dish with Pam.
- In a large skillet, melt butter over medium high heat.
- Add onions, carrots and bell pepper; cook and stir until tender.
- Add squash and zucchini. Cook until crisp tender. In a medium bowl, mix two cups Pepperidge Farm breadcrumbs, soups, sour cream and mayonnaise.
- Combine soup mixture and squash mixture.
- Add seasoned salt to taste.
- Pour mixture into prepared baking dish.
- Sprinkle cheese evenly over all.
- Toss remaining cup of breadcrumbs in melted butter.
- Sprinkle evenly over cheese layer.
- Bake 45 minutes or until crumbs are golden and mixture is bubbly.

234.   Molasses Baked Beans Recipe

Serving: 20 | Prep: | Cook: 190mins | Ready in:

Ingredients

- Ingredients:
- 2 pounds of dry navy beans
- 5 quarts water, divided
- 1 can (28-oz) diced tomatoes, un-drained (No salt added)
- 1 ½ cups ketchup
- 1 cup margarine or butter, melted
- 2 large onions, quarter
- ½ cup packed brown sugar
- ½ cup molasses
- 1 Tbs. salt
- 1 Tbs. liquid smoke or barbecue sauce

Direction

- Preheat oven at 350.
- Place beans and 2 ½ qts. Water in a 6-qt Dutch oven; bring to a boil and boil for 2 minutes. Remove from the heat; soak for 1 hour. Drain and rinse beans; return to pan with remaining water. Bring to a boil. Reduce heat; cover and simmer for 1 hour or until beans are tender. Drain, reserving cooking liquid. Return beans to pan; add remaining ingredients and mix well. Cover and bake at 350 for 2 to 2 ½ hours or until beans reach desired consistency. Add some of the reserved cooking liquid if too thick.
- Serving Size: 3/4 cup
- Nutrition Values: Calories per serving: 308, Fat: 10g, Cholesterol: 25mg, Sodium: 729mg. Carbohydrate: 47

235.   Moroccan Spiced Spaghetti Squash Recipe

Serving: 4 | Prep: | Cook: 20mins | Ready in:

Ingredients

- 1 (3 1/2- to 4-pound) spaghetti squash
- 1/2 stick (4 tablespoons) unsalted butter, cut into pieces
- 2 garlic cloves, minced
- 1 teaspoon ground cumin

- 1/2 teaspoon ground coriander
- 1/8 teaspoon cayenne
- 3/4 teaspoon salt
- 2 tablespoons chopped fresh cilantro or flat-leaf parsley,

Direction

- Two ways to cook the squash:
- To cook the squash in a microwave:
- Pierce squash (about an inch deep) all over with a small sharp knife to prevent bursting.
- Cook in an 800-watt microwave oven on high power (100 percent) for 6 to 7 minutes.
- Turn squash over and microwave until squash feels slightly soft when pressed, 8 to 10 minutes more.
- Cool squash for 5 minutes.
- To roast the squash,
- Two methods:
- If you'd like to roast the squash whole, pierce it all over with a small sharp knife to prevent bursting and bake it in a 375°F oven for one hour.
- If you are good with a big, sharp knife, you can save some time by cutting the squash in half lengthwise, scooping out the seeds and roasting the halves face-down in an oiled baking pan for about 40 minutes in a 375°F oven.
- Meanwhile, melt the butter in a small saucepan over medium heat.
- Add the garlic and cook, stirring, until it is barely golden.
- Stir in spices and salt and remove from heat.
- If you have microwaved or roasted your squash whole, carefully halve it lengthwise (it will give off a lot of steam) and remove the seeds.
- Carefully halve squash lengthwise (it will give off steam) and remove and discard seeds.
- Working over a bowl, scrape squash flesh with a fork, loosening and separating strands as you remove it from skin.
- Toss with the spiced butter and cilantro.

236. My Famous Green Beans Recipe

Serving: 10 | Prep: | Cook: 45mins | Ready in:

Ingredients

- 2 Large Bags of Whole frozen green beans
- 6 Large red potatoes
- 1 Pound of Meaty Hickory smoked bacon Chopped (2 Inch Pieces)
- 1 Large red onion Chopped
- 1 Medium yellow sweet onion Chopped
- 2 Large cloves of garlic Crushed
- 2 Tablespoons of parsley
- 2 Tablespoons of Chopped chives
- 1 Tablespoon of red pepper flakes
- 1 Tablespoon of sea salt
- 1 Tablespoon of cracked pepper
- Dressing:
- 1 Tablespoon sugar
- 1 Teaspoon of thyme
- 1 Teaspoon of apple cider vinegar
- 1 Teaspoon of Grey Poupon Country Dijon mustard
- 1 Teaspoon olive oil

Direction

- Meats and Onions and Spices:
- Combine Bacon, Red Onion, Yellow Onion, Garlic, Parsley, Chives, Red Pepper Flakes, Sea Salt and Cracked Pepper in A Large Skillet and Fry Until Bacon Starts to Turn Brown and Onions Become Transparent and Lightly Browned! Dump Into Medium Roaster Pan...
- Green Beans:
- In Another Large Pot Add Your 2 Large Bags of Green Beans and 2 Cups of Water and Enough Salt and Pepper to Taste, Boil Until Tender But Not Mush! Dump Into Same Roaster Pan...
- Potatoes:
- Wash Your Potatoes and Cut Off The Ends, Poke A Few Holes with A Knife and Put Into

The Microwave On High for 15 Minutes, Make Sure to Check Them Sometimes They Cook Faster...They Are Done When The Are Easy To Push The Knife Through But Not Done to A Mush, Still A little Firm You Don't Want Them to Break!

- Then Thick Slice The Potatoes and Pan Fry Them In The Bacon Grease Left In The Pan Until Lightly Browned On Both Sides...When Done Add Them to The Roaster Pan As Well!
- Mix Together the...
- Dressing:
- 1 Tablespoon Sugar
- 1 Teaspoon of Thyme
- 1 Teaspoon of Apple Cider Vinegar
- 1 Teaspoon of Grey Poupon Country Dijon Mustard
- 1 Teaspoon Olive Oil
- After Preparing All of These Ingredients Separately and Putting Into The Roaster Pan, Pour Over The Dressing and Lightly Tossing It Together Being Careful Not to Break The Potatoes or The Beans...You Are Ready to Serve!!!
- You May Salt and Pepper Them More If You Like...
- So Very good...These Are the Best Green Beans I've ever eaten...Enjoy and Let Me Know How You like Them!

237. Napa Style Roasted Vegetables Recipe

Serving: 8 | Prep: | Cook: 120mins | Ready in:

Ingredients

- 1/2 c. olive oil
- 2 c. each carrots, butternut squash,white potatoes, red potatoes, and red onion. all peeled and cut into 1 1/2 inch pieces
- 4 c yukon gold potatoes, unpeeled, cut into 1 1/2 pieces
- 2 t. fine sea salt, divided

- 16 pieces of fresh thyme, rinsed and cut into 2 inch pieces
- 1 t. of crushed red pepper flakes
- 2 c. apples, cored, peeled and cut into wedges
- 8 stems of flat leaf parsley, coarsely torn

Direction

- Preheat oven to 400degrees
- Pour olive oil into a large bowl. Add chopped vegetables and toss to evenly coat.
- Add 1 t. fine sea salt, thyme, and red pepper flakes, toss again. Transfer to 12 x 18 inch sheet pan
- Roast for 30 minutes. Remove from oven and stir in apple wedges. Return to oven and bake 30 minutes more. Stir and bake for 20 minutes more.
- Transfer to a serving dish. Garnish with parsley and remaining sea salt

238. New Years Day Green Beans Recipe

Serving: 8 | Prep: | Cook: 190mins | Ready in:

Ingredients

- 1 Small ham, bone in
- 15 small red potatoes
- 1 onion chopped
- 1 tablespoon garlic minced
- 1-2 pounds of fresh green beans.. snapped
- salt to taste
- Lots of black pepper
- 2 or more quarts of water

Direction

- In a large pot add ham, onion, garlic, salt and pepper
- Cover with water and bring to boil
- Lower heat and simmer for at least 1 1/2 hours
- Add potatoes and green beans

- Cook until the green beans and potatoes are done
- Serve with hot corn bread and lots of butter...
- Turns out better if lots of black pepper is used. I don't wait for New Year's...
- Enjoy!

239. North African Spiced Carrots Recipe

Serving: 6 | Prep: | Cook: 15mins | Ready in:

Ingredients

- 1 tablespoon extra-virgin olive oil
- 4 cloves garlic minced
- 2 teaspoons paprika
- 1 teaspoon ground cumin
- 1 teaspoon ground coriander
- 3 cups sliced carrots
- 1 cup water
- 3 tablespoons lemon juice
- 1/8 teaspoon salt
- 1/4 cup chopped fresh parsley

Direction

- Heat oil in a large nonstick skillet over medium heat.
- Add garlic, paprika, cumin and coriander.
- Cook stirring until fragrant but not browned.
- Add carrots, water, lemon juice and salt.
- Bring to a simmer.
- Reduce heat to low then cover and cook until almost tender.
- Uncover and simmer stirring often until carrots are just tender and the liquid is syrupy.
- Stir in parsley.
- Serve hot or at room temperature.

240. Not Really Esquites Recipe

Serving: 4 | Prep: | Cook: 12mins | Ready in:

Ingredients

- 4 fresh ears of corn, leaves pulled back, silks removed
- 2 Tbsp butter
- 2 Tbsp arbol chili powder, dried chili de arbol (Ground in a spice grinder)
- 2 limes, juiced
- 1 jalapeno pepper, cut in half, seeded
- 1/2 cup queso cotija, crumbled (parmesan will work)
- 8 cups water

Direction

- In a large shallow pan bring the water to a boil. Add the butter and the jalapeno. Once the butter is melted submerge the corn in the water. Reduce the heat to a simmer and cook for 12 minutes.
- Remove the corn from the water. Coat the corn with lime juice, a few sprinkles of chili powder, and crumbled queso cotija. Eat it while it's hot.

241. Not Rolled Rolled Cabbage Recipe

Serving: 8 | Prep: | Cook: 60mins | Ready in:

Ingredients

- 1-1/4 pounds ground beef
- 1/2 cup plain bread crumbs
- 1 egg
- 1 teaspoon salt
- 1/4 teaspoon black pepper
- 1 medium head green cabbage, shredded (12 to 14 cups)

- 1 can (16 ounces) jellied or whole-berry cranberry sauce
- 5 gingersnap cookies, crumbled (about 1/4 cup crumbs)
- 1 tablespoon lemon juice
- 1 jar (28 ounces) spaghetti sauce

Direction

- In a medium bowl, combine the ground beef, bread crumbs, egg, salt, and pepper. Form the mixture into 1-inch meatballs (about 1 tablespoon each).
- Place half the shredded cabbage in a soup pot then add the meatballs. Spread the cranberry sauce over the meatballs, sprinkle with gingersnap crumbs and lemon juice then add the remaining cabbage. Pour the spaghetti sauce over the mixture and do not stir.
- Bring to a boil then reduce the heat to low and simmer uncovered for 20 minutes. Stir gently, being careful not to break up the meatballs. Simmer for another 40 minutes, stirring halfway through.
- NOTE: If you like this on the sweeter side, add a tablespoon or two of dark brown sugar.

---

242. Onion Gruyere Pie Recipe

Serving: 8 | Prep: | Cook: 40mins | Ready in:

Ingredients

- 1 pound thinly sliced Vidalia or other sweet onions
- 4 tablespoons butter
- 2 eggs, beaten
- ½ cup sour cream
- dash of: salt, pepper, garlic powder and Tabasco
- 1 cup grated gruyere cheese
- 1 refrigerated prepared pie-crust, or use your own crust recipe (I used Jetts Mamas Easy pie

crust from this site - fantastic, flakey, delicious crust!)
- ¼ cup fresh grated parmesan cheese

Direction

- In a large skillet, sauté sliced onions in butter until nicely golden brown - do this over low to medium low heat, and it will take about 15 minutes.
- In bowl, mix together eggs, sour cream and seasonings.
- Remove onions from heat and add egg mixture to sautéed onions.
- Add gruyere cheese and gently stir mixture to blend ingredients.
- Pour into a 10-inch glass pie plate lined with a pie crust (I like to pre-bake my crust for 8 minutes at 350 degrees before adding the filling).
- Top mixture with the parmesan cheese.
- Bake at 350 degrees for 20 minutes; reduce heat to 325 degrees and bake another 15 minutes.
- Note: if you want to omit the pie crust, just pour the filling into a well-buttered 10-inch glass pie plate and bake as directed.

---

243. Onion Pie Recipe

Serving: 8 | Prep: | Cook: 35mins | Ready in:

Ingredients

- 1 pound thinly sliced vidalia onions
- 4 tablespoons butter
- 2 eggs, beaten
- ½ cup sour cream
- dash each of: salt, pepper, garlic and Tabasco
- 1 cup grated gruyere cheese
- 1 pie crust (I usually use the refrigerated crusts)
- ¼ cup fresh grated parmesan cheese

Direction

- In a large skillet, sauté sliced onions in butter until nicely golden. In bowl, mix together eggs, sour cream and seasonings; add egg mixture to sautéed onions. Add gruyere cheese and gently stir mixture to blend ingredients. Pour into a 10-inch glass pie plate lined with a pie crust (I like to pre-bake my crust for 8 minutes at 350 degrees before adding the filling). Top quiche with the parmesan cheese. Bake at 350 degrees for 20 minutes; reduce heat to 325 degrees and bake another 15 minutes.
- Note: if you omit the pie crust, just pour the filling into a well-buttered 10-inch glass pie plate as bake as directed.

244. Oven Fried Cauliflower Recipe

Serving: 8 | Prep: | Cook: 100mins | Ready in:

Ingredients

- 1 cup mayonnaise
- 1 medium cauliflower broken into flowerets
- 1 cup Italian seasoned breadcrumbs

Direction

- Place mayonnaise in a large heavy duty plastic bag.
- Add cauliflower then seal and shake to coat.
- Place breadcrumbs in a large heavy duty plastic bag.
- Add half of cauliflower mixture then seal and shake to coal.
- Spread in a single layer onto a lightly greased baking sheet.
- Repeat with remaining cauliflower mixture and breadcrumbs.
- Bake at 350 for 1 hour.

245. Oven Fried Zucchini Sticks Recipe

Serving: 4 | Prep: | Cook: 10mins | Ready in:

Ingredients

- canola oil cooking spray
- 1/2 cup whole-wheat flour
- 1/2 cup all-purpose flour
- 2 tablespoons cornmeal
- 1 teaspoon salt
- 1/2 teaspoon freshly ground pepper
- 1 1/2 pounds zucchini (about 3 medium), cut into 1/2-by-3-inch sticks
- 2 egg whites, lightly beaten

Direction

- Preheat oven to 475°F.
- Coat a large baking sheet with cooking spray.
- Combine flours, cornmeal, salt and pepper in a large sealable plastic bag.
- Dip zucchini in egg white, shake in the bag to coat, and arrange, not touching, on the baking sheet. Coat all exposed sides with cooking spray.
- Bake on the centre rack for 7 minutes. Turn the zucchini and coat any floury spots with cooking spray. Continue to bake until golden and just tender, about 5 minutes more. Serve hot.

246. Oven Fried Zucchini In A Crunchy Parmesan Crust Recipe

Serving: 4 | Prep: | Cook: 15mins | Ready in:

Ingredients

- 1 tablespoon extra-virgin 0live oil
- 1/4 cup fine dried bread crumbs
- 1/3 cup grated imported parmesan cheese
- 1/2 teaspoon dried rosemary, crumbled
- 2 to 3 dashed cayenne pepper

- 1/2 teaspoon salt
- 1/4 teaspoon freshly ground black pepper
- 1 large egg
- 4 small green or golden zucchini squash

Direction

- Preheat the oven to 400 degrees F. Lightly grease a heavy baking sheet with the oil and set aside.
- In a shallow dish, combine the bread crumbs, Parmesan cheese, rosemary, cayenne, salt and pepper, and mix well. In a second shallow dish, lightly beat the egg.
- Trim the ends of the squash. Cut each squash in half lengthwise. Lay the halves flat and cut in half lengthwise again. Then cut the strips in half crosswise. Dredge each piece first in the egg and then in the Parmesan mixture, coating evenly. Arrange well-spaced in a single layer on the prepared baking sheet.
- Bake in the oven for 5 to 7 minutes, then turn the squash over and bake 5 to 7 minutes longer, or until crisp and lightly browned. Serve hot or at room temperature.

247. Pa Dutch Old Fashioned Green Beans And Bacon Recipe

Serving: 4 | Prep: | Cook: 30mins | Ready in:

Ingredients

- 3/4 lb. green beans
- 8 slices bacon
- 2 medium potatoes, pared and cut into 1/2 in. pieces
- 1 small onion, sliced
- 1/4 cup water
- 1/2 tsp salt

Direction

- Cook green beans in a small amount of boiling, salted water 10 to 15 min. or until just tender.
- Dice the bacon and fry until crisp. Add green beans and remaining ingredients to bacon and cook, covered, about 15 min. or until potatoes are tender.

248. Palak Paneer Recipe

Serving: 4 | Prep: | Cook: 20mins | Ready in:

Ingredients

- 1lb fresh spinach, chopped
- 8oz Paneer*(recipe follows, or, semi firm tofu can be substituted), cubed
- 3T olive oil
- 1T butter
- 1 onion, diced
- 4-6 cloves garlic, minced
- 2 large tomatoes, diced(or sub 14oz can, partially drained)
- 2tsp ground cumin
- 1-2T fresh ginger, grated(or 1T ground)
- 2t pepper flakes, or powder, or to taste
- 1t turmeric
- 1t coriander
- 2-3T cream, half and half, or milk(optional)

Direction

- Heat olive oil in large stir fry pan, or wok over medium heat. Add onion.
- Cook about 3 minutes, alone.
- Add butter, garlic, cumin, pepper, turmeric and coriander
- Add paneer cubes and carefully brown on all sides.
- Remove from pan.
- Add spinach, tomatoes and ginger to pan and toss while cooking down
- If using cream, add now, and stir just to combine.
- Add cheese back to pan and toss till warmed

- **Here's a simple recipe for Paneer:
- 1q whole fat or 2% milk
- Juice from 2 lemons
- Salt and cumin (about 1tsp or so, each, maybe a bit more salt)
- Heat milk, salt and cumin over medium heat and simmer for about 5 minutes, stirring often.
- Remove from heat and add lemon juice, 1/2 lemon at a time, stirring constantly. Curds will separate from whey while stirring. It will take on a cottage cheese type consistency.
- When whey is only slightly cloudy and curds are defined, pour into cheesecloth over large bowl/dish to strain.
- When mostly done draining, and cooling, carefully squeeze out as much of the liquid as you can, and mold curds into "block" type shape. (Think "cream cheese":)
- Place in shallow bowl, then cover the cloth covered cheese block with heavy object (I used my cast iron Dutch oven).
- Let rest, there, a couple hours, till all that's going to come out is out :)
- Refrigerate at least several hours before using in a recipe such as above...the longer it sets, the firmer it will be

---

249. Pan Fried Cabbage Recipe

Serving: 6 | Prep: | Cook: 12mins | Ready in:

Ingredients

- 1 head cabbage(cut into slices)
- 1 large onion,sliced
- 1 cup celery, chopped
- 1 cup sliced smoked sausage(you can also use bacon or ham if you prefer!)
- 6 tablespoons butter
- 3 tablespoons(more if needed) olive oil(you could sub vegetable oil)]
- 1/4 cup soy sauce
- 1 teaspoon cracked black pepper

- salt to taste

Direction

- Heat oil in large skillet. Add sausage (or other meat), onions, and celery and cook until sausage is lightly browned.
- Add cabbage and stir well.
- Continue cooking on med/high heat for 3 to 4 minutes, stirring often to prevent sticking.
- Add butter, sour sauce, and black pepper, cover, lower heat to low/med.
- Cook for 2 to 3 minutes.
- Taste, add salt if needed.

---

250. Paneer Butter Masala Recipe

Serving: 3 | Prep: | Cook: 25mins | Ready in:

Ingredients

- 125 grams paneer (cottage cheese)
- 1 tomato (grind to a fine paste)
- 1 Tsp tomato puree
- 2 onions (grind to fine paste)
- 1 tsp cumin powder
- 1 tsp Dhania Powder (coriander powder)
- 1 tsp ginger garlic paste
- 3 cloves
- 1 tsp cashews
- 1 cinnamon stick
- 1/2 tsp garam masala powder (http://www.recipedelights.com/basics/GaraMMasala.htm)
- 1/4 tsp chilli powder
- 3 Tsp yogurt
- coriander leaves
- 4-5 Tsp butter
- salt

Direction

- Grind cloves, cinnamon to fine powder

- Heat oil, fry few paneer cubes on medium heat until golden brown. Set the paneer pieces aside.
- Grate remaining paneer and keep it aside
- Heat oil or butter, fry onions, ginger garlic paste, for 3 minutes.
- Add tomato paste and puree and simmer for 5 minutes.
- Add cashews, Dhania powder, Cumin powder, garam masala powder, salt, chilli powder, extra butter and masala powder from step 1.
- Add yogurt and stir until gravy becomes thick. Add fried paneer cubes, grated paneer add 1/2 -1 cup water and simmer for 5 minutes, until all the flavour is absorbed into paneer.
- Serve hot garnished with coriander leaves.

---

251. Papas Potato Cabbage Casserole Recipe

Serving: 6 | Prep: | Cook: 45mins | Ready in:

Ingredients

- 3 med. potatos scrubbed
- 8 oz. bacon chopped
- 1/2 cup sliced onion
- 2 TBSP all-purpose flour
- 1/2 tsp dried thyme
- 1/2 tsp salt
- 1 (12 Oz.) can of beer
- 1/2 cup milk
- 6 cups shredded green cabbage
- 1 cup shredded swiss cheese

Direction

- Combine potatoes with water cook until tender. About 30 min. Cut potatoes into slices.
- Fry bacon in skillet until crisp. Remove bacon with slotted spoon reserving 2 TBSP of pan drippings.
- Preheat oven to 375 degrees. Spray a 3 qt. round baking dish with cooking spray.

- Sauté onion in reserved drippings until tender. Stir in flour, thyme and salt. Add beer and milk and mix well. Cook over low heat. Stirring continually, until sauce has thickened.
- Layer cabbage, potatoes, bacon, Swiss and beer sauce one half at a time in baking dish. Bake, covered for 30 min. remove cover. Bake until cabbage is tender, about 20 min.

---

252. Parmesan Celery Recipe

Serving: 4 | Prep: | Cook: 15mins | Ready in:

Ingredients

- 1 bunch fresh crisp celery, cleaned, and sliced on a thin diagonal
- 1/4 cup onion slivers
- 1 medium clove garlic, pressed,
- 1 cup chicken broth
- 4 slices crisp, crumbled bacon, or 1/2 cup minced ham
- 1 cup shredded swiss cheese
- 2 tbs grated parmesan cheese

Direction

- Wash and slice celery on the diagonal into medium thin slices.
- Mix with onion and garlic. Simmer in broth about 10 minutes until tender crisp.
- Drain, but save 2 tbsp. broth.
- Turn into flat casserole, top with bacon or ham and cover with Swiss cheese.
- Sprinkle Parmesan over all.
- Bake at 350* for 10 to 15 minutes.
- Sprinkle with Paprika when out of oven.
- Heat darkens Paprika and this keeps it bright red.

253. Parmesan Portobellos N Marinara Sauce Recipe

Serving: 6 | Prep: | Cook: 25mins | Ready in:

Ingredients

- 1 16-ounce ounce jar marinara sauce
- 2 T garlic
- 2 T italian seasoning
- 6-8 large portobello mushrooms
- 1 cup grated parmesan cheese
- 1 cup mozzarella cheese

Direction

- Preheat oven to 375 degrees.
- Coat a 9-by13-inch glass baking dish with non-stick cooking spray.
- Stir seasoning and garlic into sauce
- Spread 3/4 cup marinara sauce in the bottom of the dish.
- Trim the mushrooms so they fit in one layer; use the trimmed pieces to fill in where needed.
- Pour the remaining sauce over the mushrooms.
- Sprinkle with Parmesan then Mozzarella
- Sprinkle with a little more Italian seasoning
- Cover the dish with foil and bake for 20-25 minutes.
- Let stand a couple of minutes before serving.

254. Parmesan Veggie Stir Fry Ci Recipe

Serving: 4 | Prep: | Cook: 10mins | Ready in:

Ingredients

- 1/2 lb sugar peas
- 8oz fresh mushrooms, chunked
- 2 large green onions or 1 leek, cut in 1 inch pieces
- 1 large red pepper, sliced in strips
- 2 cloves garlic, minced

- 1T butter
- 1T olive oil
- juice from 1/2 lemon
- 1/2 cup fresh Parmesan, shredded
- fresh basil leaves, coarsely chopped
- salt and fresh ground pepper

Direction

- Add butter and olive oil to a stir fry skillet over medium high heat.
- As soon as butter begins to melt, add garlic then all veggies and toss to coat.
- Cook for only about 3-5 minutes so veggie are warm but still crisp.
- Add lemon juice, salt and pepper and basil and toss, again.
- Remove from heat and add cheese to top after placing in serving dish or add to each individual serving on plates.

255. Pepperoni Zucchini Boats Recipe

Serving: 4 | Prep: | Cook: 15mins | Ready in:

Ingredients

- 2 Tablespoons butter
- 2 medium zucchini
- 1/3 cup diced onion
- 1 teaspoon italian seasoning
- 12 slices pepperoni sausage, diced
- 1 cup Italian cheese blend, divided
- 1/2 cup grated Asiago or parmesan cheese

Direction

- Preheat oven to 375 degrees F (190 degrees C).
- Melt butter in skillet.
- Cut zucchini in half lengthwise. With a metal spoon, scoop out most of the insides and place into a skillet. Transfer the zucchini shells to a baking sheet.

- Place the skillet over medium heat, and stir in onion, Italian seasoning and pepperoni. Cook about 3 minutes. Remove from heat, and spoon cooked mixture into zucchini shells. Top with Italian cheese blend then sprinkle with grated cheese.
- Bake in preheated oven for 12 minutes.

256. Peruvian Grilled Yucca With Huancaina Sauce Recipe

Serving: 4 | Prep: | Cook: 35mins | Ready in:

Ingredients

- 1 whole yucca
- salt
- 4 tablespoons melted butter
- ****
- 4 tablespoons canola oil
- 1/2 red onion, diced
- 1 aji amarillo, rib and seeds removed, diced
- 1 clove garlic
- salt and pepper
- 5 ounces fresh mozzarella cheese
- 1 hard-boiled egg, plus chopped hard-boiled egg, for garnish
- 1/2 cup heavy cream
- nicoise olives, for garnish, optional
- cilantro leaves, for garnish, optional

Direction

- Peel yucca and cut into 4 cylinders; then split in half and remove the root. Place yucca in a large pot. Add enough water to cover yucca and season with salt. Bring to a boil and simmer until fork tender, about 30 minutes.
- Remove from heat and allow to cool. Brush with butter and place on grill. Cook about 3 to 4 minutes per side. Remove and season with salt.
- Meanwhile, in a skillet, heat 2 tablespoons oil over medium heat.

- Add onion, ají, and garlic. Season with salt and pepper and sauté until onion becomes translucent.
- Remove from heat and add to blender. Add cheese and hard-boiled egg and blend. Slowly drizzle in heavy cream and remaining 2 tablespoons oil until sauce consistency. Adjust salt before serving.
- Serve yucca with huancaina sauce, garnished with hard-boiled egg, olives, and cilantro.

257. Pickled Blackeyed Peas Recipe

Serving: 12 | Prep: | Cook: 12mins | Ready in:

Ingredients

- 4 cups of cooked blackeyed peas
- 1 cup oil
- 1/2 of cider vinegar
- 1/2 cup of thinly sliced onions
- 1/2 teaspoon of salt
- several grinds of black pepper
- 6 cloves of chopped garlic, very fine
- 2 jalapeno peppers, minced
- extra Tabasco sauce if desired

Direction

- Combine all ingredients.
- Place in covered container.
- Resist eating for two days.
- Dig in. (the longer they sit, the better they taste!)

258. Pickled Jalapenos Recipe

Serving: 6 | Prep: | Cook: 5mins | Ready in:

Ingredients

- 3 cups rice wine vinegar

- 3 tablespoons sugar
- 1 teaspoon white peppercorns
- 1 teaspoon coriander seeds
- 1 teaspoon mustard seeds
- 1/2 teaspoon cumin seeds
- 2 tablespoons kosher salt
- 3 jalapenos, sliced in half lengthwise
- 3 tablespoons fresh cilantro
- Special Equipment:
- 1 (8-ounce) jar

Direction

- Combine the vinegar, sugar, peppercorns, seeds, and salt in a medium saucepan and bring to a boil. Let boil for 2 minutes, and then remove from the heat and let sit until cooled to room temperature.
- Place the jalapenos, stem side up, into the jar and pour enough cooled vinegar mixture over them to cover. Pack the cilantro into the jar. Cover and refrigerate for at least 24 hours and up to 4 days.

259.   Pinto Beans Recipe

Serving: 12 | Prep: | Cook: 180mins | Ready in:

Ingredients

- 1 lb. package dried pinto beans, soaked, rinsed and drained
- Approx 4 quarts water
- 1/2 yellow onion, chopped
- 3 garlic cloves, minced
- 4 chicken bouillon cubes
- 1 large palmful of chili powder (approx 2 tbs)
- 1 large palmful of cumin (approx 1 1/2 tbs)
- 1 Tbs garlic powder
- 1 bay leaf
- 1 Tbs dried parsley
- kosher salt and pepper to taste
- (1-2 Tbs pickled or fresh jalapenos, chopped - optional)

Direction

- Put beans in large pot, and add about 4 quarts of water over high heat.
- Add bouillon cubes, onion and garlic and bring to a boil.
- Reduce to low heat and add chili powder, cumin, garlic powder and bay leaf. (You can add jalapenos, if you like it spicy.)
- Simmer over low heat (you want a very slight bubbling), with lid partially over pot, for 2 hours.
- Add parsley, salt and pepper to taste (I use a couple of Tbsp. of salt and a couple of Tsps. of pepper)
- If it becomes too salty, add hot water to pot.
- Great served with Mexican food, or over rice. Awesome with cornbread, as its own meal!
- Enjoy!

260.   Popeye Spinach With Sesame Dressing Recipe

Serving: 5 | Prep: | Cook: 3mins | Ready in:

Ingredients

- 1 lb fresh spinach, washed
- 6 Tbs toasted sesame seeds
- 2 tsp suagr
- 3 Tbs soy sauce
- 2 Tbs rice wine vinegar
- 1 Tbs dashi or chicken broth

Direction

- To make dressing:
- First toast the sesame seeds in a 350 F oven for 6 mins. Remove. Let cool.
- Bring to boil an inch of dashi flavored water or chicken broth in a sauté pan. When it simmers and 1/4 tsp. salt.
- Put in spinach, stalk sections first then leaves. Simmer for 1-3 mins and rinse right away in cold water.

- Squeeze firmly but lightly. Mix spinach with dressing and form into small individual mounds or one large log. Keep cold till serve time.
- Just before serving slice log with a scissors into smaller squares.

261. Potato Tomato And Onion Casserole Recipe

Serving: 6 | Prep: | Cook: 30mins | Ready in:

Ingredients

- 2Tbs olive oil
- 2lg. russet potatoes,peeled and cut into thin rounds
- 6lg. plum or beefsteak tomatoes,thinly sliced
- salt to taste
- 1c grated pecorino romano cheese
- 2Tbs minced fresh marjoram leaves
- 1/2c dry white wine such as Pinot Grigio
- 2 med. red onins,cut into thin rounds.

Direction

- Preheat oven to 375
- Brush olive oil on a 9x13" casserole dish. Starting with the potatoes, make three alternating layers of potatoes, tomatoes and onions. Sprinkle each layer with salt and 1/3c cheese and marjoram
- Pour wine carefully into dish on one side. Cover with foil and bake 25-30 mins. Uncover the dish and continue baking till the top is nicely browned.

262. Pumpkins Kadu Bouranee With Yogurt Sauce Recipe

Serving: 6 | Prep: | Cook: 25mins | Ready in:

Ingredients

- 1.5 - 2 pounds fresh pumpkin or squash
- 1/4 cup corn oil
- Sweet Tomato Sauce:
- 1 teaspoon crushed garlic
- 1 cup water
- 1/2 teaspoon salt
- 1/2 cup sugar
- 1 4oz can tomato sauce
- 1/2 teaspoon ginger root, chopped fine
- 1 teaspoon freshly ground coriander seeds
- 1/4 teaspoons black pepper
- yogurt Sauce:
- 1/4 teaspoon crushed garlic
- 1/4 teaspoon salt
- 3/4 cup plain yogurt

Direction

- Peel the pumpkin and cut into 2-3 inch cubed pieces, set aside.
- Heat oil in a large frying pan that has a lid. Fry the pumpkins on both sides for a couple of minutes until lightly browned.
- Mix together ingredients for sweet tomato sauce in a bowl and then add to pumpkin mixture in frying pan. Cover and cook for 20-25 minutes over low heat until the pumpkin is cooked and most of the liquid has evaporated.
- Mix together the ingredients for the yogurt sauce.
- To Serve: Spread half the yogurt sauce on a plate and lay the pumpkins on top. Top with remaining yogurt and any cooking juices left over.

263. Quick Spicy Kimchee Low Carb Tyler Style Recipe

Serving: 8 | Prep: | Cook: 27mins | Ready in:

Ingredients

- 1 head napa cabbage, 1 to 1 1/2 pounds

- 1/4 cup kosher salt
- 1/2 cup rice vinegar
- 1 tablespoon granular Splenda or equivalent liquid Splenda
- 2 tablespoons chili paste
- 2 teaspoons crushed red pepper flakes
- 2 teaspoons ginger root, grated
- 2 cloves garlic, chopped fine
- 2 green onions, sliced fine
- 2 tiny Thai bird chiies, seeded and halved

Direction

- Chop the stem end off the cabbage and then cut it into quarters lengthwise.
- Cut the quarters into 1/2-inch chunks. Place in a large colander and add the salt; mix well.
- Place over a bowl or in the sink and let drain, covered, about 2 hours until wilted.
- In a large bowl, mix the vinegar and Splenda.
- Add the remaining ingredients except the Thai chilies.
- Rinse the salt off the cabbage well.
- Drain then add to the vinegar mixture.
- Pack into a clean quart canning jar, packing down the cabbage tightly.
- Tuck in the Thai bird chilies deep into the cabbage.
- Add enough water to cover the cabbage.
- Cover and refrigerate at least 4 hours and preferably overnight. This will get hotter as it ages.
- I love this stuff and it will clear your sinuses.

---

264. RED CABBAGE WITH APPLES Recipe

Serving: 4 | Prep: | Cook: 20mins | Ready in:

Ingredients

- 1 TB oil
- 1 head red cabbage (approx 2#), cored and thinly shredded

- 1/2 c. + 2 tsp water
- 1 large tart apple, cored and coarsley chopped
- 1 TB packed light brown sugar
- 1/2 tsp caraway seed (optional)
- 1 tsp. salt
- 1/4 tsp. black pepper
- 2 tsp flour
- 1 TB cider vinegar

Direction

- In a large pot, heat oil over medium heat. Add the cabbage and 1/4 c. Of water. Cover and cook 5-7 minutes, stirring occasionally until wilted. Stir in 1/4 c. Water, apple, brown sugar, if using caraway seed, salt and pepper. Cover and cook for 7-10 minutes, stirring often until cabbage is almost done.
- Meanwhile in a small cup mix flour with remaining 2 tsp. Of water; add vinegar. Add to the cabbage, stirring to coat. Cook and stir for 2-3 minutes. Serve immediately.

---

265. Ratatouille My Way Recipe

Serving: 8 | Prep: | Cook: 60mins | Ready in:

Ingredients

- 1 medium eggplant cut in medium sized cubes (don't bother to peel)
- 2 zucchini, scrubbed and cut in medium chunks
- 2 yellow squash, scrubbed and cut in chunks
- 1 full head of garlic, most of the outer peel pulled off
- 2 large yellow or red onions cut in coarse wedges, ends removed
- 1 8 oz. box of white button mushrooms or crimini, wiped down left whole (on the small side, don't aim for huge mushrooms here, you don't want to cut them; that is more work)
- 1 green pepper, seeded and cut in medium chunks

- 1 red pepper seeded and cut in medium chunks
- 1 yellow pepper seeded and cut in medium chunks
- 2 lbs. of roma tomatoes stem ends removed and halved
- extra virgin olive oil
- sea salt
- fresh ground black pepper
- fresh marjoram if available (I mysteriously kill mine each year)
- several sprigs of fresh thyme leaves
- a handful of parsley, stemmed and coarsely chopped
- two long pieces of lemon rind, juice of one lemon
- sprinkle of crushed red pepper flakes
- few shavings of parmesan if you must gild the lily

Direction

- Line a large sheet pan with foil.
- Preheat oven to 450 degrees while you prep the veggies.
- Toss the eggplants, zucchini, yellow squash in a scant amount of oil, you don't want them drenched.
- Put on sheet pan, don't crowd and sprinkle with sea salt and ground black pepper.
- Trim the end of the garlic bulb and rub generously with oil.
- Toss peppers and onion and mushrooms with scant oil and put on the other end of the sheet pan. Again, don't crowd.
- If there is too much for your sheet pan, fix up another sheet pan and plan to rotate the pans while cooking.
- DON"T ROAST THE TOMATOES.
- Roast the veggies in hot oven for about 20 minutes. You want each to maintain their shape but to get a tiny bit of char on the surface.
- Don't cook the garlic to mush, you want to be able to just squeeze it from the bulb.
- Finally dump all the veggies into a stock pot, including the prepped tomatoes, squeeze the

garlic out of the bulb into the pot, the thyme leaves, the marjoram, the lemon rind and the lemon juice and a sprinkle of red pepper flakes.
- Cook over low heat until the tomatoes give up their juice and stir only enough to combine, you don't want to break down the veggies anymore if at all possible.
- At service, fish out lemon rind and thyme branches if you left them whole. Garnish with chopped fresh parsley and long shavings of parmesan.

---

266. Ratatouille Recipe

Serving: 8 | Prep: | Cook: 30mins | Ready in:

Ingredients

- Large onion
- 2 zucchini (unpeeled)
- 3 potatoes peeled and quartered
- 3 green peppers
- 2 tomatoes
- 1 jalapeno pepper
- 5 mini eggplants
- olive oil and salt

Direction

- Combine all ingredients and cook over medium heat until vegetables are cooked through.

---

267. Red Cabbage Recipe

Serving: 4 | Prep: | Cook: 40mins | Ready in:

Ingredients

- medium head red cabbage, cored
- 1 onion, chopped
- 1 T oil

- 1 c [water
- dash salt
- 3 T vinegar
- 3 T sugar
- 1 T flour

Direction

- Shred the cabbage into strips about ¼" by 1 or 2 inches. Chop onion; heat oil in medium sized pot; cook onion until soft. Add cabbage, water, and salt; cover and simmer on very low heat about 30-40 minutes until limp but not mushy. [There should be very little water left at this point. If there's more than a few tablespoons present, drain most of it off, either reserving it for soup or discarding it.] Finish by stirring in vinegar and sugar. Taste test to see if it needs more salt/sugar/vinegar. Sprinkle flour across cabbage while quickly blending to avoid lumping. Turn up heat and cook, stirring, until thickened.

---

268. Red Lentil Patties Vegetarian Meatballs Recipe

Serving: 6 | Prep: | Cook: 5mins | Ready in:

Ingredients

- • 1 cup red lentils, uncooked
- • 2 and 1/2 cups water
- • 1/2 cup fine bulgur, uncooked
- • 2 tablespoons extra virgin olive oil, plus more for drizzling
- • 1 medium onion, finely diced
- • 1 tablespoon tomato paste
- • 1tbspoon red pepper paste
- • 2tbspoon pomegranade molasses
- • 2tbspoon lemon juice
- • 1 teaspoon salt or more, depending on taste
- • 1 tablespoon paprika, plus more for dusting
- • 1 tablespoon ground cumin (or up to 2 tablespoons if you prefer)
- • 1/2 cup flat leaf parsley, finely chopped
- • ¾ cup fresh mint ,finely chopped
- • 3 scallions, finely sliced

Direction

- Wash the lentils in a large bowl until water runs clear. In a medium saucepan, bring water to a boil. Add lentils, and simmer until soft (but not overly mushy), about 15 minutes while stirring occasionally. Mix in bulgur; turn off the heat, cover the pot, and let it rest until the residual liquid is absorbed by the bulgur, about 15 minutes or longer.
- While the lentils cook, bring a skillet to medium heat and with olive oil and sauté diced onions until tender and translucent, about 8-10 minutes. Add in tomato paste; red pepper paste stir and turn off heat.
- Use the resting time of the lentils mixture and onions cooking to chop scallions and parsley.
- Once the lentils and bulgur are cooked, it should be moderately moist and not completely dry, like cookie dough. Add salt, onions, paprika, cumin, fresh onions, lemon juice, pomegranate molasses and most of the parsley and scallions, fresh mints into the mixture and stir to combine.
- At this point, the lentil and bulgur mixture should resemble thick cookie dough when stirred. If it still seems too damp, add more bulgur and let the mixture rest longer. The bulgur should no longer be hard, but soft and melded in to the mix.
- When the lentil-and-grain mixture is cool enough to handle, use your hands to knead it together. With a bowl of water at your side, wet your hands and mold the lentil and bulgur mixture into mini golf-ball sized balls (or any shape you prefer) and place on a platter. A tablespoon is a good amount for each ball. Garnish with remaining scallions and parsley and drizzle with good extra virgin olive oil ,the lettuce leaves and onions, then drizzle over the dressing..
- Note Turkish red pepper paste is available from Turkish and Middle Eastern food stores.

- Red lentils and bulgur can be purchased in bulk food bins, which are probably the least expensive. Sometimes they are also available in the international food aisle.

269. Refrigerator Pickled Beets And Onions Recipe

Serving: 6 | Prep: | Cook: 7mins | Ready in:

Ingredients

- 1/2 cup apple cider vinegar
- 1/2 cup water
- 2/3 cup granulated sugar
- 1/4 teaspoon salt
- 1/2 teaspoon ground cinnamon
- 1 large sweet onion, peeled and thinly sliced
- 2 cans sliced beets, undrained

Direction

- In saucepan, combine vinegar, water, sugar, salt, cinnamon and juice from canned beets to a boil.
- Reduce heat and simmer 5 to 7 minutes.
- Pour over sliced beets and onion.
- Cover and chill overnight. (Stir occasionally if you think of it!)

270. Remys Ratatouille Recipe

Serving: 6 | Prep: | Cook: 240mins | Ready in:

Ingredients

- Piperade (bottom layer):
- ½ red bell pepper, seeds and ribs removed
- ½ yellow bell pepper, seeds and ribs removed
- ½ orange bell pepper, seeds and ribs removed
- 2 tablespoons extra-virgin olive oil
- 1 teaspoon minced garlic

- ½ cup finely diced yellow onion
- 3 tomatoes (about 12 ounces total weight), peeled, seeded and finely diced, juices reserved
- 1 sprig fresh thyme
- 1 sprig flat-leaf parsley
- ½ bay leaf
- kosher salt
- For the vegetables:
- 1 medium zucchini (4 to 5 ounces) sliced in 1/16-inch-thick rounds
- 1 Japanese eggplant (4 to 5 ounces) sliced into 1/16-inch-thick rounds
- 1 yellow (summer) squash (4 to 5 ounces) sliced into 1/16-inch-thick rounds
- 4 roma tomatoes, sliced into 1/16-inch-thick rounds
- ½ teaspoon minced garlic
- 2 teaspoons extra-virgin olive oil
- ⅛ teaspoon fresh thyme leaves
- kosher salt and freshly ground black pepper
- For the vinaigrette:
- 1 tablespoon extra-virgin olive oil
- 1 teaspoon balsamic vinegar
- Assorted fresh herbs (such as thyme flowers, chervil, thyme)
- kosher salt and freshly ground black pepper

Direction

- Make the piperade, preheat oven to 450 F. Line a baking sheet with foil.
- Place pepper halves on the baking sheet, cut side down. Roast until the skins loosen, about 15 minutes. Remove the peppers from the oven and let rest until cool enough to handle. Reduce the oven temperature to 275 F.
- Peel the peppers and discard the skins. Finely chop the peppers, then set aside.
- In medium skillet over low heat, combine oil, garlic, and onion and sauté until very soft but not browned, about eight minutes.
- Add the tomatoes, their juices, thyme, parsley, and bay leaf. Bring to a simmer over low heat and cook until very soft and little liquid remains, about 10 minutes. Do not brown. (Note: I like to place the herbs in a metal tea

infuser -- that way, when it's time to discard the herbs, I simply lift out the infuser and save myself the trouble of fishing around for a soggy bay leaf.)

- Add the peppers and simmer to soften them. Discard the herbs, then season to taste with salt. Reserve a tablespoon of the mixture, then spread the remainder over the bottom of an 8-inch oven-proof skillet.
- To prepare the vegetables, arrange the sliced zucchini, eggplant, squash, and tomatoes over the piperade in the skillet.
- Begin by arranging eight alternating slices of vegetables down the center, overlapping them so that ¼ inch of each slice is exposed. This will be the center of the spiral. Around the center strip, overlap the vegetables in a close spiral that lets slices mound slightly toward center. All vegetables may not be needed. Set aside.
- In a small bowl, mix the garlic, oil and thyme, then season with salt and pepper to taste. Sprinkle this over vegetables.
- Cover the skillet with foil and crimp edges to seal well. Bake until the vegetables are tender when tested with a paring knife, about two hours. Uncover and bake for another 30 minutes. (Lightly cover with foil if it starts to brown.)
- If there is excess liquid in pan, place it over medium heat on stove until reduced. (At this point it may be cooled, covered and refrigerated for up to two days. Serve cold or reheat in 350 F oven until warm.)
- To make the vinaigrette, in a small bowl whisk together the reserved piperade, oil, vinegar, herbs, and salt and pepper to taste.
- To serve, heat the broiler and place skillet under it until lightly browned. Slice in quarters and lift very carefully onto plate with an offset spatula. Turn spatula 90 degrees as you set the food down, gently fanning the food into fan shape. Drizzle the vinaigrette around plate.
- NOTE: Can also make individual servings in small skillets.

271. Rich Creamed Corn Recipe

Serving: 4 | Prep: | Cook: 15mins | Ready in:

Ingredients

- 2 c. fresh corn (see below)
- 1/2 t. sugar (see below)
- 2 T. butter
- 1/2 c. heavy cream
- salt and pepper

Direction

- Cut the kernels off the cob, then using the back of the knife, scrape the cob (this is always the way to do it -- you get all the milk that way). The sooner you do this after it's picked, the better the corn will be.
- Melt the butter in a sauté pan, then add the corn (only use the sugar if using frozen corn). As you stir the corn, gently mash some of the kernels, and cook over medium heat for about five minutes.
- Add the cream, and cook, stirring frequently, until the starch from the corn thickens the cream. Salt and pepper to taste.
- You can make an alternative version by turning the heat up high after adding the cream so it will caramelize. Excellent either way.

272. Rich Squash Casserole Recipe

Serving: 6 | Prep: | Cook: 120mins | Ready in:

Ingredients

- 1 c grated gruyere cheese
- 1 c ricotta cheese
- 1/2 c plain bread crumbs

- 1 Tbs cornstarch
- 1-1/4 tspdried basil
- 1-1/2 tsp dried thyme
- 3/4 tsp each salt and black pepper
- 1 Tbs olive oil
- 1 pkg (8oz) sliced mushrooms
- 1 large onion,chopped
- 3 large summer squash,slice 1/4" thick
- 2 large zucchini,slice 1/4" thick

Direction

- Stir together Gruyere, ricotta, bread crumbs, cornstarch, basil, 3/4 tsp. of thyme and 1/2 tsp. each of salt and pepper; set aside
- Heat olive oil in large skillet over med-high heat. Add mushrooms and onion, sprinkle with remaining 3/4 tsp. thyme and 1/4 tsp. each salt and pepper. Cover, cook 6 mins, stirring occasionally.
- Coat slow-cooker with cooking spray. Layer 1/3 of squash in bottom. Add 1 c mushroom mixture over squash; sprinkle 2/3 c ricotta mixture on top. Later with another 1/3 squash, rest of mushroom mixture and another 2/3 c ricotta mixture. Place remaining squash and ricotta mixture on top.
- Cover, cook for 2 hours on high or 4 hours on low. Serve immediately

273. Roasted Asparagus Recipe

Serving: 4 | Prep: | Cook: 10mins | Ready in:

Ingredients

- 1 lb asparagus spears (thicker spears are best)
- 1-3 tbsp olive oil
- 2 clove garlic minces or 3 tbsp minced garlic in jar
- Kosher or sea salt
- Fresh grated black pepper
- lemon juice

Direction

- Preheat oven to 400
- Rinse asparagus and cut off tough ends only
- Lay asparagus spears in single layer on baking sheet lined with foil
- Drizzle oil, pepper, salt & garlic over asparagus
- Roll back and forth to evenly distribute seasonings
- Roast in oven approximately 10 minutes until lightly browned and tender when pierced with fork (return to cover for a few more minutes if still tough - watch not to overcook)
- Remove to plate and drizzle with lemon juice before serving
- WARNING: Make at least a double batch

274. Roasted Autumn Vegetables Recipe

Serving: 4 | Prep: | Cook: 45mins | Ready in:

Ingredients

- 1 large sweet potato ("garnet yam" or other), peeled and chopped into bite-sized pieces
- 3-4 medium red or yukon gold potatoes (or 1 russet potato, peeled), chopped into bite-sized pieces
- 1 acorn or butternut squash, or 2 delicata squash, peeled, seeded, and chopped into bite-sized chunks
- 1 large yellow onion, chopped fine
- 2-3 shallots, chopped fine
- About 5 garlic cloves, coarsely chopped
- olive oil
- Freshly ground black pepper
- salt
- Some fresh thyme and rosemary, chopped (or a few pinches of dried, crumbled between your fingers)
- red pepper flakes (optional), to taste
- Optional: 1 bunch kale

- Optional: goat cheese (6-8 ounces)

Direction

- Preheat oven to 400 degrees Fahrenheit. Assemble all vegetables except kale in large baking pan, drizzle generously with olive oil, and sprinkle with pepper and salt, herbs, and red pepper flakes to taste. Toss together until thoroughly covered with olive oil and herbs. Bake until vegetables are fork-soft, about 45 minutes.
- If using kale, prepare it while the other vegetables are roasting. Clean it, remove tough stems, and tear the leaves into bite-sized pieces. Steam it for about 10 minutes until tender, then drain.
- When other vegetables are soft, if desired, mix steamed kale in with the rest of the vegetables. If adding goat cheese, crumble over the top of the vegetables and place under broiler until the goat cheese is melted and slightly browned, about 5 minutes.

275. Roasted Cabbage Wedges Recipe

Serving: 6 | Prep: | Cook: 25mins | Ready in:

Ingredients

- 1 tsp. salt
- 1/4 tsp. pepper
- 1 tsp. sugar
- 1 medium head green cabbage
- 3 TBSP. vegetable oil
- 2 tsp. balsamic vinegar

Direction

- Adjust oven rack to upper middle position. Place rimmed baking sheet on rack and heat oven to 450 degrees F. Combine salt, pepper, and sugar in small bowl. Quarter cabbage through core and cut each quarter in to 1-inch

wedges, leaving core intact. You'll have about 16 wedges. Brush cabbage wedges all over with oil and sprinkle with salt mixture.
- Arrange cabbage wedges on hot baking sheet and roast until cabbage is tender and lightly browned around edges, about 25 minutes. Drizzle cabbage with vinegar.
- Serve with Chicken Paprikash and Egg Noodles with Caraway and Brown butter; both posted on my page.

276. Roasted Cauliflower & Garlic Recipe

Serving: 2 | Prep: | Cook: 30mins | Ready in:

Ingredients

- 1/2 head cauliflower, broken/cut into floret pieces
- 6 cloves garlic, peeled
- olive oil to drizzle
- sea salt & black pepper (freshly ground), to taste

Direction

- Preheat oven to 400F.
- Arrange cauliflower pieces and garlic on a baking sheet or glass pan. Drizzle with olive oil. Season with salt & pepper. Place in oven for 15 minutes. Remove and flip. Place back in oven for another 15 minutes. Enjoy!

277. Roasted Cauliflower Popcorn Recipe

Serving: 4 | Prep: | Cook: 60mins | Ready in:

Ingredients

- 1 large head cauliflower or equal amount of pre-cut commercially prepped cauliflower

- 4 tablespoons olive oil
- 1 teaspoon salt, to taste

Direction

- Preheat oven to 400 degrees F.
- Trim the head of cauliflower, discarding the core and thick stems; cut florets into pieces about the size of Ping-Pong balls.
- In a large bowl, combine the olive oil and salt, whisk, then add the cauliflower pieces and toss thoroughly.
- Line a baking sheet with parchment for easy clean-up (you can skip that, if you don't have any) then spread the cauliflower pieces on the sheet and roast/bake in oven for 1 hour, turning 3 or 4 times, until most of each piece has turned golden brown.
- (The browner the cauliflower pieces turn, the more caramelization occurs and the sweeter they'll taste).
- Serve immediately and enjoy!
- Where I got it: I originally heard about this recipe at Gail's Recipe Swap, where Josh posted it and many folks tried and loved it.
- Note: if you already like cauliflower, you might consider doubling this recipe. One regular-size (what *is* regular, anyhow?) head of cauliflower barely makes enough for three people with this recipe, because the veggie does shrink down during the cooking. Make sure you get a *large* head or do two heads. Believe me, it'll all disappear off the dinner plates! :)

278. Roasted Cauliflower Recipe

Serving: 5 | Prep: | Cook: 30mins | Ready in:

Ingredients

- 1 head cauliflower
- olive oil
- salt & pepper

Direction

- Preheat your oven to 400 F.
- Rinse the cauliflower and separate it into florets. Place it on a baking pan.
- Drizzle the florets with olive oil and season with salt and pepper.
- Roast the cauliflower for 25 to 30 minutes or until golden.
- Enjoy!

279. Roasted Green Beans Recipe

Serving: 4 | Prep: | Cook: 25mins | Ready in:

Ingredients

- 2 lbs green beans
- 1 tablespoon olive oil
- 1 teaspoon kosher salt
- 1/2 teaspoon fresh ground pepper

Direction

- Preheat oven to 400°F.
- Wash, dry well, and trim green beans.
- Put green beans on a baking sheet, and drizzle with olive oil (alternately, use an olive-oil spray).
- Sprinkle with salt and pepper to taste.
- Ensure all the beans are evenly coated, and spread them out into 1 layer.
- Roast for 20-25 minutes, stirring the beans after 15 minutes, until beans are fairly brown in spots and somewhat shrivelled.
- Serve hot or at room temperature.

280. Root Vegetables Casserole Recipe

Serving: 8 | Prep: | Cook: 40mins | Ready in:

Ingredients

- 1 large rutabaga or a yellow turnip, about 2-1/4 pounds, trimmed, peeled, cut in chunks
- 2 medium purple-topped turnips, trimmed, peeled, cut in chunks
- 1 large sweet potato, peeled, cut in chunks
- 3 medium carrots, peeled, cut in chunks
- Sauce: (or use ready made béchamel)
- 1 tablespoon unsalted butter
- 2 big leeks (only the white part)
- 1 tablespoon flour
- 1/3 cup milk
- 1/3 cup apple cider
- 1/4 pound good melting cheese ,Cheddar or gruyere, cut in chunks
- Grated fresh Parmesan

Direction

- Bring water to a boil in a large pot or Dutch oven. Add the rutabaga chunks as they're prepped, even if water's not yet boiling. Once it comes to a boil, cook for about 10 minutes before adding the turnips, sweet potato and carrots. Drain.
- In a large skillet or Dutch oven, melt the butter on medium, add the leeks and cook, stirring often, till soft. Set aside.
- If making the sauce:
- In the skillet or Dutch oven used for the leeks, melt the butter on medium. Stir in the flour, removing all the lumps. A spoonful at a time at first, slowly stir in the milk, stirring all the time to remove all the lumps, not adding more till the lumps are stirred out. (Press with the back of a spoon if needed.) Add the apple cider. Stirring often, cook till the sauce thickens. Turn the heat off and stir in the cheese, the sautéed leeks and the cooked root vegetables.
- Transfer to a baking dish.
- Preheat oven to 375ºF and bake for 30 minutes or until hot and bubbly throughout. Top with Parmesan and bake another 15 minutes.

281. Rudolph Moms Black Cherry Yam Casserole Recipe

Serving: 6 | Prep: | Cook: 30mins |Ready in:

Ingredients

- 2 (15-ounce) cans cut yams, drained
- 1 cup brown sugar, packed
- 1 1/2 tablespoons cornstarch
- 1 teaspoon grated orange zest
- 1/2 teaspoon salt
- 1/2 teaspoon ground cinnamon
- 1/4 teaspoon ground ginger
- 1 cup apricot nectar
- 2 (16-ounce) cans pitted dark sweet cherries, drained
- 2 tablespoons butter
- Grease a 13 x 9-inch pan. Arrange drained yams in pan.

Direction

- In a saucepan, stir brown sugar, cornstarch, orange zest, salt, cinnamon, and ginger; stir in apricot nectar until smooth. Cook, stirring constantly, until simmering; boil 2 minutes, then remove from heat. Add pitted, dark sweet cherries and butter.
- Pour cherry mixture over yams.
- Bake, uncovered, 30 minutes at 375°F (190°C).
- Makes 12 servings

282. Rutabaga Gratin With Fennel And Leeks Recipe

Serving: 6 | Prep: | Cook: 45mins |Ready in:

Ingredients

- 1 fennel bulb
- 1 large leek
- 2 cloves roasted garlic, mashed

- 2-3 large rutabagas
- 1 tbsp fresh chopped thyme
- 1 c grated manchego (or gruyere if you can't find manchego)
- 1/2 c heavy cream
- 1/4 c dry white wine
- butter
- 1/2 sprig fresh thyme
- salt and pepper to taste

Direction

- Remove green tops and damaged outer leaves from fennel bulb and slice on mandoline to achieve thickness of ~1/8". Repeat for leeks. Allow slices to sit in a bowl of water 5-10 minutes to ensure there is no sand stuck in them. Strain and allow to drain on paper towels.
- Peel and clean rutabagas and slice on mandoline to achieve thickness of ~1/8".
- Heat about 1 tbsp. butter in a large, heavy skillet over medium heat until butter melts. Add fennel and leeks and stir to coat. Reduce heat to low and cook until fennel and leeks are caramelized, stirring occasionally. Salt and pepper lightly to taste. Preheat oven to 375 degrees.
- In a medium saucepan, gently heat cream, sprig of thyme, wine, and roasted garlic mash over low heat for 10 minutes, stirring occasionally. Do not scald. Strain cream mixture through a fine mesh strainer and discard solids.
- Butter a 9x9" casserole or similarly sized oval dish on its bottom and sides.
- Layer 1/3 of sliced rutabaga in the bottom of the baking dish, overlapping slightly. Season lightly with salt and pepper.
- Spread half of caramelized fennel and leek mixture over rutabaga slices in an even layer. Dot with 1 tbsp. butter and sprinkle with 1 tsp. chopped fresh thyme. Pour half of the cream mixture over layer.
- Repeat layers, using the remaining fennel and leek mixture. Top with another overlapping layer of sliced rutabagas.

- Dot top layer with another tbsp. butter and sprinkle with the last tsp. of chopped thyme. Cover with grated Manchego and pour remaining cream mixture over casserole. The liquid should just barely cover the top layer of rutabaga slices.
- Bake, uncovered, 45-60 minutes or until top is golden to dark brown and rutabagas are easily pierced with a fork.

---

283. SPINACH WITH OLIVE OIL AND GARLIC Recipe

Serving: 4 | Prep: | Cook: 5mins | Ready in:

Ingredients

- 1 pound bag fresh spinach
- 2 cloves garlic
- 3 tablespoon olive oil
- 1 pat of real butter (optional)
- salt to taste
- fresh ground pepper to taste..

Direction

- In a large flat skillet heat oil and butter if using.
- Mince the garlic fine and add, do not let it get brown or it will be bitter.
- Add the spinach, stir, and lid for about 4 minutes.
- Stir again, tossing to mix all.
- Cook to your desired doneness. I do not let it cook for long or it will lose that bright green color.
- Salt and pepper to taste.
- I hope you like it as much as we do
- Enjoy

284. Sauted Potatoes And Fish Cakes Gamja Chae Bokkeum Recipe

Serving: 4 | Prep: | Cook: 10mins | Ready in:

Ingredients

- 2 medium potatoes
- 1 package (3-4 0z) square fish cakes
- 1/2 green pepper, seeded, halfed, sliced
- 1/4 carrot, skined, juliened
- 1/2 onions, sliced
- 1 tablespoon minced garlic
- 1 tablespon salt
- 1 teaspoon sesame seed oil
- 1 teaspoon toasted sesame seed
- a pinch of black pepper

Direction

- Peel the potatoes and wash and cut them into julienne strips.
- Soak the potato in the water about 10 minutes to remove starch.
- Meantime, cut the fish cakes into julienne strips. Drain water from potatoes using a colander
- In a heated pan, add 2 TBS of olive oil and add the potato strips. Stir it with a wooden spoon for 1 minute.
- Add fish cakes, carrots, onions, garlic green pepper. Add ½ tsp. to1 tsp. of salt (depends on your taste) and lower the heat over medium heat and sauté until potato strips are fully cooked.
- Add sesame oil and sesame seed, turn off the heat.
- Garnish with green onion.

285. Sauteed Brussels Sprouts With Onions And Lemon Zest Recipe

Serving: 6 | Prep: | Cook: 15mins | Ready in:

Ingredients

- About 2 lbs Brussels sprouts, washed, brown spots removed, cut in halves
- 1 large onion, thinly sliced
- 1 tbsp butter
- 1 tbsp olive oil
- juice of 1 lemon
- zest of 1 lemon
- 1 tsp herbs de Provence (The mixture typically contains rosemary, marjoram, basil, bay leaf, thyme, and sometimes lavender flowers and other herbs.)
- salt & pepper to taste

Direction

- In a non-stick skillet over medium heat, melt the butter and olive oil and add herbs de Provence and a minute later, the onions. Sauté the onions until they are golden-brown salting them lightly in the end.
- Add the Brussels sprouts and the lemon juice and sauté for about 7-8 minutes until the green color becomes brighter and more intense. Add the lemon zest and mix well in the pan reducing the heat to low. Cook for 1 more minute and remove from heat.
- Season with salt and pepper to taste and serve immediately.

286. Sauteed Kale Recipe

Serving: 4 | Prep: | Cook: 10mins | Ready in:

Ingredients

- 1 1/2 pounds young kale, stems and leaves coarsely chopped

- 3 tablespoons olive oil
- 2 cloves garlic, finely sliced
- 1/2 cup vegetable stock or water
- salt and pepper
- 2 tablespoons red wine vinegar

Direction

- Heat olive oil in a large saucepan over medium-high heat. Add the garlic and cook until soft, but not colored. Raise heat to high, add the stock and kale and toss to combine. Cover and cook for 5 minutes. Remove cover and continue to cook, stirring until all the liquid has evaporated. Season with salt and pepper to taste and add vinegar.

---

287.   Scalloped Brussel Sprouts Recipe

Serving: 8 | Prep: | Cook: 45mins | Ready in:

Ingredients

- 2 lb. brussel sprouts
- 2 tbsp. butter
- 1 onion, chopped
- 1/4 tsp. Dried thyme
- 1/4 cup flour
- 2 cups milk, warmed
- 1 ½ cups shredded gruyere cheese
- 3/4 tsp. salt
- 1/4 tsp. pepper
- TOPPING:
- 1 ½ cups bread crumbs
- ½ cup shredded gruyere, cheddar or gouda cheese
- 2 tbsp. butter, melted

Direction

- Trim Brussels sprouts; cut X in base of each. In saucepan of boiling salted water, cover and cook Brussels sprouts until tender-crisp, 7 to 9 minutes. Drain and chill under cold water;

press out excess water with towel. Cut in half if large; place in greased shallow 8-cup casserole dish.
- In saucepan, melt butter over medium heat; cook onion and thyme, stirring occasionally, until onion is softened, about 5 minutes. Sprinkle with flour, cook, stirring, for 1 minute. Add milk; cook, stirring, until thickened, 6 to 8 minutes. Remove from heat; stir in cheese, salt and pepper. Pour over Brussels sprouts.
- TOPPING: In bowl, stir together bread crumbs, cheese and melted butter (Make ahead and cover and refrigerate Brussels sprouts mixture and topping separately for up to 24 hours.)
- Cover and bake Brussels sprouts mixture in 375 F oven for 30 minutes. Uncover and sprinkle with topping; bake until golden and bubbling, about 20 minutes. Serves 8

---

288.   Sesame Brussels Sprouts Recipe

Serving: 4 | Prep: | Cook: 10mins | Ready in:

Ingredients

- 1 pound fresh Brussels sprouts
- 2 Tbsp sesame seeds (Can use toasted)
- 1/4 Cup soy sauce (I used reduce sodium)
- 1 Tbsp EVOO (extra virgin olive oil)
- 2 Tbsp sugar
- Dash of salt

Direction

- Wash Brussels sprout thoroughly, remove discolored leaves.
- Cut off stem ends and slash the bottom end with a shallow X.
- Place sprouts in a small amount of boiling water, cover, reduce heat, and simmer for ~ 8 minutes, or until tender.
- Drain sprouts, set aside.

- Brown sesame seeds in hot oil. Remove from heat; add soy sauce, sugar, salt (optional), stirring will.
- Pour over warm Brussels sprouts, tossing gently.
- Serve immediately.

289. Skinny Potatoes Recipe

Serving: 6 | Prep: | Cook: 40mins | Ready in:

Ingredients

- 4 Large potatoes - washed, peeled and sliced paper thin.
- 4 oz. Low Fat cream cheese.
- 8 oz. Fat Free Half n' Half
- 3/4 cup Low Fat/low sodium chicken broth.
- 1/2 cup Fresh Grated parmesan cheese.
- 2 green onions (white and green parts) - chopped fine.
- 2 tsp. kosher salt.
- 1 tsp. bacon salt

Direction

- Pre-heat oven to 400*
- Thoroughly butter a 13"x9" casserole dish.
- Layer the potatoes evenly in the bottom of the casserole dish.
- In a separate microwave safe bowl, mix together the remaining ingredients.
- Microwave on high for 60 seconds. Stir well and pour evenly over the potatoes.
- Bake uncovered on the middle rack for 40 minutes. Remove from oven, cover and let sit for 15 minutes. Serve warm.

290. Slow Cooker Kishke Dumplings Recipe

Serving: 12 | Prep: | Cook: 60mins | Ready in:

Ingredients

- .
- 2 celery stalks
- 2 medium carrots, peeled
- 1 large spanish onion
- 1/2 cup duck fat, melted and cooled, or canola oil
- 1 1/2 cups all-purpose flour
- 1 teaspoon sweet paprika
- 2 teaspoons kosher salt
- 1 teaspoon freshly ground black pepper

Direction

- Grate the celery, carrots, and onion in a food processor fitted with a grating blade or by hand on the coarse side of a box grater.
- Mix the celery, carrots, onion, fat, flour, paprika, salt, and pepper in a large bowl by hand or in a mixer until the mixture forms a ball and clings together.
- Place a large sheet of parchment paper on a work surface.
- Roll the dough on the parchment into a log shape about 1 1/2 inches thick and 12 inches long.
- Roll the parchment paper around the log.
- . Wrap the parchment-wrapped kishke log with several layers of plastic wrap to form a waterproof package.
- Place a large saucepan filled with several inches of water over medium heat.
- Bring the water to a simmer.
- Poach the kishke in the water for 1 hour until the kishke feels firm and solid.
- . Carefully remove the kishke and allow it to cool completely before unwrapping or slicing.
- Kishke may be made up to 3 days before serving and stored, covered, in the refrigerator.
- It may also be frozen for up to 3 months.
- Reheat kishke in a covered casserole in the oven at 350°F.

291. Smoky Baked Limas Recipe

Serving: 6 | Prep: | Cook: 400mins | Ready in:

Ingredients

- 1 pound dried small lima beans
- 1 large white onion chopped
- 1/2 pound smoked sausage
- 1/4 cup lightly packed brown sugar
- 2 tablespoons dijon-style mustard
- 1 teaspoon worcestershire sauce
- 1 garlic clove crushed
- 1/4 cup molasses
- 1/4 cup ketchup
- 1/8 teaspoon ground cloves
- 1 teaspoon salt
- 1/8 teaspoon freshly ground black pepper

Direction

- In 4 quart saucepan combine beans and 2 quarts water then boil 2 minutes.
- Remove from heat and cover then let stand 1 hour then add onion and bring to a boil.
- Cover then reduce heat and simmer 1-1/2 hours.
- Cut several slices smoked sausage and set aside then dice remaining sausage.
- Drain beans and reserve liquid.
- Combine all ingredients except beans and mix well then gently stir in drained cooked beans.
- Bake at 300 for 2 hours adding reserved bean liquid as needed.
- Garnish with reserved sliced sausage.

292. Sour Cream And Mushroom Pie Recipe

Serving: 6 | Prep: | Cook: 30mins | Ready in:

Ingredients

- 12-16 oz. fresh mushrooms
- 9 inch pie shell
- 3 tbs. butter or margarine, divided
- 1/2 cup chopped onion
- 3 large eggs
- 1 cup sour cream
- 1 tsp. salt
- 1/2 tsp. tarragon leaves, crushed
- 1/4 tsp. ground black pepper
- 1/4 cup swiss cheese, shredded

Direction

- * Preheat oven to 425°F.
- * Rinse, pat dry and slice mushrooms (makes about 4 cups); set aside.
- * Roll pastry 1/8-inch thick; fit into 9 inch pie pan; turn under and flute edges; prick with fork tines. Bake for 5 minutes; remove from oven.
- * In a large skillet, melt 1 tbs. of the butter. Add onion; sauté until tender, about 5 minutes. Remove from skillet, set aside.
- * Melt remaining 2 tbs. of butter in skillet; add mushrooms. Sauté until tender, about 5 minutes; set aside.
- * In a medium bowl, lightly beat eggs. Add sour cream, salt, tarragon, and black pepper; mix well.
- * Reserve 1/3 of the mushrooms; add remaining sautéed mushrooms and onion to sour cream mixture; mix well.
- * Pour into partially baked pie shell. Sprinkle with cheese. Bake until a knife inserted in the center comes out clean, 20 to 25 minutes.
- * Heat reserved sautéed mushrooms until hot. Arrange on top of pie. Let pie stand 5 minutes before cutting.
- ****When I made the rustic tart, I reduced everything to 2/3: 2 T butter, 1 lb. mushrooms, etc. I then rolled the crust out with a rolling pin as large as I could make it, piled the mushroom-onion mixture in the middle, and pulled the edges up around the filling. I baked it for only 35 minutes. ****

293. Southern Asparagus Casserole Recipe

Serving: 8 | Prep: | Cook: 30mins | Ready in:

Ingredients

- 2 cans (14.5 oz)asparagus, drain and reserve one cup juice (buy the cheap cans of cut spears)
- 1 cup asparagus juice from can
- 2 cups grated cheddar
- 6 eggs boiled, sliced
- 1/3 cup flour
- 1/2 tsp black pepper
- 1/2 sleeve Ritz crackers
- butter to top

Direction

- Drain asparagus and reserve one cup liquid
- Layer one can asparagus in square baking pan
- Add three boiled eggs, sliced
- Add one cup grated cheddar
- Repeat layers
- Mix flour with juice and pepper
- Pour over asparagus, eggs
- Top with crumbled Ritz crackers and dot with butter.
- Bake uncovered at 350 for about 30 minutes
- Serve as side with a variety of main dishes.

294. Southern Collard Greens Theyre Not Just For New Years Anymore Recipe

Serving: 6 | Prep: | Cook: 180mins | Ready in:

Ingredients

- 1-1/2 quarts water
- 1-1/2 pounds ham hocks
- 4 pounds collard greens, rinsed and trimmed

- 1/2 teaspoon crushed red pepper flakes (optional)
- 1/4 cup vegetable oil
- salt and pepper to taste
- Optional: 4 to 6 garlic cloves, crushed and chopped

Direction

- Optional: In the large pot, sweat the garlic before adding the water and ham hock.
- Place the water and the ham hock in a large pot with a tight-fitting lid. Bring to a boil. Lower the heat to very low and simmer covered for 30 minutes.
- Add the collards and the hot pepper flakes the pot. Simmer covered for about 2 hours, stirring occasionally.
- Add the vegetable oil and simmer covered for 30 minutes.

295. Southern Collards Recipe

Serving: 8 | Prep: | Cook: 150mins | Ready in:

Ingredients

- 1 1/2 quarts water possibly a little more
- 1 1/2 - 2 lbs pounds ham hocks
- 4 pounds collard greens, rinsed and trimmed
- 1/2 teaspoon crushed red pepper flakes (optional)
- 1/4 cup vegetable oil
- salt and pepper to taste
- dash of sugar
- MUST HAVE A GOOD pepper sauce!!!!!!!

Direction

- MAKE SURE TO WASH YOUR COLLARDS SEVERAL TIMES IN YOUR SINK BEFORE COOKING.....
- Place the water and the ham hock in a large pot with a tight-fitting lid. Bring to a boil.

Lower the heat to very low and simmer covered for 30 minutes.

- Add the collards and the hot pepper flakes the pot. Simmer covered for about 2 hours, stirring occasionally.
- Add the vegetable oil and simmer covered for 30 minutes.
- EAT YOUR COLLARDS WITH PEPPER SAUCE (THIS IS PEPPERS BOTTLED IN VINEGAR, WHICH HAS SAT ON A SHELF FOR A FEW MONTHS) WITH CHOPPED ONION ON TOP OR BOTH!

296. Southern Corn Pudding Recipe

Serving: 4 | Prep: | Cook: 45mins |Ready in:

Ingredients

- 3 cups fresh corn, (can use frozen niblets, but fresh is best)
- 3 eggs
- 1 cup heavy cream
- 2 tablespoons sugar
- 1 tablespoon flour
- 1 teaspoon salt
- 1 teaspoon baking powder
- 1/4 pound melted butter

Direction

- Beat eggs, add heavy cream and slowly add the dry ingredients. Add corn and stir in melted butter.
- Pour the mixture into a small greased casserole dish and bake at 350 degrees for 45 minutes.
- Serves 4.

297. Southern Smothered Green Beans Recipe

Serving: 8 | Prep: | Cook: 45mins |Ready in:

Ingredients

- FRESH SNAP green beans OR 2 CANS OF green beans
- seasoning (I USE NATURES seasoning)
- black pepper
- 1 LARGE yellow onion DICED (OR YOU CAN USE green onions)
- water
- SMOKED pork (YOU CAN ALSO YOU ham, ham hocks OR A pork chop)
- I COOKED THESE FOR SUPPER TONIGHT AND TOOK A PICTURE TO SHARE WITH YOU.

Direction

- SAUTEE THE ONION WITH YOUR MEAT AND ABOUT ONE TABLESPOON OF OIL.
- ADD THE GREEN BEANS (IF YOU ARE USING CAN GREEN BEANS, DRAIN THE WATER OFF AND ADD WATER TO THE CAN WHILE BEANS ARE STILL IN CAN, POUR THIS WATER OFF AND ADD MORE WATER, THIS GETS RID OF THE CANNED TASTE)
- ADD 2 CUPS OF WATER
- COOK ON A MEDIUM HEAT UNTIL TENDER FOR ABOUT 45 MINUTES TO AN HOUR, BRING TO A BOIL THEN BACK DOWN TO A MEDIUM HEAT
- YOU CAN ALSO, ADD NEW POTATOES OR SMALL RED POTATOES

298. Southern Style White Beans Recipe

Serving: 9 | Prep: | Cook: 180mins |Ready in:

Ingredients

- 4 cups dried, white beans, rinsed and drained
- 1 ham hock
- 1 teaspoon salt
- 1/4 teaspoon ground black pepper

Direction

- Fill a Dutch oven with 4 inches of water.
- Add white beans and ring to a boil over medium high heat on stovetop.
- Add ham hock, salt, and pepper.
- Reduce heat to low and simmer covered, for 3 hours, or until desired degree of tenderness.
- Add water as needed to keep beans covered during cooking.

299. Southwestern Fried Corn Recipe

Serving: 6 | Prep: | Cook: 8mins |Ready in:

Ingredients

- 1/4 pound mesquite-smoked or regular bacon, cut into small pieces
- 1/4 cup green onions, sliced
- 1/4 cup red bell pepper chopped
- 2 can (11-ounces) super sweet yellow and white corn, drained
- 1/4 cup purchased ranch salad dressing
- 1 teaspoon fresh lime juice
- 1/2 teaspoon cumin
- 1/4 teaspoon crushed red pepper flakes
- 1 Tablespoon fresh cilantro, chopped
- 2 lime slices (garnish)
- 2 fresh cilantro sprigs (garnish)

Direction

- Cook bacon until crisp
- Drain on paper towels and discard bacon drippings.
- In same skillet, add cooked bacon, onions, bell pepper and corn.

- Reduce heat to low and cook for 5 minutes or until thoroughly heated.
- Stir occasionally.
- In small bowl, add the salad dressing, lime juice, cumin and red pepper flakes.
- Mix well.
- Add dressing mixture to corn mixture and mix well.
- Remove skillet from heat.
- Stir in chopped cilantro.
- Garnish with lime slices and cilantro sprigs.

300. Spanish Style Grilled Vegetables With Breadcrumb Picada Recipe

Serving: 6 | Prep: | Cook: 20mins |Ready in:

Ingredients

- On The Grill:
- 3 large red bell peppers (about 1 1/2 pounds), stemmed, seeded, quartered
- 4 large Japanese eggplants (about 1 1/4 pounds), trimmed, cut lengthwise into 3 slices
- 4 medium green or yellow zucchini (preferably 2 of each; about 1 pound), trimmed, cut lengthwise into 1/3-inch-thick slices
- extra-virgin olive oil (for grilling)
- ~~~~
- For The Dish:
- 6 tablespoons extra-virgin olive oil, divided
- 2 garlic cloves, finely chopped
- 1/2 teaspoon dried crushed red pepper flakes
- 1/2 cup panko (Japanese breadcrumbs)*
- 2 tablespoons sherry wine vinegar
- 1/4 cup chopped fresh Italian parsley
- 2 tablespoons chopped fresh oregano

Direction

- Prepare grill (medium heat).

- Arrange vegetables on baking sheets. Brush with oil; sprinkle with salt and pepper.
- Grill peppers, skin side down and without turning, until blackened and blistered, moving occasionally for even cooking, about 10 minutes. Enclose in plastic bag. Let stand until skins loosen, about 30 minutes.
- Grill eggplants and zucchini until charred and tender, turning and rearranging for even browning, 5 to 6 minutes. Place on foil lined baking sheet.
- Peel peppers. Transfer to sheet with eggplants and zucchini.
- Heat 3 tablespoons olive oil in medium skillet over medium heat. Add garlic and crushed red pepper; stir until fragrant, about 30 seconds.
- Add breadcrumbs; stir until golden, about 3 minutes. Season breadcrumb picada to taste with salt; scrape into small bowl.
- Place vinegar in another small bowl; whisk in 3 tablespoons oil. Mix in parsley and oregano. Season to taste with salt.
- Arrange vegetables on platter. Spoon herb dressing over; sprinkle with breadcrumbs.

301.   Spicy Chick Peas Recipe

Serving: 6 | Prep: | Cook: 30mins | Ready in:

Ingredients

- 1 cup chopped onion
- 3 garlic cloves, coarsely chopped
- 1-2 small chiles, coarsely chopped
- 1 Tbsp ghee or canola oil
- 2 tsp tamarind concentrate
- 1 cup chopped tomatoes
- 1/2 cup water
- 1 Tbsp grated fresh ginger
- 1/2 tsp salt
- 2 cups of cooked garbonza beans (chick peas)

Direction

- Sauté onions, garlic, and chilies in ghee or oil until onions are tender- about 10 minutes.
- Dissolve the tamarind paste in the water.
- Puree the onion mixture, tamarind liquid and all the remaining ingredients except the chickpeas.
- Add this mixture to a non-reactive, heavy saucepan.
- Add the chick peas and simmer, uncovered, on low heat for 20-30 minutes, until the sauce becomes thick and dark.
- Serve at room temperature or hot.

302.   Spicy Chickpeas In Grilled Eggplant Purses Recipe

Serving: 2 | Prep: | Cook: 20mins | Ready in:

Ingredients

- 1 big glossy eggplant, slice 1/8-inch thick
- 1 can chickpeas, rinse and drained
- 1/2 onion, finely diced
- 1/4 tsp minced ginger
- 1 clove of garlic, minced
- 1 Tbp tomato paste
- spoonfuls tomato sauce
- 1 big pod of tamarind* (original recipe calls for dry mango powder)
- 1/4 turmeric powder
- 1/2 tsp coriander seed powder
- 1 tsp cumin seed, crushed
- 1 tsp garam marsala
- paprika to taste
- some scallions
- some cherry tomatoes, halved
- salt and pepper

Direction

- 1 Tamarind, crack the pod and soak the pulp in 1/2 cup of hot-warm water for 30 minute. Throw away the seed but save the pulp and liquid

- 2 Soak the sliced eggplant in a big pot of tap water, add in 1 tablespoon of salt, for 30 minutes... in order to release the brown (bitter) juice from the eggplant
- 3 Take out about 30% of the chickpeas, mash them and set aside.
- 4 Pre-heat a medium-size skillet, dry roast cumin and coriander powder over very low heat for a minute. And put them aside.
- 5 Using the same pan, heat some oil, sauté the onion for 2 minutes over medium heat. Add garlic and ginger, fry over low heat for 1 minute, then add tomato paste fry for another minute. Add whole chickpeas, cumin, coriander powder, garam marsala, turmeric and paprika, sauté another 3 minutes over medium heat. Add mashed peas, tamarind pulp plus its juice, and tomato sauce as needed, bring the whole thing to boil, then lower the heat let it simmer for 2 - 3 minutes. Taste and season. Scoop the chickpeas in a big bowl and let them cool off.
- 6 Pre-heat the grill, brush oil, grill eggplant over medium to medium-high heat, take about 2 minutes on each side.
- In a small pot bring some water to boil, blanch the scallion for 5 seconds or so, drain immediately. Set them aside.
- On a slice of eggplant spoon in some chickpea mixture, curl up the sides of eggplant and tight it with scallion.
- Place halved cherry tomatoes on a serving plate, sprinkle salt and pepper to taste. Arrange the eggplant "purses" on top to serve.

---

303. Spicy Couscous Moroccan Recipe

Serving: 2 | Prep: | Cook: 20mins | Ready in:

Ingredients

- 1 tablespoon olive oil
- 1 medium onion, chopped

- 2 whole star anise pods
- salt to taste
- 3 cloves garlic, peeled and chopped
- 1/2 red bell pepper, chopped
- 2 dried hot red peppers, diced
- 1/2 teaspoon ground black pepper
- 4 large fresh mushrooms, chopped
- 1 tablespoon lemon juice
- 1/4 cup chopped dates
- 1 teaspoon ground cinnamon
- 1 cup uncooked couscous
- * 1 1/2 cups vegetable stock

Direction

- Heat oil in a medium saucepan over medium heat,
- Sauté onion until tender.
- Season with anise pods
- Mix in garlic, red bell pepper, dried hot red peppers, and black pepper. Continue to cook and stir until vegetables are tender.
- Stir mushrooms and lemon juice into the vegetable mixture.
- Mix in dates and cinnamon, and simmer over low heat for about 10 minutes.
- Place couscous in a medium saucepan, and cover with vegetable stock. Bring to a boil. Reduce heat to low. Cover, and simmer 3 to 5 minutes, until all moisture has been absorbed.
- Fluff couscous with a fork, mix into the vegetables, and serve.

---

304. Spicy Curried Chickpeas Recipe

Serving: 4 | Prep: | Cook: 10mins | Ready in:

Ingredients

- 2 tablespoons vegetable oil
- 2 onions, minced
- 2 cloves garlic, minced
- 2 teaspoons fresh ginger root, finely chopped

- 1/4 teaspoon ground cloves
- 1 teaspoon ground cinnamon
- 1 teaspoon ground cumin
- 1 teaspoon ground coriander
- salt, to taste
- 1 teaspoon cayenne pepper
- 1 teaspoon ground turmeric
- 2 (15-ounce) cans garbanzo beans (chickpeas)
- 1 cup chopped fresh cilantro (optional)

Direction

- Heat oil in a large frying pan over medium heat, and fry onions until tender.
- Stir in garlic, ginger, cloves, cinnamon, cumin, coriander, salt, cayenne and turmeric.
- Cook for 1 minute over medium heat, stirring constantly.
- Mix in garbanzo beans and their liquid.
- Continue to cook and stir until all ingredients are well-blended and heated through.
- Remove from heat.
- Stir in cilantro just before serving.

---

305. Spicy Herbed Cauliflower Cheese Recipe

Serving: 4 | Prep: | Cook: 10mins | Ready in:

Ingredients

- 1 medium head cauliflower, chopped
- 1/4 cup skim milk powder
- 3 tbsp flour
- 1/4 tsp salt
- 1/2 tsp garlic powder
- 1/2 tsp oregano
- 1/4 tsp basil
- 1/4 tsp cayenne pepper
- 1/8 tsp coarse ground black pepper
- 1 1/2 cups skim milk
- 1/3 cup shredded low-fat old Cheddar
- 1 tbsp Dijon mustard

Direction

- Steam the cauliflower until just tender, 3 - 4 minutes. Transfer to a medium bowl and keep warm.
- In a medium saucepan, whisk together the dry milk powder, flour, salt, herbs and spices.
- Place pan over medium heat, and slowly whisk in the skim milk until no lumps remain.
- Cook, whisking, over medium heat for 5 minutes.
- Stir in the cheese and cook until melted.
- Whisk in the mustard.
- Pour sauce over the cooked cauliflower in the serving dish and toss to combine well.
- Serve immediately.

---

306. Spicy Roasted Roots Recipe

Serving: 8 | Prep: | Cook: 90mins | Ready in:

Ingredients

- 3 carrots, chopped
- 3 parsnips, chopped
- 3 tbsp olive oil
- 1 butternut squash, chopped
- 2 red onions, sliced
- 2 leeks, sliced
- 3 garlic cloves, roughly chopped
- 2 tbsp mild curry paste

Direction

- Preheat oven. Put the carrots and parsnips in a large roasting tin or on a large baking tray, drizzle with 1 tbsp. oil and cook for 40 minutes.
- Add the butternut squash, red onions, leeks and garlic to the roasting tin or baking trey. Season, then drizzle over the remaining 2 tbsp. olive oil.
- Roast for 45 min until the root vegetables are tender and golden. Stir in curry paste and

return to the oven for 10 min to continue roasting, then serve. Enjoy!

307. Spiffy Spiced Roasted Carrots Recipe

Serving: 6 | Prep: | Cook: 35mins | Ready in:

Ingredients

- 2 pounds very fresh baby carrots
- 1 1/2 teaspoons sweet paprika
- 1 teaspoon ground cumin
- 1/2 teaspoon salt
- 1/2 teaspoon ground ginger
- 1/4 teaspoon ground cinnamon
- 1/4 teaspoon garlic powder
- 1/8 teaspoon cayenne pepper
- 1/4 teaspoon black pepper
- 1 tablespoon olive oil, plus more for drizzling
- 2 tablespoons lemon juice
- 1 tablespoon honey

Direction

- Preheat oven to 400°F.
- Put carrots, paprika, cumin, salt, ginger, cinnamon, garlic powder, cayenne, black pepper and 1 tablespoon of the oil into a large bowl and toss to coat.
- Transfer carrots to a large rimmed baking sheet and spread out in a single layer.
- Roast, tossing halfway through, until just tender, 30 to 40 minutes.
- Remove carrots from oven and transfer to a large bowl.
- Add lemon juice and honey and toss well.
- Drizzle with a bit more oil, if you like, then serve.

308. Spinach Artichoke Gratin Recipe

Serving: 6 | Prep: | Cook: 25mins | Ready in:

Ingredients

- vegetable oil spray
- 16 ounces fat free cottage cheese
- egg substitute equivalent to 2 eggs
- 3 tablespoons shredded or grated parmesan cheese
- 1 tablespoon fresh lemon juice
- 1/8 teaspoon white pepper
- 1/8 teaspoon nutmeg
- 2 10 ounce packages frozen chopped spinach, thawed and drained
- 3 medium green onions, thinly sliced (green part only)
- 10 ounce package frozen artichoke hearts, thawed and drained
- 2 tablespoons shredded or grated parmesan cheese

Direction

- Preheat the oven to 375*.
- Lightly spray a 1 1/2 quart baking dish with vegetable oil spray.
- In a food processor or blender, process the cottage cheese, egg substitute, 3 tablespoons Parmesan, lemon juice, pepper, and nutmeg until smooth.
- Squeeze the moisture from the spinach. Put the spinach in a large bowl.
- Stir in the cottage cheese mixture and green onions.
- Spread half the mixture in the baking dish.
- Cut the artichoke hearts in half. Pat dry with paper towels. Place in single layer on the spinach mixture. Sprinkle with 2 tablespoons Parmesan.
- Cover with the remaining spinach mixture.
- Bake, covered for 25 minutes.

309. Spinach Gnocchi Recipe

Serving: 6 | Prep: | Cook: 10mins | Ready in:

Ingredients

- 1 10-oz. package chopped spinach, defrosted and undrained
- 1 cup flour
- 1 cup Italian-seasoned breadcrumbs
- 1 egg
- 1/2 cup parmesan cheese, grated
- 1/4 tsp. salt
- onion Sauce:
- 1 cup chopped onion
- 1 stick butter
- grated Parmesan

Direction

- Mix together first six ingredients in food processor, if available.
- If not, mix with a standard or hand mixer.
- Form into a large ball, take off about 1/4 cup and roll on a well-floured board into the shape of a pretzel log.
- Slice diagonally in one-inch sections.
- Place on parchment paper-lined cookie sheet.
- Repeat until all of the spinach mixture is cut into one-inch sections.
- Brown chopped onions in butter.
- While onions are browning, place water in a three-quart saucepan.
- When the water starts to boil, add gnocchi.
- When the gnocchi float, they're done.
- Drain well.
- Place gnocchi on a serving platter, sprinkle liberally with grated Parmesan cheese and then spoon browned onions on top.
- Serve warm.
- The gnocchi can be prepared ahead of time and frozen.
- No need to defrost before placing in boiling water.
- Make the browned onion sauce while the gnocchi is cooking.

310. Spinach Pauline Recipe

Serving: 4 | Prep: | Cook: 20mins | Ready in:

Ingredients

- 2 (10 oz.) pkgs. frozen chopped spinach
- 6 Tbsp. grated onion
- 1/3 cup melted butter, divided
- 1/4 tsp. salt
- 1/4 tsp. pepper
- 6 Tbsp. heavy cream
- 6 Tbsp. grated parmesan cheese
- 2 Tbsp. cream cheese
- 2 dashes Tabasco sauce
- Italian bread crumbs

Direction

- Cook spinach according to package directions in unsalted water. Drain real well.
- In a medium skillet, sauté onions in 1/4butter. Add spinach, salt and pepper. Pour in milk. Add cheeses and Tabasco sauce. Mix well. Before serving, Place in baking dish and top with Italian bread crumbs and drizzle with remaining butter. Bake at 375* for 10-15 minutes.
- Freezes well.

311. Spinach Risotto Recipe

Serving: 6 | Prep: | Cook: 35mins | Ready in:

Ingredients

- 5 cups of lower-sodium chicken broth
- 1 tbsp of olive oil
- 2 medium leeks, trimmed, cleaned and sliced in half moons
- 1 1/2 cups of arborio rice
- 1/4 of dry white vermouth
- 1/2 tsp of salt

- 3/4 tsp of white pepper-I like the peppery zest against the creamy rice
- 1/4 tsp of thyme leaves, fresh stripped off the step
- 2 long strips of lemon peel
- 6 cups of fresh tender baby spinach leaves
- 1/3 cup of half and half
- 1/4 cup of freshly grated parmesan cheese

Direction

- Heat the broth in a medium sauce pan to a very low simmer.
- Heat oil in large heavy bottom skillet.
- Add leeks and cook until limp over low-medium heat.
- Add Arborio rice and toast in the oil and leeks for a few minutes.
- Add wine and cook until nearly evaporated.
- Add the lemon peel to the pot.
- Add ladles of warm stock to barely cover the rice and stir gently, cooking over low heat until the liquid is nearly completely absorbed.
- Add another ladle and continue until the stock is used and the rice is not quite tender to the tooth. There is still a bit of bite in each grain.
- Season with salt, pepper, thyme.
- Fish out the long lemon pieces and discard.
- Add spinach, half and half, stir once or twice to wilt the spinach into the rice.
- Remove from heat and stir in the cheese. The rice will warm and melt the cheese into unctuous goodness.

---

312.   Spinach Stuffed Onions Recipe

Serving: 8 | Prep: | Cook: 40mins | Ready in:

Ingredients

- 4 large red onions
- 1 1/2 lb. fresh spinach, stems removed
- 3 Tbsp melted butter
- 1/3 cup of half and half

- 1 tsp of beef base concentrate (from a jar not a cube)
- 1/2 tsp of white pepper
- 1/4 tsp of nutmeg or more to taste
- Grated Parmesan or gruyere cheese

Direction

- Peel onions and cut in half horizontally;
- Steam in colander over boiling water for about 12 minutes or until tender but not soft and mushy. You want an onion cup to stuff.
- Cool; remove the center of the onions and dice.
- Leave shells intact.
- Wash spinach and cook for one minute; using only the water that clings to the leaves.
- Drain and chop.
- Sauté spinach and chopped onion in melted butter.
- Add half and half, beef base and seasoning.
- Cook until most liquid evaporates.
- You want it fairly dry, not soupy.
- Fill onion shells with spinach mixture.
- Sprinkle generously with cheese.
- Bake in greased shallow pan at 350 degrees until piping hot and thoroughly heated, about 15-20 minutes.

---

313.   Spinach And Potatoes Aloo Palak Recipe

Serving: 8 | Prep: | Cook: 35mins | Ready in:

Ingredients

- 2 to 3 lbs fresh chopped spinach
- 3 onions
- 3 to 4 potatoes small cubed
- 3 med tomatoes
- 1/2 cup+ vegetable oil
- 1 cup plain yoghurt
- 1/4 tsp tumeric
- 1/2 tsp cumin powder
- 1/2 cup water

- 1/4 tsp cardomon powder
- 1/4 tsp coriander powder
- pinch of cinnamon
- salt and pepper
- 1 cup cream

Direction

- Chop onions and sauté in a bit of the oil till light brown.
- Blend onions with yoghurt and set aside.
- Chop tomatoes and cook with the 1/2 cup oil and turmeric for 5 to 7 minutes.
- Add remainder of spices and cook about 5 minutes more.
- Add the onion and yoghurt mixture plus the water and cook about 10 to 15 minutes stirring often.
- Add the spinach and simmer stir often about 15 minutes.
- Add the potatoes and continue to cook and simmer until potatoes are tender; stirring often.
- When tender add the cream and cook low for only a few minutes longer.

---

314. Spinach With Chickpeas And Fresh Dill Recipe

Serving: 6 | Prep: | Cook: 15mins | Ready in:

Ingredients

- 2 tablespoons olive oil
- 1 large onion, thinly sliced
- 1 1/2 cups canned chickpeas, drained
- 1 pound spinach
- 1/2 cup minced fresh dill
- 2 lemons, juiced
- salt and pepper to taste

Direction

- In a large skillet, heat olive oil over medium heat.

- Add onion, and sauté until soft.
- Add chickpeas, and toss to coat in oil.
- Clean spinach and cut away thick stems
- Add undrained spinach and dill to skillet, and cook until spinach is tender.
- Stir in lemon juice, and season with salt and pepper to taste
- Serve warm.

---

315. Squash Casserole Recipe

Serving: 6 | Prep: | Cook: 55mins | Ready in:

Ingredients

- 6 cups of diced yellow squash and zucchini
- vegetable oil
- 1 Large onion, Chopped
- 4 tablespoons of butter
- 1/2 cup sour cream, mouth watering yet???
- 1 teaspoon House seasonings, hold on, ingredients below =)
- 1 cup grated cheddar cheese
- 1 cup crushed butter crackers, I used Ritz but you can use whatever your heart desires
- NOW preheat your oven to 350 degrees F
- HOUSE SEASONING:
- 1 cup of salt
- 1/4 cup of black pepper
- 1/4 cup of Guess...lol! garlic powder

Direction

- Sauté the squash in a little vegetable oil over medium heat until it has completely broken down, around 15 to 20 minutes.
- Line a colander with a clean tea towel (don't ask I don't know what that is but I believe a paper towel might work).
- Place the cooked squash in the lined colander. Squeeze excess moisture from the squash. Now set that aside for now.
- In a medium size skillet, sauté the onion in butter for 5 minutes. Remove from the pan &

mix all the ingredients together except the cracker crumbs, they go on top later =)
- Pour mixture into a buttered casserole dish & top with cracker crumbs ;)
- Bake for 25 to 30 minutes
- Now devour it like I did....ENJOY, Thanks PAULA DEAN!!!

316. Squash With Dill Tejfeles Tokfozelek Recipe

Serving: 6 | Prep: | Cook: 20mins | Ready in:

Ingredients

- 2 1/2 lb yellow squash (green squash can be used but peel it)
- 1 tsp. salt
- 2 T butter
- 1 onion, minced
- 1/4 tsp paprika
- 1/4 tsp sugar
- 1 tsp vinegar or lemon juice
- Sprig fresh or dried dill
- 2 tsp flour
- 1/4 C hot water
- 3 T sour cream
- 1 bay leaf (optional)

Direction

- Pare squash, cut in half lengthwise, and remove seeds, then half crosswise into pieces about 3" long.
- Place pieces flat on board and cut into thin strips, place in bowl and sprinkle with salt. Let stand about 1 hour.
- Lift out of bowl and dry with paper towels.
- Melt butter in skillet, add onion and cook until tender, add squash, paprika, sugar, vinegar and snipped dill, cover and cook 10 -12 min. Or until tender.
- Sprinkle flour over top of squash, gently stir, then cook 2-3 min.
- Pour in water and cook about 1 min.

- Gently stir in sour cream.
- Serve at once.

317. Stir Fried Green Beans With Coconut Recipe

Serving: 4 | Prep: | Cook: 20mins | Ready in:

Ingredients

- Stir Fried green beans with coconut
- 4 tablespoons butter
- 1 teaspoon black mustard seeds
- 3 ounces onion finely chopped
- 1 teaspoon freshly grated ginger
- 1 teaspoon salt
- 1 teaspoon freshly ground black pepper
- 1 pound fresh green beans thinly sliced on the diagonal
- 1/4 teaspoon paprika
- 1 ounce unsweetened shredded coconut
- 2 tablespoons freshly chopped coriander
- 2 tablespoons lemon juice

Direction

- Heat butter in a large frying pan or wok over moderate heat.
- Add mustard seeds and fry for 30 seconds.
- Stir in the onions, ginger, salt and pepper and mix well.
- Add green beans and paprika and stir fry 5 minutes.
- Add coconut and coriander then reduce heat to low.
- Cover and cook 10 minutes stirring from time to time until beans are tender.
- Sprinkle with lemon juice and serve immediately.

318. Stir Fried Cabbage Recipe

Serving: 4 | Prep: | Cook: 15mins |Ready in:

Ingredients

- 1 tablespoon vegetable oil
- 2 cloves garlic, minced
- 3 cups sliced green cabbage (1/2 small head)
- 3 cups sliced red cabbage (1/2 small head)
- 2 small carrots, sliced (about 1 cup)
- 1 medium yellow onion, sliced (about 1 cup)
- 2 medium red or yellow bell peppers, julienned (about 2 cups)
- 1/4 cup reduced-sodium soy sauce
- 2 teaspoons ground ginger
- 1/4 cup water
- 2 tablespoons cornstarch

Direction

- In a wok or large nonstick skillet, heat oil over medium heat.
- Add garlic and cook, stirring constantly, for I minute.
- Stir in green cabbage, red cabbage, carrots, onion, bell peppers, soy sauce, and ginger. Cover and cook, stirring occasionally, until vegetables are crisp-tender, about 10 minutes.
- In a small bowl, combine water and cornstarch. Mix well. Add cornstarch mixture to wok, stirring until sauce thickens, about I minute. Serve immediately.
- VARIATION
- Use leftover cooked chicken to make a tasty main dish. Add I cup chicken to the wok in Step 3. Proceed as recipe directs.

319. Stir Fry Broccoli Stems Recipe

Serving: 4 | Prep: | Cook: 20mins |Ready in:

Ingredients

- Large, thick stems from 4 bunches broccoli
- 1 T oil
- 1 T minced garlic
- 1/4 cup diagonally sliced green onion for garnish (optional)
- 1 tsp sesame seeds
- 1 tsp sesame oil
- 1 T salt & a pinch of salt to taste

Direction

- First cut off the ends of the broccoli stalks, which might be kind of brown if the broccoli has been in the fridge for a while.
- Use a sharp knife to cut away the smaller ribs and leftover pieces of leaves. Then use a sharp vegetable peeler to peel the stems carefully, then cut them into thin julienne strips about 2 inches long.
- Place in a colander and sprinkle with the salt. Set aside for 10 minutes to drain, then rinse with cold water and gently squeeze out excess liquid.
- Heat the pan over medium-high heat for one minute, add the oil and heat 10 seconds, then add the garlic and cook about 30 seconds. Then add the broccoli stems and start to stir-fry.
- Continue to cook the broccoli stems until they are starting to brown but are still crisp, about 6 minutes.
- Sprinkle sesame seeds and Sesame oil, taste to salt: Mix gently and remove from heat.
- Serve hot, garnished with green onions if desired.

320. Stuffed Artichokes Recipe

Serving: 4 | Prep: | Cook: 30mins |Ready in:

Ingredients

- 1 cup panko bread crumbs

- fresh basil and cilantro chopped
- ½ cup grated Pecorino-romano cheese
- 1 tablespoon parsley,
- 5 cloves chopped galic
- salt & freshly ground pepper to taste
- 6 tablespoons olive oil
- 4 artichokes

Direction

- Combine bread crumbs, Pecorino-Romano Cheese, parsley, basil, cilantro, salt, pepper, and 2 tablespoons of the olive oil in a medium bowl. Mix together well.
- Cut stems off artichokes, flush with bottom.
- Cut pointy leaves off the top of the artichokes.
- Take out fuzzy center in artichoke
- Spread leaves of each artichoke out and push stuffing in between them.
- In a pot just large enough to fit the artichokes, add the sliced garlic cloves, 2 tablespoons of the olive oil and the artichokes. Drizzle the remaining 2 tablespoons of olive oil over the top of the artichokes.
- Turn heat on to medium and cook until sizzling about 1-2 minutes. Add water to reach half way up the sides of the artichokes.
- Cover and cook until the artichokes are tender and a leaf is easily pulled out, about 45 minutes. If liquid is evaporating too quickly add a little more water.
- Transfer to a serving platter, drizzle a little of the liquid from the pot over the artichokes and serve. Surround with roasted red peppers aioli.

321. Stuffed Eggplant Baked In A Delightful Yogurt Sauce Recipe

Serving: 4 | Prep: | Cook: 45mins | Ready in:

Ingredients

- 1 large eggplant
- 1/2 pound lean ground beef
- 6 ounce can tomato paste
- 1 egg slightly beaten
- 2 tablespoons finely chopped onion
- 2 tablespoons finely chopped green pepper
- 1 clove garlic, minced
- 1/2 teaspoon salt
- 1/4 teaspoon ground black pepper
- 1/2 cup dry red wine
- 1/2 cup plain whole milk yogurt
- 1 8 ounce can tomato sauce
- 1/2 cup shredded mozzarella cheese

Direction

- Preheat oven to 350.
- Cut eggplant in half and scoop out pulp leaving shell intact.
- Finely dice eggplant pulp.
- In a skillet brown eggplant in oil and add beef turning until browned.
- Drain off any fat if necessary.
- Stir in tomato paste, egg, onion, green pepper, garlic, salt, pepper red wine and yogurt.
- Heat thoroughly but do not boil.
- Spoon mixture into eggplant halves then top with tomato sauce and mozzarella cheese then place in baking dish and bake for 45 minutes until bubbly and eggplant is tender.

322. Stuffed Eggplant Recipe

Serving: 4 | Prep: | Cook: 55mins | Ready in:

Ingredients

- 1 large eggplant
- 1/2 pound lean ground beef
- 6 ounce can tomato paste
- 1 egg slightly beaten
- 2 tablespoons finely chopped onion
- 2 tablespoons finely chopped green pepper
- 1 clove garlic, minced
- 1/2 teaspoon salt

- 1/4 teaspoon ground black pepper
- 1/2 cup dry red wine
- 1/2 cup plain whole milk yogurt
- 8 ounce can tomato sauce
- 1/2 cup shredded mozzarella cheese

Direction

- Preheat oven to 350 degrees.
- Cut eggplant in half, scoop out pulp, leaving shell intact.
- Finely dice eggplant pulp.
- In a skillet, brown eggplant in oil and add beef, turning until browned.
- Drain off any fat if necessary.
- Stir in tomato paste, egg, onion, green pepper, garlic, salt, pepper red wine and yogurt.
- Heat thoroughly, but do not boil.
- Spoon mixture into eggplant halves, top with tomato sauce and mozzarella cheese.
- Place in baking dish and bake for 45-55 minutes until bubbly and eggplant is tender.

---

323.   Stuffed Green Beans Recipe

Serving: 4 | Prep: | Cook: 20mins | Ready in:

Ingredients

- can of green beans-drained
- 1/2 cup of bread crumbs
- 1/4 cup of grated cheese, ramano parmisian whatever you like.
- minced garlic- but I have used garlic salt in a pinch
- olive oil

Direction

- Combine first 4 ingredients and mix around (but don't smoosh the beans)
- Then add approximately 1/4 a cup of olive oil, enough so that it wets all the ingredients.

- This measurements are approximate so if you like more or less of anything it still will work out.
- Bake for about 20-30 minutes on 350.
- Enjoy

---

324.   Stuffed Red Peppers For Sukkah Recipe

Serving: 6 | Prep: | Cook: 45mins | Ready in:

Ingredients

- 3 large red bell peppers
- 1/2 cup extra virgin olive oil
- 3 cloves garlic, finely chopped
- 1/4 lb. shredded cheese, such as fontina or Monterey Jack
- 4 oz. breadcrumbs or matzah meal
- 2 Tbs. chopped Italian parsley
- 1/2 tsp. dried thyme
- 1 tsp. fine sea salt
- 1 tsp. pepper
- 4 small zucchini, finely chopped

Direction

- Cut the peppers in half lengthwise and remove their seeds and cores.
- In a large bowl, combine 1/4 cup olive oil, garlic, cheese, 2 oz. breadcrumbs, thyme, salt and pepper.
- Mix well, then add the zucchini, tossing well to coat the zucchini.
- Stuff the peppers generously with the zucchini mixture.
- Lightly oil the bottom of a baking dish and place the stuffed peppers in it.
- Sprinkle the remaining olive oil, breadcrumbs and chopped Italian parsley over the peppers.
- Bake in a preheated 400-degree oven about 45 minutes, until the peppers are tender and the surface of the stuffing is nicely browned. Serve warm or at room temperature.

325. Stuffed Tomatoes Recipe

Serving: 8 | Prep: | Cook: |Ready in:

Ingredients

- 8 oz. grape (cherry) tomatoes
- 4 oz goat cheese
- 2 oz. mayonnaise (Hellmann's)
- 1 garlic clove, crushed
- 1 Tbl mixed herbs, crushed (your choice)
- salt and black pepper

Direction

- Wash tomatoes and drain
- Carefully remove 1/2" slice from top of each and reserve
- Scoop out seeds with a small melon baller or other scoop
- Mix goat cheese, mayonnaise, garlic and herbs in a small bowl
- Add salt and pepper to taste
- Spoon mixture into pastry bag and pipe into tomatoes
- Cap with reserved tops and arrange on a serving plate or tray.

326. Summer Squash Casserole Recipe

Serving: 68 | Prep: | Cook: 30mins |Ready in:

Ingredients

- 2 pounds yellow squash,sliced (6)cups
- 1/4 cup chopped onion
- 1 can cream of chicken soup(und)
- 1 cup sour cream
- 1 cup shredded carrot
- 1 8oz package herb-seasoned stufing mix
- 1/2 cup butter

Direction

- Cook slice squash and onion in sauce pan with salted water for about 5 minutes
- Drain
- Combine cream of chicken soup, sour cream
- Stir in shredded carrots
- Fold in squash and onion
- Combine melted butter and stuffing mix
- Spread half stuffing mix in the bottom of a baking pan
- Spoon vegetable mixture on top
- Sprinkle remaining stuffing on top
- Bake 350 degree
- 30 to 40 Minutes

327. Summertime Coleslaw Recipe

Serving: 8 | Prep: | Cook: 120mins |Ready in:

Ingredients

- 1 cup mayonnaise
- 2 tablespoons vinegar
- 2 tablespoons sugar
- 1 1/2 teaspoons McCormick® Season-All® Seasoned salt
- 1 teaspoon McCormick® ground mustard
- 1 teaspoon McCormick® celery Seed
- 4 cups shredded green cabbage
- 3 cups shredded red cabbage
- 1 cup shredded carrots

Direction

- In a small bowl, combine mayonnaise, vinegar, sugar, Season-All, ground mustard and celery seed.
- In a large bowl, toss cabbage and carrots together.
- Add mayonnaise mixture and mix well.
- Refrigerate 2 hours or until ready to serve.
- Stir again just before serving.

328.   Sweet Potato Casserole Recipe

Serving: 6 | Prep: | Cook: 40mins | Ready in:

Ingredients

- 2 1/2 pounds sweet potatoes; scrubbed
- 2 large eggs; lightly beaten
- 3 tablespoons unsalted butter; melted
- 2 tablespoons packed dark brown sugar
- 1 teaspoon kosher salt
- 1/2 teaspoon ground cinnamon
- 1/2 teaspoon ground ginger
- 1 pinch freshly ground nutmeg
- freshly ground black pepper; to taste
- 8 ounces crushed pineapple in juice; drained
- 1/4 cup pecans; coarsely chopped

Direction

- Preheat oven to 400.
- Put the sweet potatoes on a baking sheet and pierce each one 2-3 times with a fork.
- Bake for 45 to 60 minutes or until tender.
- Put aside to cool.
- Turn the oven down to 350.
- Scoop the sweet potato out of their skins and into a medium bowl.
- Discard the skins.
- Mash the potatoes until smooth.
- Add the eggs, butter, sugar and spices.
- Whisk until smooth, add pineapple and mix well.
- Butter an 8x8 inch casserole.
- Pour the sweet potato mixture into the pan and sprinkle with the pecans.
- Bake for 30 to 40 minutes or until a bit puffy.
- Serve immediately.
- Notes: Casserole can be made a day or two ahead up to the point of adding the nuts and baking it. Cover and refrigerate and when ready to serve, add nuts and bake as directed.

329.   Sweet Potato Gnocchi With Maple Cinnamon Sage Brown Butter Recipe

Serving: 8 | Prep: | Cook: 90mins | Ready in:

Ingredients

- For the Gnocchi:
- 2 pounds sweet potatoes
- 2/3 cup whole milk ricotta cheese
- 1 1/2 teaspoons salt
- 1 teaspoon ground cinnamon
- 1/4 teaspoon freshly ground black pepper
- 1 1/4 cups all-purpose flour, plus 1/3 cup for the work surface
- For the Maple cinnamon sage Brown Butter:
- 1/2 cup unsalted butter (1 stick)
- 20 fresh sage leaves
- 1 teaspoon ground cinnamon
- 2 tablespoons maple syrup
- 1 teaspoon salt
- 1/2 teaspoon freshly ground black pepper

Direction

- For the Gnocchi:
- Preheat the oven to 425 degrees F.
- Pierce the sweet potato with a fork. Bake the sweet potatoes until tender and fully cooked, between 40 to 55 minutes depending on size. Cool slightly.
- Cut in half and scoop the flesh into a large bowl. Mash the sweet potatoes and transfer to a large measuring cup to make sure the sweet potatoes measure about 2 cups.
- Transfer the mashed sweet potatoes back to the large bowl.
- Add the ricotta cheese, salt, cinnamon, and pepper and blend until well mixed.
- Add the flour, 1/2 cup at a time until a soft dough forms.
- Lightly flour a work surface and place the dough in a ball on the work surface.
- Divide the dough into 6 equal balls.

- Roll out each ball into a 1-inch wide rope.
- Cut each rope into 1-inch pieces.
- Roll the gnocchi over the tines of a fork.
- Transfer the formed gnocchi to a large baking sheet.
- Continue with the remaining gnocchi.
- Meanwhile, bring a large pot of salted water to a boil over high heat.
- Add the gnocchi in 3 batches and cook until tender but still firm to the bite, stirring occasionally, about 5 to 6 minutes.
- Drain the gnocchi using a slotted spoon onto a baking sheet.
- Tent with foil to keep warm and continue with the remaining gnocchi.
- For the Brown Butter sauce:
- While the gnocchi are cooking melt the butter in a large sauté pan over medium heat.
- When the butter has melted add the sage leaves.
- Continue to cook, swirling the butter occasionally, until the foam subsides and the milk solids begin to brown.
- Remove the pan from the heat.
- Stir in the cinnamon, maple syrup, salt, and pepper. Careful, the mixture will bubble up. Gently stir the mixture.
- When the bubbles subside, toss the cooked gnocchi in the brown butter.
- Transfer the gnocchi to a serving dish and serve immediately.

330. Sweet Potatoes Extraordinaire Recipe

Serving: 12 | Prep: | Cook: 35mins | Ready in:

Ingredients

- 3 large sweet potatoes, baked
- 1 1/2 cups white sugar
- 3 eggs, beaten
- 1/2 cup butter, melted
- 1 cup evaporated milk

- 1 teaspoon ground cinnamon
- 2 cups miniature marshmallows
- 1 cup flaked coconut
- Topping
- 1/2 cup packed brown sugar
- 1 cup chopped pecans
- 1/2 cup butter, melted

Direction

- Generously butter a 9x13 inch baking dish or casserole.
- Bake the sweet potatoes until soft. Peel and mash (this may be done ahead and kept in the refrigerator until you're ready to prepare the casserole).
- Mix mashed potatoes together with sugar, eggs, butter, evaporated milk, cinnamon, marshmallows and coconut; place the mixture into the baking dish.
- In a small bowl, mix together brown sugar, pecans and butter; spread the topping over the casserole.
- Bake 30-35 minutes at 400 degrees.

331. Swiss Chard Sicilian Style Recipe

Serving: 6 | Prep: | Cook: 15mins | Ready in:

Ingredients

- 1 large bunch (1 1/4 pounds) swiss chard, washed and trimmed
- 1 tablespoon olive oil
- 1 small onion, chopped
- 1/4 cup golden raisins
- salt to taste
- 2 tablespoons pignoli nuts (pine nuts), toasted

Direction

- Cut ribs and stems from chard, cut in 1/2" pieces and set aside.

- Cut leaves into 2" pieces and place in colander to drain.
- In Dutch oven heat oil on medium heat.
- Add onion and chard ribs/stems.
- Cook until tender stirring occasionally, 7 to 9 minutes.
- Add drained chard leaves, raisins and 1/4 teaspoon salt.
- Cover and cook 2 to 3 minutes OR until leaves are tender.
- Remove Dutch oven from heat and stir in pignoli.

332. Szechuan Green Bean Recipe

Serving: 4 | Prep: | Cook: 10mins | Ready in:

Ingredients

- 1 pound green beans, washed and trimed.
- 1 tablespoon garlic, chopped
- 1 tablespoon ginger, chopped
- 2 scallions (spring onions, green onions), white parts only, tinly sliced
- 1/2 teaspoon chili garlic sauce
- 1 tablespoon dark soy sauce
- 1/2 teaspoon sugar
- 1/4 teaspoon salt, or to taste
- pepper to taste, optional
- 2 tablespoons canola oil or peanut oil for stir-frying, or as needed

Direction

- Wash the long beans, drain thoroughly, and trim the tops and bottoms.
- Cut the long beans on the diagonal into slices approximately 2 inches long.
- Chop the garlic, ginger and white part of the scallions.
- Heat 1 tablespoon oil over medium heat. Add the green beans and stir-fry until they start to shrivel or "pucker" and turn brown (5 - 7 minutes).

- Remove the green beans and drain in a colander or on paper towels.
- Heat 1 tablespoon oil in the wok on high heat. Add the garlic, ginger and scallions. Stir-fry for a few seconds, then add the chili sauce and stir-fry for a few more seconds until aromatic.
- Add the green beans and the remaining ingredients. Mix together and serve with steamed rice.

333. Taiwanese Pickeled Cabage Recipe

Serving: 6 | Prep: | Cook: | Ready in:

Ingredients

- 1 fresh Cabage
- 1 cup of shredded carrot
- water
- 6 tbs salt
- 1 cup sugar
- 4 cups vinegar
- 3 fresh chilli

Direction

- Cut cabbage into bite size or just tear it with your hand like when you prepare salad greens
- Put the cabbage in a big container put salt and water just to cover it
- Leave it for 1 hour, excess water should come out by now (the water might double) if not leave it for another 30 mins, drain
- Mix vinegar, sugar than pour into your cabbage, add shredded carrots, chilly mix well, taste it should be sour a little sweet and not too salty if the taste is perfect store it in jar or a container with lid
- Store it in the fridge for at least 2 hours or overnight, bon apetit!

334. Tex Mex Summer Squash Casserole Recipe

Serving: 8 | Prep: | Cook: 40mins | Ready in:

Ingredients

- 2-1/4 pounds summer squash quartered lengthwise and thinly sliced crosswise
- 2/3 cup finely chopped yellow onion
- 4 ounce can chopped green chiles
- 4-1/2 ounce can chopped jalapenos drained
- 1/2 teaspoon salt
- 2-1/4 cups grated extra-sharp cheddar cheese, divided
- 1/4 cup all-purpose flour
- 3/4 cup mild salsa
- 4 scallions thinly sliced for garnish
- 1/4 cup finely chopped red onion for garnish

Direction

- Preheat oven to 400.
- Coat rectangular baking dish with cooking spray.
- Combine squash, onion, chilies, jalapenos, salt and 3/4 cup cheese in a large bowl.
- Sprinkle with flour and toss to coat.
- Spread mixture in the prepared baking dish and cover with foil.
- Bake for 45 minutes.
- Spoon salsa over the casserole and sprinkle with remaining cheese.
- Bake uncovered for 30 minutes.
- Sprinkle with scallions and red onion.

335. Texas Corn With Onions And Peppers Recipe

Serving: 8 | Prep: | Cook: 20mins | Ready in:

Ingredients

- 2 pound bag frozen corn kernels thawed
- 1 large yellow onion finely diced

- 1 green bell pepper
- 1 red bell pepper
- 1 pickled jalapeno pepper
- 4 tablespoons chili powder
- 1 tablespoon ground cumin
- 1 tablespoon garlic powder
- 1 tablespoon hot paprika
- 16 ounces unsalted butter
- 1 bunch cilantro

Direction

- Thaw and drain frozen corn kernels.
- Heat a large skillet over medium high and add 4 ounces of butter.
- Add chili powder, paprika, cumin and garlic powder and fry 30 seconds to release oils.
- Add finely diced onions, peppers and jalapenos then sauté until onions caramelize.
- Remove mixture from skillet and set aside.
- Add remaining butter and stir in thawed corn kernels.
- Sauté corn 8 minutes until corn is hot and beginning to soften.
- Return onion and pepper mixture to skillet and combine well with corn.
- Remove from heat and add chopped cilantro and stir well then serve hot.

336. Thai Coleslaw Claim Jumper Recipe

Serving: 4 | Prep: | Cook: | Ready in:

Ingredients

- 1/2 head napa cabbage, thinly sliced
- 1/2 zucchini, julienned
- 2 jumbo carrots, julienned
- 2 green onions, sliced
- 1 tablespoon toasted sesame seeds
- 3 tablespoons shaved coconut
- 3 tablespoons roasted unsalted peanuts
- 2 tablespoons toasted almonds

- --THAI COLESLAW DRESSING--
- 8 ounces Thai sweet chili sauce (Lingham's brand is good)
- 8 ounces orange juice
- 1/2 ounce honey
- 1/2 teaspoon fresh ginger, chopped fine
- 1/2 teaspoon light brown sugar
- 1 teaspoon cilantro, chopped fine
- 1 tablespoon sesame oil

Direction

- For salad: Combine cabbage, zucchini, carrots, onions, sesame seeds, coconut, peanuts and almonds in large bowl. Chill until ready to use.
- For dressing: Place ingredients in a mixing bowl and whisk together. Slowly add sesame oil while whisking. Pour desired amount, about 1/4 cup, over chilled salad vegetables. Serve.

---

337. Thai Green Rice Recipe

Serving: 4 | Prep: | Cook: 30mins | Ready in:

Ingredients

- 12fl oz/340ml basmati rice
- 50g/2oz creamed coconut
- 4 cloves garlic
- 2 large or 3 medium-sized fresh green or red chillies
- 4cm cube root ginger
- 20g fresh coriander
- 1½ tbsp groundnut or other flavourless oil
- 3 x 2in/5cm pieces cinnamon stick
- 6 whole cloves
- 15 black peppercorns
- 1½ oz/40g unsalted cashew nuts, halved
- 2 medium onions, peeled and finely sliced
- 4oz/110g fresh peas, or frozen and defrosted
- 1½ level tsp salt, or to taste
- 15fl oz/425ml hot water
- 2 tbsp lime juice

Direction

- Begin by dissolving the creamed coconut in the boiling water, then place it in a food processor with the garlic, chillies, ginger and coriander stalks, whizzing until everything is finely chopped.
- Leave this aside while you heat the oil over a gentle heat in the frying pan, then add the cinnamon sticks, cloves, peppercorns and cashew nuts to the pan and sauté everything gently for about 1 minute. Next, add the onions and continue to cook over a medium heat until they become softened and pale gold in colour, which will take 8-10 minutes. Next add the rice, then stir once and cook for another 2-3 minutes. After that, add the coconut mixture, give everything a stir, and cook for a further 2-3 minutes. Now add the peas, salt and hot water, bring it all up to a gentle simmer, and then cover with the lid. Turn the heat to low and let everything cook very gently for 8 minutes; use a timer here, and don't lift the lid.
- Then remove the pan from the heat, take the lid off and cover the pan with a cloth for 10 minutes before serving. Finally, remove the pieces of cinnamon, sprinkle in the lime juice and the finely chopped coriander leaves, then fork the rice gently to separate the grains. Garnish with the reserved whole coriander leaves.
- ENJOY! :)

---

338. Three Bean Casserole Recipe

Serving: 8 | Prep: | Cook: 45mins | Ready in:

Ingredients

- 1 pound italian sausage out of casing
- 2 medium stalks of celery, sliced about 1 cup
- 1 medium onion chopped
- 1 large green pepper chopped

- 1 large clove garlic, crushed
- 2 21 oz. cans baked beans in tomato sauce
- 2 15 oz. cans (1 light, 1 dark) kidney beans drained
- 1 8 oz. can tomato sauce (ketchup can be substituted)
- 1/4 cup spicy brown mustard
- 1/4 cup molasses
- 2 tablespoons honey
- 1/4 teaspoon red pepper sauce
- 1 teaspoon vinegar
- salt and pepper to taste

Direction

- Heat oven to 400 F. Cook the sausage breaking into small pieces, celery, onion, pepper and garlic about 10 minutes in 10 inch skillet, stirring frequently until the sausage is done; drain. Mix sausage mixture and remaining ingredients in ungreased 3 quart casserole. Bake uncovered about 45 minutes, stirring once, until hot and bubbly.

---

339. Tiny Ham Stuffed Tomatoes Recipe

Serving: 6 | Prep: | Cook: |Ready in:

Ingredients

- 1 pint cherry tomatoes
- 2 cans deviled ham
- 3 tablespoons sour cream
- 2 tablespoons horseradish
- fresh parsley for garnish

Direction

- Thinly slice tops of cherry tomatoes then remove pulp and drain shells upside down on paper towels.
- In a small bowl combine ham, sour cream and horseradish.
- Stuff tomatoes and refrigerate.

- Garnish with parsley before serving.

---

340. Tomato Blue Cheese Salad Recipe

Serving: 6 | Prep: | Cook: |Ready in:

Ingredients

- 3 large ripe tomatoes, chopped into bite-size pieces
- 1 sweet onion, diced (not too fine - medium pieces are nice)
- 1 tsp or so of Jane's Crazy Mixed Up salt (if you can't get this in your area, use a mixture of sea salt, onion powder, garlic powder and a little dried parsley)
- 2 to 4 ounces best creamy blue cheese, cut into small chunks (if you can get some Maytag Blue, that's my favorite...the creamier, the better)
- French dressing (honey French is excellent with this, as is the Lite version of that dressing)

Direction

- Place the chopped tomatoes and onions into a serving bowl. Sprinkle with the Jane's Crazy Mixed Up Salt and gently stir.
- Allow it to set 5 or 10 minutes before continuing. If you want, you can drain off any excess liquid from the tomatoes before continuing.
- Add the chunks of blue cheese.
- Pour in just enough French dressing to moisten it at bit (you don't want your veggies floating in a lot of dressing - just a touch is best).
- Gently stir to combine everything.
- Serve immediately, or cover and chilled until you are ready to serve. I like to eat this immediately, when the flavors are the freshest.
- You can serve this over a bed of lettuce, too, if desired.

341. Tomato Fritters Greek Style Recipe

Serving: 4 | Prep: | Cook: 15mins | Ready in:

Ingredients

- tomato fritters are a delightful appetizer or side dish. The combination of herbs can be adjusted to include dill, parsley, basil, mint, or oregano, depending on taste preference. (Lenten, Vegan)
- 4 ripe medium tomatoes, finely chopped
- 2 medium zucchini, grated
- 1 medium onion, grated
- 1 1/2 - 2 cups of self-rising flour
- 1/2 bunch fresh parsley, finely chopped
- 1/2 bunch fresh mint or fresh basil, finely chopped
- salt
- pepper
- sunflower or canola oil for frying

Direction

- Combine all ingredients except flour in a bowl.
- Add enough flour to make a thick batter.
- Heat 1/2 to 3/4 inch of oil in a non-stick frying pan. When the oil is hot, drop the batter by tablespoonfuls into the oil and fry until browned.

342. Tzatziki Greek Turkish Recipe

Serving: 2 | Prep: | Cook: 60mins | Ready in:

Ingredients

- 4 cucumbers
- 3 cloves garlic, peeled and minced

- 1 tablespoon olive oil
- salt and pepper, to taste
- 2 cups yogurt, or yogurt and sour cream mixed
- In a small bowl, mash the garlic with the olive oil, salt and pepper
- Stir in the cucumbers and yogurt
- Serve as a dip with crackers or raw vegetables

Direction

- Peel and seed the cucumbers, and put through a fine grater (not a blender)
- Allow to drain in a colander until the juices have stopped running
- Chill, covered, for 1 hour or more
- ENJOY!

343. Tzimmes With Sausage Recipe

Serving: 12 | Prep: | Cook: 240mins | Ready in:

Ingredients

- 2 very large sweet potatoes
- 4 medium white potatoes
- 4 large carrots
- 1 box pitted prunes
- 1 cup orange juice
- 1 cup brown sugar
- 1/2 stick butter or margarine cut up
- 1 lb ring kielbasa turkey sausage sliced
- salt, pepper, cinnamon and honey to taste

Direction

- Peel vegetables and uniformly coarse chunk or cube them.
- I like to use the crock-pot but one can use a large covered casserole for oven baking; If using a casserole or Dutch oven for baking add everything and bake 350 about one hour or until tender but not overly soft.

- Correct seasoning and sweeten with some honey to taste.
- If using a crock-pot, cook high 4 to 6 hours or longer at low.
- However add the sliced turkey sausage the last 2 hours of crock-pot cooking since the sausage is already precooked.
- Correct seasoning and sweetness.
- Yield 12 servings.
- Extras freeze well.
- Notes Tastes even better when reheated.
- Remember to spoon the liquids in bottom of casserole dish over the mixture gently.
- Variations. Omit meat for a vegetarian dish.
- Try adding sweetened canned chunk pineapple if desired and use the liquid to replace some of the orange juice.
- Or add a small piece of brisket if desired to replace the turkey sausage and cook the full time in the crock-pot until meat is fork tender.

---

344. Unexpected Turnip Casserole Recipe

Serving: 8 | Prep: | Cook: 45mins | Ready in:

Ingredients

- 1 large or 2 medium turnips, peeled and chopped into pieces
- 2 carrots, peeled and chopped into pieces (optional)
- 2 small macintosh apples, peeled and chopped into pieces
- 2 extra large or 3 large eggs, separated
- 1/2 tsp salt
- 1/2 tsp pepper
- 1 tsp nutmeg
- 2 tbsp brown sugar
- Add a bit more sugar and nutmeg if you find you end up with a huge heaping mound of mashed veggies
- 1/2 cup breadcrumbs
- 2 tbsp butter

Direction

- Preheat oven to 350 degrees
- Peel turnip, cut up into pieces, and boil turnip until tender
- Mash turnip (and carrots/apples if you are using)
- Mix in egg yolks, nutmeg, salt, pepper, brown sugar
- Beat egg whites in separate dish until soft peaks form
- Mix in the egg whites - this is what makes the turnip lighter than your normal turnip dishes (as well as the carrots and/or apples if that's what you've chosen to add)
- Smooth turnip mixture evenly over bottom of greased casserole dish
- Melt butter and add breadcrumbs, and sprinkle mixture over top
- Bake for 35 to 40 minutes

---

345. Unusual Layered Corn Casserole Recipe

Serving: 8 | Prep: | Cook: 35mins | Ready in:

Ingredients

- 1 white onion
- 2 tablespoons vegetable oil
- 1 pound ground beef
- 1 teaspoon salt
- 1 teaspoon freshly ground black pepper
- 1/4 teaspoon cinnamon
- 1 pound can corn
- 1/4 pound sliced salami
- 1 pound fresh tomatoes
- 1 teaspoon oregano
- 1/2 pound gouda cheese shredded
- 2 tablespoons breadcrumbs
- 1 tablespoon butter

Direction

- Preheat oven to 400.

- Chop onion and sauté in oil until soft.
- Add beef and brown then drain and place mixture in bottom of large casserole dish.
- Season with salt, pepper and cinnamon then rinse corn and drain well.
- Layer over beef mixture then cut salami slices into thin strips and layer over corn.
- Peel tomatoes then slice and layer over salami and season with salt, pepper and oregano.
- Combine cheese and breadcrumbs then layer over tomatoes and dot with butter.
- Bake 35 minutes then allow to cool 5 minutes before serving.

346. VERY HOT KIMCHEE Recipe

Serving: 8 | Prep: | Cook: 6mins | Ready in:

Ingredients

- 1 lg. head napa cabbage
- salt
- water
- 5 habanero peppers, finely chopped, with seeds
- 4 garlic cloves, minced
- 4 green onions, julienned
- 1/2 lg. Daikon (Chinese radish), julienned
- 1 small fresh ginger (1/2" thick), grated
- 1/4 tsp. cayenne pepper (or to taste)

Direction

- Cut cabbage into 1-inch slices.
- Dissolve about 1-2 tablespoons salt in enough water to cover cabbage slices in a glass or plastic bowl.
- Leave cabbage to soak in salted water for about 12 to 24 hours at room temperature.
- Rinse cabbage well, drain, & set aside.
- Combine peppers, green onions, garlic, ginger, daikon and mix with 1 tablespoon salt & cayenne pepper.

- Pack cabbage in a large glass gallon jar, cover with water and gently stir in chopped pepper mixture.
- Refrigerate for several days before serving.
- Keeps well if stored in refrigerator.
- Remove kimchee from liquid before serving.

347. Vegetable Slaw Recipe

Serving: 6 | Prep: | Cook: | Ready in:

Ingredients

- 2 cups red cabbage
- 3 cups green cabbage
- 1/2 cup julienned carrots
- 1 cup sliced celery
- 1/2 red pepper, sliced thin
- 1/2 green pepper, sliced thin
- 1/2 yellow pepper, sliced thin
- 1/2 red onion, sliced thin
- 2 tablespoons mustard seeds
- 1 tablespoon celery seeds
- 1/4 cup red wine vinegar
- 1/2 cup extra-virgin olive oil
- salt & pepper to taste
- 3 tomatoes cut into wedges (add last)

Direction

- Add all ingredients together, toss very gently and serve. (* I don't know how many this salad will serve. My guess would be 6 - 8, but it may be more).

348. Vegetable And Shrimp Tempura (for Beginners)

Serving: 4 | Prep: | Cook: 5mins | Ready in:

Ingredients

- vegetables, cut into serving pieces (e.g. pepper, asparagus, zucchini, green beans, broccoli, sweet potato 1/4 inch thick)
- large shrimp (16-20 count), peeled, deveined
- vegetable oil
- Tempura batter mix (or make your own -see instructions below)
- about 2 tablespoons of flour, for dredging shrimp
- tempura sauce (buy this or make your own)

Direction

- PREPARING THE INGREDIENTS: Make 3-4 slits on the underside of each shrimp without cutting all the way through. This will allow them to lay flat. Prepare all vegetables you are using, laying them on a plate or cutting board with the shrimp. Lightly dredge shrimp in the flour IF you want a slightly thicker coating on the shrimp.
- HEATING THE OIL: The right temperature is very important in this recipe. Heat 2 inches of oil in the frying pan to 350F-360F. If you don't have a thermometer, use one of these tests to ensure the right temperature. 1) Put a drop of batter into the hot oil. If it sinks, then floats to the top immediately, sizzling, the oil is ready. 2) Put a popcorn kernel in the oil. When the kernel pops, the oil has reached the right temperature.
- MAKING THE BATTER: Mix the tempura batter according to package directions in a bowl that will be able to lie on the ice water bowl. DO NOT mix well. Batter should be lumpy and not thick. Note 1 - to make your own batter. Place the tempura batter bowl on top of the ice and water bowl. The batter must be kept very cold to ensure a crispy coating when frying. If batter is too thin, add a bit more flour.
- FRYING: Start with the vegetables like peppers, beans and sweet potatoes first. One at a time, use tongs (I use my fingers) to dip each piece of vegetable in batter and place in hot oil. Don't crowd the pan. Do only 5-6 pieces at once, depending on the size of the pan.

Separate the pieces so they don't stick together. Fry for a few minutes, gently turning once. Remove to a plate lined with a paper towel to absorb the oil.
- Bring oil back to 350-360F. Remove any floating batter from the oil with a slotted spoon. Repeat with asparagus, broccoli or zucchini. These will only need about 2 minutes.
- Again, allow oil to return to the right temperature, then repeat with the shrimp. You can sprinkle on some extra batter over the shrimp to add an additional lacy layer (this can be messy though!).
- PLATING: Arrange the vegetables and shrimp on a plate (or individual plates) in a nice arrangement and serve with tempura sauce.
- Notes
- Make your own batter: Mix 1 cup flour, 1 tablespoon cornstarch, 1 1/2 cups cold seltzer/club soda and 1/2 teaspoon salt in a bowl. Continue with instructions above.

---

349. Veggie Jack Salad Recipe

Serving: 6 | Prep: | Cook: 60mins | Ready in:

Ingredients

- 2 medium cucumbers(or zucchini) sliced
- 2 medium tomatoes, wedged or cubed(or 1 pint cherry or grape tomatoes)
- 2 green onions, sliced
- 6oz monterey jack cheese, cubed
- 2T dressing quality olive oil
- 2t balsamic vinegar
- dash of sugar
- 1-2T fresh herbs(basil, cilantro,oregano, thyme, chives, parsley, etc(any combination you like)
- salt and pepper

Direction

- Combine veggies and cheese in large bowl and set aside.

- Whisk together oil and vinegar, add sugar, salt and pepper and whisk well.
- Add herbs and mix to "break" herbs and combine.
- Pour dressing over veggies and toss to coat.
- Refrigerate at least 1 hour.

350. Veggie Filled Eggplant Crepes Recipe

Serving: 10 | Prep: | Cook: 30mins | Ready in:

Ingredients

- 1 medium sized eggplant
- 1/2 cup oil, or more if necessary
- 1 cup flour, seasoned to taste with salt and pepper
- 3 eggs, beaten
- 1/3 cup finely grated carrot
- 1/2 cup bread crumbs
- 1/4 cup chopped parsley
- 1/4 teaspoon onion powder
- 1/4 cup water
- mozzarella cheese, thinly sliced, one slice per crepe
- italian seasoning
- 1 tablespoon grated mozzarella cheese
- 1 can (14 1/4 oz.) salt free stewed tomatoes
- /3 cup water

Direction

- Peel the eggplant.
- Cut lengthwise into 1/4 inch slices.
- In a large Teflon-coated skillet over medium heat a few tablespoon of oil.
- Dredge a slice of eggplant in the flour seasoned with salt and pepper; shake off excess. Dip in the egg, allowing the excess to drip back into the bowl. Dredge the eggplant in the flour a second time, shaking off the excess.

- Add the coated eggplant slices to the skillet, a few at a time, and brown on both sides - adding more oil if necessary.
- Using a slotted spatula, remove the eggplant crepes from the skillet and drain on paper towels.
- Repeat until all of the eggplant has been cooked.
- Prepare the stuffing while the crepes cool; put the grated carrot in a bowl.
- Add the breadcrumbs, parsley, and onion powder; mix together.
- Add the remaining beaten egg and the 1/4 cup of water. Stir well to blend.
- If too dry add an additional teaspoon or more of water, the mixture should be spreadable.
- Preheat the oven to 350 degrees.
- Divide the filling among the eggplant slices. Spread the filling evenly over two thirds of each slice, then top the filling with a thin slice of mozzarella cheese.
- Arrange the rolls seam side down in a 6 1/2 X 10 1/4 inch baking pan.
- Sprinkle with Italian seasoning and grated mozzarella cheese.
- Pour the stewed tomatoes over and around the rolls.
- Add 1/3 cup of water.
- Cover with foil and bake for 15 minutes, then uncover and bake for an additional 15 minutes until hot and bubbly.

351. Vidalia Onions And Beef Bouillon On The Grill Recipe

Serving: 4 | Prep: | Cook: 45mins | Ready in:

Ingredients

- 4 large vidalia onions
- 4 Knorr extra large beef bouillon cubes (these are worth buying – they're the best for this recipe!)
- 4 tablespoons butter

- 4 cloves of peeled garlic, each clove cut in half
- heavy duty aluminum foil (a must!)
- garlic croutons, optional
- grated swiss cheese, optional

Direction

- Peel onions without cutting off the root end; cut off about 1 inch of the top of the onion.
- Removing as little as possible, cut the root end into a nice flat surface so the onion will remain upright while cooking.
- Using a potato peeler or knife, dig a small cone shaped section from the center of each onion (be careful not to cut through to the root end!).
- Cut the onion into quarters from the top down, stopping within an inch of the root end. Place a bouillon cube in the center of each onion, and place chunks of butter around the bouillon.
- If you are using the garlic, place 1 half in each of 2 quartered sections of the onion.
- Wrap each onion separately in heavy duty aluminum foil. Seal the foil well so moisture can't escape during baking, letting the yummy broth evaporate. Place the foil packages directly on the grill grate, or in a baking pan in a 425 degree oven. Bake until onions are soft, about 45 minutes to 1 hour.
- To serve, place each onion in an individual bowl and open foil package (don't burn yourself with the steam!). Remove onion and all the broth from inside the foil. Serve warm.
- To create instant onion soup, carefully open the tops of each foil packet when onions are done, throw in some croutons and top with grated Swiss cheese, then place the opened packets back on the grill (or in the oven) and continue to cook until the cheese melts (this should only take a few minutes).

352.   Wild Mushroom And Matzo Strata Recipe

Serving: 12 | Prep: | Cook: 50mins | Ready in:

Ingredients

- 1   pound shiitake mushrooms
- 1   pound black trumpet mushrooms
- 2   pounds portobello mushrooms
- 2   pounds oyster mushrooms
- 3/4 cup olive oil
- 1/2 cup chopped shallots
- kosher salt and freshly cracked black pepper
- 2   large Spanish onions sliced
- 3   Tablespoons chopped fresh rosemary leaves
- 8   pieces matzo
- 8   large eggs
- 2 Tablespoons fresh thyme leaves

Direction

- Preheat the oven to 350 degrees F and set the rack to the center of the oven.
- Lightly oil a 9-by-13-by-3-inch or a 10-by-12-by-3-inch baking pan.
- Remove the stems from all the mushrooms, wipe clean if necessary, and cut into slices.
- Keep the different varieties separate.
- Heat 2 tablespoons of olive oil in a large heavy skillet over medium heat and sauté 2 tablespoons of the chopped shallots until softened.
- Add a single layer of mushrooms (one variety at a time), season with salt and pepper, and cook until well browned.
- Set aside to drain on paper towels.
- Repeat this procedure for each of the 4 varieties of mushrooms.
- Wipe out the skillet, then heat the remaining 4 tablespoons of oil and add the sliced onions.
- Season with salt, pepper, and rosemary and sauté until well browned.
- Set aside to drain.
- Soak the sheets of matzo briefly in cool water until soft.

- Lightly beat the eggs with the thyme leaves. Season with salt and pepper.
- Spread the onions in a single layer on the baking pan.
- Cover them with a single layer of soaked matzo, filling in any spaces with broken pieces of matzo.
- Add a layer of mushrooms, then another of matzo.
- Continue layering mushroom varieties with matzo, ending with a layer of mushrooms.
- Pour the egg mixture over the top layer, making sure it covers the top completely and reaches the corners of the pan.
- Bake for 50 to 55 minutes or until an inserted knife comes out clean.
- Remove from oven and let rest for 10 to 15 minutes before cutting.
- Serve hot.
- Note: mushrooms are expensive bur use a mixed variety for best flavor and texture

353. Zucchini Bake Recipe

Serving: 8 | Prep: | Cook: 25mins | Ready in:

Ingredients

- 1/2 cup chopped onion
- 3 cups zucchini, peeled and shredded
- 1/3 cup canola oil
- 1 cup "Jiffy" Mix or Bisquick
- 1/2 cup grated cheese
- 4 beaten eggs
- 1/2 teaspoon italian seasoning

Direction

- Preheat the oven to 350 degrees. Soften onion and zucchini in a bit of water, drain and sauté 10 minutes.
- Mix them with all the other ingredients and put into buttered casserole dish. Bake at 350 degrees about 25 minutes, to a golden color. This is almost like a quiche.

354. Zucchini Casserole Recipe

Serving: 6 | Prep: | Cook: 40mins | Ready in:

Ingredients

- 3-1/2 - 4 cups shredded zucchini or I have also taken 5-6 zucchini's and thinly sliced them on a mandolin
- 1/2 carrot, shredded (optional)
- 1/2 tsp. salt
- 3/4 -1 cup egg substitute
- 1/2 cup dry bread crumbs
- 1/4 cup all-purpose flour
- 2 tsp. italian seasoning
- a squirt of Italian salad dressing (I prefer Kraft)
- 1/2 lb. sliced fresh mushrooms
- 1 onion, either sliced or chopped (I cut the onion in half and then slice it lengthwise not across)
- 2 tsp. Olive or canola oil
- 1-15 oz. can pizza sauce, divided
- 3/4 cup or 1 whole green or yellow pepper either sliced or chopped
- 1/4 cup sliced ripe olives, drained
- Note: I like to add 2 garlic cloves, minced or finely chopped
- 1-1/2 cups shredded mozzarella cheese, divided
- 3/4 cup romano cheese, grated
- Note: I mix the two cheeses together.
- (I'm sure low fat mozzarella cheese would work just fine)

Direction

- Place shredded zucchini in a fine sieve or colander over a plate. Sprinkle with a little salt and toss. Allow this to stand for 15 minutes then rinse and drain well.
- In a bowl, combine the zucchini, shredded carrot (optional) egg substitute, bread crumbs,

flour, Italian seasoning and Italian Salad Dressing.

- Spread in an 11" x 7" baking dish coated with non-stick cooking spray.
- Bake, uncovered at 350 F for 25 minutes.
- In a non-stick skillet, sauté mushrooms and onions in oil.
- Spread half of the pizza sauce over zucchini mixture then sprinkle with the mushrooms, onion, green pepper, olives and half of the cheeses.
- Top with remaining pizza sauce and blended cheeses.
- Bake 15 minutes longer or until hot and bubbly.
- Serves 4 - 6

355. Zucchini Parmesan Recipe

Serving: 6 | Prep: | Cook: 55mins | Ready in:

Ingredients

- 1 1/2 lbs lean ground beef
- 1, 26 oz can, favorite sphaghetti or tomato sauce
- 6 1/2 cups sliced 1/2 inch thick zuchinni-about 4 medium
- 1 cup grated parmesan cheese
- 3 cups shredded mozzarella cheese
- italian seasoning to taste
- fresh basil leaves for garnish
- Additional tomato sauce for topping pieces

Direction

- Cook ground beef in skillet and drain off fat.
- Add the tomato sauce and seasoning to taste
- In a 3 qt. baking dish layer zucchini, half the meat sauce mixture and half the cheeses
- Repeat layers but leave out the remaining mozzarella cheese
- Cover and bake 350F about 45 minutes.

- Uncover, add the remaining mozzarella cheese and bake 5 minutes more
- Let stand 5 minutes before cutting into squares.
- Garnish each piece with additional sauce and basil leaves

356. Zucchini Rice Casserole Recipe

Serving: 1012 | Prep: | Cook: 60mins | Ready in:

Ingredients

- 1 1/2 cups long-grain brown rice
- 3 cups reduced-sodium chicken broth
- 4 cups diced zucchini and/or summer squash (about 1 pound)
- 2 red or green bell peppers, chopped
- 1 large onion, diced
- 3/4 teaspoon salt
- 1 1/2 cups low-fat milk
- 3 tablespoons all-purpose flour
- 2 cups shredded pepper Jack cheese, divided
- 1 cup fresh or frozen (thawed) corn kernels
- 2 teaspoons extra-virgin olive oil
- 8 ounces chicken or turkey sausage, casings removed
- 4 ounces reduced-fat cream cheese (Neufchâtel)
- 1/4 cup chopped pickled jalapeños

Direction

- Preheat oven to 375°F. Pour rice into a 9-by-13-inch baking dish. Bring broth to a simmer in a small saucepan. Stir hot broth into the rice along with zucchini (and/or squash), bell peppers, onion and salt. Cover with foil. Bake for 45 minutes. Remove foil and continue baking until the rice is tender and most of the liquid is absorbed, 35 to 45 minutes more. Meanwhile, whisk milk and flour in a small saucepan. Cook over medium heat until bubbling and thickened, 3 to 4 minutes.

Reduce heat to low. Add 1 1/2 cups Jack cheese and corn and cook, stirring, until the cheese is melted. Set aside.

- Heat oil in a large skillet over medium heat and add sausage. Cook, stirring and breaking the sausage into small pieces with a spoon, until lightly browned and no longer pink, about 4 minutes.5. When the rice is done, stir in the sausage and cheese sauce. Sprinkle the remaining 1/2 cup Jack cheese on top and dollop cream cheese by the teaspoonful over the casserole. Top with jalapeños.
- Return the casserole to the oven and bake until the cheese is melted, about 10 minutes. Let stand for about 10 minutes before serving.

---

357. Zucchini Supper Casserole Recipe

Serving: 6 | Prep: | Cook: 40mins | Ready in:

Ingredients

- 3-1/2 cups shredded zucchini
- 1/2 tsp. salt
- 3/4 -1 cup egg substitute
- 1/2 cup dry bread crumbs
- 1/4 cup all-purpose flour
- 2 tsp. italian seasoning
- 1/2 lb. sliced fresh mushrooms
- 2 garlic cloves, minced
- 2 tsp. olive or canola oil
- 1-15 oz. can pizza sauce, divided
- Note: you can use your favourite spaghetti sauce as well
- 3/4 cup chopped green pepper
- 1/4 cup sliced ripe olives, drained
- 1-1/2 cups shredded mozzarella cheese, divided
- (I'm sure low fat mozzarella cheese would work just fine)

Direction

- Place shredded zucchini in a colander over a plate; sprinkle with salt and toss.
- Let stand for 15 minutes.
- Rinse and drain well.
- In a bowl, combine the zucchini, egg substitute, bread crumbs, flour and Italian seasoning.
- Spread in an 11" x 7" baking dish coated with non-stick cooking spray.
- Bake, uncovered, @ 350 F for 25 minutes.
- In a non-stick skillet, sauté' mushrooms and garlic in oil.
- Spread half of the pizza sauce over zucchini mixture.
- Sprinkle with the mushrooms, green pepper, olives and half of the cheese.
- Top with remaining pizza sauce and cheese.
- Bake 15 minutes longer or until hot and bubbly.
- Serves 6

---

358. Zucchini Tomato Gratin Recipe

Serving: 8 | Prep: | Cook: 30mins | Ready in:

Ingredients

- 2 tablespoons olive oil plus oil for baking dish
- 1 small red onion
- 3 medium zucchini or summer squash
- 3 plum tomatoes
- 3 cloves garlic minced
- 1/2 teaspoon salt
- 1/4 teaspoon freshly ground black pepper
- 1 tablespoon fresh thyme
- 3 ounces gruyere cheese grated

Direction

- Preheat oven to 350.
- Lightly oil round baking dish.
- Slice onion into rounds then slice zucchini and tomatoes 1/2" thick.

- In large skillet over medium heat warm 2 tablespoons oil and sauté onion and garlic 5 minutes.
- Place zucchini slices on edge around sides of baking dish.
- Place tomato slices against zucchini then add some of the sautéed onion garlic mixture.
- Repeat with zucchini, tomato and onion garlic mixture to form alternating rows.
- Place remaining vegetables in center then sprinkle with salt, pepper, thyme and cheese.
- Bake 25 minutes then serve warm.

359. Zuchini Ribbons With Garlic And LemonPepper Recipe

Serving: 6 | Prep: | Cook: 5mins | Ready in:

Ingredients

- zucchini Ribbons with lemon and garlic
- 4 medium zucchini
- 2 tablespoons butter
- 1 or 2 garlic cloves
- 1 tsp grated lemon zest
- 2 tsp minced fresh tarragon
- salt and pepper

Direction

- With a vegetable peeler, cut 4 medium zucchini into long, thin ribbons.
- Melt 2 Tablespoon butter in a skillet; add zucchini, 1 grated garlic clove, and 1 teaspoon grated lemon zest.
- Sauté, stirring, until tender, 2 minutes.
- Sprinkle with 2 teaspoon minced fresh tarragon.
- Season to taste with salt and pepper.

360. Aubergines With Cheese Recipe

Serving: 4 | Prep: | Cook: 50mins | Ready in:

Ingredients

- 2 large aubergines
- 1 lb tomatoes
- 1 onion
- 5-7 tbl spoons olive oil or a really good glug for the more experienced cook
- 175g/6oz kosher dutch or cheddar cheese thinly sliced
- salt and ground black pepper

Direction

- Slice aubergines into 1cm/ 1/2 inch rounds
- Sprinkle them with salt and leave to drain for 30min.
- Rinse well and pat dry
- Meanwhile place the tomatoes in a bowl and cover with boiling water
- Leave for 3 or 4 min or till they are easy to peel
- Peel and chop
- Slice onions and gently fry till golden, set aside
- Gently brown aubergines
- Preheat oven to 190C/375F/gas 5
- Oil a casserole dish and begin with a layer of aubergine
- Sprinkle some onion
- Then tomatoes and then cheese
- Continue with layers ending with a layer of cheese
- Bake for 30-40min or until the cheese is brown and bubbly

361. Bourbon Walnut Sweet Potato Mash Recipe

Serving: 8 | Prep: | Cook: 90mins | Ready in:

Ingredients

- 4 pounds red-skinned sweet potatoes (yams)
- 1/2 cup whipping cream
- 6 tablespoons (3/4 cup) butter
- 1/4 cup pure maple syrup
- 2 tablespoons bourbon
- 1 1/2 teaspoons ground cinnamon
- 1 teaspoon ground allspice
- 3/4 teaspoon ground nutmeg
- 1 cup walnuts, toasted, chopped

Direction

- Preheat oven to 350°F. Roast potatoes on rimmed baking sheet until tender, 1 to 1 1/2 hours. Cool slightly. Scoop flesh into large bowl; discard skins. Mash hot potatoes until coarse puree forms.
- Heat cream and butter in heavy small saucepan over low heat until butter melts, stirring occasionally. Gradually stir hot cream mixture into hot potatoes. Stir in syrup, bourbon, and all spices. Season with salt and pepper.

---

362. Easy Crockpot Stuffed Bell Peppers Recipe

Serving: 6 | Prep: | Cook: 47mins |Ready in:

Ingredients

- 6 green peppers washed, topped and seeded
- 1 1/2lb-2 ground beef
- 1c cooked rice
- 1sm. onion chopped
- 1tsp salt
- 1/8 black pepper
- dash of basil
- 1/2c ketchup
- 1 8oz can of tomato sauce with or w/o seasoning
- cheese(optional)
- bacon (optional)

Direction

- Heat brown beef in a skillet. Combine meat and next 6 ingredients. Stuff bell peppers. Arrange bell peppers in large crock pot. Can be stacked. Pour tomato sauce over peppers. Cooker on low for 6-7 hours or on high for 3-4 hours
- My sister makes two different batches the ones listed on top and then she adds bacon on top of a few and when they're just about done she adds cheese.
- These are really great and she's a better cook.

---

363. Korean Kimchi Recipe

Serving: 10 | Prep: | Cook: 30mins |Ready in:

Ingredients

- 5 heads of Chinese cabbage
- 2 white radishes
- 2 green onions
- 2 cups of hot red pepper powder
- 4 tablespoons of salt
- 4 tablespoons of sugar
- 5 cloves of garlic
- 1 root of fresh ginger
- 1 cup of tiny salted shrimp
- Fresh oysters optional

Direction

- Carefully cut cabbage in half lengthwise. If the cabbage is unusually large, cut in half again, making 4 lengthwise quarters.
- Sprinkling liberally with coarse salt and letting it sit for four hours, or by soaking overnight, then turn occasionally
- Julienne the radishes finely -chop the green onions and mince or crush the garlic and ginger.
- Mix the salted shrimp juice into the red pepper powder. (To take out some of the kimchi fire, reduce the amount of red pepper powder.)

Add radish strips and knead well with hands. Add the remaining ingredients and mix thoroughly -- use your hands because the next step is done by hand anyway.

- Rinse the cabbage thoroughly in clean water and drain well. Pack the seasoned mixture between each leaf of the wilted cabbage.
- Fold over stuffed cabbage sections to hold in the seasonings, and fasten loosely by wrapping the outer leaf around the section. Pack the bundles in a crock or kimchi jar. Keep at room temperature a day or two, then refrigerate. Cut to bite size before serving

364.　　Korean Kimchi Pancake Recipe

Serving: 2 | Prep: | Cook: 5mins |Ready in:

Ingredients

- 1 cup kimchi, chopped
- 1 egg
- 1/2 cup of flour
- 1/3 cup of water
- salt to taste
- 2 tbs oil

Direction

- Mix all ingredients,
- On a heavy skillet add oil
- Add mixture on the cold skillet and oil as thin as possible
- Turn stove to medium heat cook for around 3 minutes
- Flip, and cook the other side for another 3 mins
- Make sure the pancake is cooked through, serve

365.　　Pineapple Topped Sweet Potatoes Recipe

Serving: 2 | Prep: | Cook: 55mins |Ready in:

Ingredients

- 2 medium sweet potatoes
- 1/4 cup drained crushed pineapple in own juice (8 ounce can)
- 1 tablespoon sunflower nuts
- 2 tablespoons brown sugar
- 1/4 teaspoon cinnamon

Direction

- Heat oven to 375 degrees, scrub potatoes, and prick all over with a fork, place in shallow baking pan do not use glass, bake 55 to 60 minutes, until tender.
- set oven to broil when potatoes are done, cut potatoes lengthwise in half, mash down the sides slightly with fork, spoon pineapple over cut sides of potato, top with brown sugar cinnamon and sunflower nuts.
- Broil with tops 4 to 6 inches from heat 2 to 3 minutes or until brown sugar is bubbly and serve....

Index

A

Apple 3,34,111

Arborio rice 144

Artichoke 3,7,11,13,142,147

Asparagus 3,4,6,7,13,14,18,67,127,136

Aubergine 7,166

Avocado 3,15,20

B

Bacon 3,4,5,6,17,18,30,37,48,49,54,83,110,111,115

Basil 5,79

Bay leaf 13

Beans 3,4,5,6,7,10,15,17,18,23,29,40,42,46,50,51,55,67,68,70,72,73,74,91,95,101,109,110,111,115,120,129,137,146,149

Beef 3,5,7,22,80,161

Brazil nut 20

Bread 3,5,7,19,73,138

Broccoli 3,4,5,6,7,15,26,27,48,84,106,147

Brussels sprouts 27,28,37,53,55,132,133,134

Buckwheat 5,99

Burger 3,29

Butter 3,4,5,6,7,14,16,20,29,30,36,37,40,67,75,76,77,116,131,151,152

C

Cabbage 3,4,5,6,7,32,33,47,49,54,63,65,74,112,116,117,123,128,147

Cake 3,4,6,27,64,132

Capers 77

Caramel 4,63

Carrot 3,4,5,6,7,26,34,49,63,69,70,87,91,104,112,142

Cashew 5,73

Cauliflower 3,4,5,6,7,17,26,35,36,37,52,56,57,85,87,90,91,92,114,128,129,141

Celery 6,117

Chard 7,152

Chayote 4,38

Cheddar 3,17,18,71,72,81,130,141

Cheese 3,4,6,7,14,15,26,37,40,48,49,92,102,106,141,148,156,166

Cherry 6,130

Chicken 128

Chickpea 4,5,7,52,60,91,139,140,145

Chinese cabbage 97,100,167

Chipotle 4,5,40,41,81

Chives 110

Chutney 60

Cider 4,42,111

Cinnamon 4,7,42,151

Coconut 7,146

Coffee 5,79

Coleslaw 4,6,7,44,46,105,107,150,154

Collar 4,5,7,43,94,136

Coriander 6,60,104

Couscous 3,4,7,23,45,140

Cranberry 4,46,47

Cream 3,4,5,6,7,26,47,48,49,53,54,67,71,83,126,135

Crumble 103

Cucumber 4,5,51,52,95

Cumin 60,117

Curd 116

Curry 3,5,38,60,91

Custard 4,44

D

Daikon 159

Dijon mustard 44,55,57,63,87,141

Dill 7,145,146

Dumplings 7,134

E

Edam 4,68

Egg 3,4,5,7,19,24,57,58,59,60,69,77,93,128,139,148,161

Emmental 92

F

Fat 65,69,71,84,109,134

Fennel 6,130

Feta 4,5,45,51,72

Fish 6,76,132,144

French dressing 156

G

Garam masala 56

Garlic
3,4,5,6,7,19,25,28,29,35,60,67,68,77,96,97,110,128,166

Gin 4,5,69,70,101

Gnocchi 7,143,151

Gratin 3,4,5,6,7,27,36,37,54,66,92,103,130,142,165

Guacamole 5,81

H

Halibut 77

Ham 7,156

Hazelnut 3,36

Heart 5,62,84

Herbs 5,75

Honey 5,73,75,85,86,87

J

Jelly 5,99

Jus 7,121,136

K

Kale 3,4,5,6,12,25,68,96,97,107,132

L

Leek 3,4,5,6,22,69,83,102,103,106,130

Lemon 4,6,7,67,104,132,166

Lentils 3,5,16,85

Lettuce 5,78

Lime 5,75,76,77

Ling 155

M

Manchego 131

Mandarin 6,105

Mango 6,106

Matzo 6,7,107,162

Mayonnaise 5,79

Meat 6,110,124

Milk 32

Mince 87,99,131

Mint 61

Molasses 6,109

Mozzarella 5,57,80,118

Mushroom 3,5,6,7,11,19,71,88,104,135,162

Mustard 3,22,60,111

N

Noodles 128

Nut 69,77,84,109

O

Oil 3,22,60,77,111,166

Okra 4,56

Olive 3,22,77,111,163

Onion
3,5,6,7,20,21,26,29,33,38,77,78,82,86,104,110,113,121,125
,132,144,154,161

P

Pancakes 6,102

Pancetta 5,72

Paneer 4,6,54,115,116

Paprika 117,128

Parmesan 3,5,6,7,13,19,22,31,34,54,57,67,73,92,93,114,115,117,118,130,142,143,144,164

Parsley 77,110

Pasta 4,67

Pear 3,26

Peas 4,5,6,7,52,91,119,139

Pecorino 148

Peel 9,21,29,34,38,58,59,66,69,77,86,93,106,119,121,125,131,132,139,144,152,157,158,159,161,162,166

Pepper 4,6,7,45,50,61,77,101,109,110,111,118,149,154,166,167

Pesto 4,56

Pickle 3,5,6,32,95,99,119,125

Pie 4,6,7,69,104,110,113,135,151

Pineapple 3,8,34,168

Plantain 4,64

Popcorn 6,128

Port 4,6,46,71,118

Potato 3,4,5,6,7,8,30,66,90,91,102,107,110,111,117,121,132,134,144,151,152,166,168

Pumpkin 5,6,84,121

Q

Quinoa 5,96

R

Raisins 4,70,77

Raita 4,51

Ratatouille 6,122,123,125

Red lentil 125

Rice 3,7,10,23,155,164

Risotto 3,7,13,143

Roast potatoes 167

Rum 3,17

S

Sage 7,151

Salad 3,4,5,7,23,51,52,62,74,77,84,96,156,160,164

Salmon 75

Salsa 3,15

Salt 11,18,60,61,65,72,77,110,111,116,126,131,156

Sauces 4,59

Sausage 7,157

Savory 5,76

Scallop 7,133

Seasoning 95,109

Seaweed 4,52

Seeds 60

Sesame oil 147

Shallot 5,72

Soup 5,71,84

Spaghetti 6,109

Spices 110

Spinach 3,4,5,6,7,11,52,54,57,68,100,120,142,143,144,145

Squash 3,4,5,6,7,10,18,30,47,53,86,104,108,109,126,145,146,150,154

Stew 6,103,107

Stuffing 3,27

Sugar 3,10,60,84,111

Swiss chard 73

T

Tabasco 42,44,63,81,113,119,143

Tamari 60,139

Tea 110,111

Tempura 7,159,160

Thyme 111

Tofu 3,21

Tomato 3,4,5,6,7,19,28,30,58,60,77,94,121,150,156,157,165

Turmeric 60

Turnip 7,158

V

Vegan 5,101,157

Vegetables 5,6,7,26,79,83,111,127,129,138

Vegetarian 6,124

Vinegar 3,22,111

W

Walnut 4,5,7,42,68,72,166

Wine 3,22

Worcestershire sauce 11,63

Y

Yam 6,130

Z

Zest 6,96,132

Conclusion

Thank you again for downloading this book!

I hope you enjoyed reading about my book!

If you enjoyed this book, please take the time to share your thoughts and post a review on Amazon. It'd be greatly appreciated!

Write me an honest review about the book – I truly value your opinion and thoughts and I will incorporate them into my next book, which is already underway.

Thank you!

If you have any questions, **feel free to contact at:** _author@limerecipes.com_

Judy Massa

limerecipes.com

Printed in Great Britain
by Amazon